SHELLY CASHMAN SERIES®

© Tom Kates/Cengage Learning

WEB DESIGN

INTRODUCTORY

Fifth Edition

Jennifer T. Campbell

CENGAGE
Learning®

Australia • Brazil • Japan • Korea • Mexico • Singapore • Spain • United Kingdom • United States

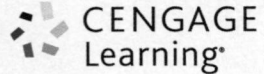

Web Design: Introductory, Fifth Edition
Jennifer T. Campbell

Senior Product Manager: Jim Gish

Content Developer: Jon Farnham

Associate Content Developer:
   Crystal Parenteau

Product Assistant: Gillian Daniels

Development Editor: Amanda Brodkin

Director of Production: Patty Stephan

Content Project Manager:
   Jennifer Feltri-George

Manufacturing Planner: Julio Esperas

Market Development Manager: Kristie Clark

Market Development Manager:
   Gretchen Swann

QA Manuscript Reviewers: Jeffrey Schwartz,
   John Freitas, Danielle Shaw

Composition: PreMediaGlobal

Art Director: GEX Publishing Services

Cover Design: Lisa Kuhn, Curio Press, LLC

Cover Photo: © Tom Kates/Cengage Learning

Library of Congress Control Number: 2014935851

ISBN-13: 978-1-285-17062-6

ISBN-10: 1-285-17062-8

Cengage Learning
20 Channel Center Street
Boston, MA 02210
USA

Cengage Learning is a leading provider of customized learning solutions with office locations around the globe, including Singapore, the United Kingdom, Australia, Mexico, Brazil, and Japan. Locate your local office at: **international.cengage.com/region**

Cengage Learning products are represented in Canada by Nelson Education, Ltd.

To learn more about Cengage Learning, visit **www.cengage.com**

Purchase any of our products at your local college bookstore or at our preferred online store at **www.cengagebrain.com**

Printed in the United States of America
1 2 3 4 5 6 7 18 17 16 15 14

Contents

Chapter 7

Appendix A

Appendix B

Appendix C

Appendix D

Preface

In this Shelly Cashman Series® *Web Design: Introductory, Fifth Edition* book, you will find an educationally sound and easy-to-follow pedagogy that artfully combines screen shots, marginal elements, and text with full color to produce a visually appealing and easy-to-understand presentation of web design. This textbook conveys useful design concepts and techniques typically not addressed in web authoring textbooks. It explains the connections between a detailed design plan that considers audience needs, web site design, and various technical issues. Students learn how to balance these elements to create a successful, responsive web site.

The book's seven chapters emphasize key written concepts and principles with numerous Design Tips boxed throughout the text. A variety of challenging research-based and hands-on activities both within and at the conclusion of each chapter test comprehension, build web research skills and design awareness, and encourage critical thinking about current issues in web design.

Objectives of This Textbook

Web Design: Introductory, Fifth Edition is intended for a one-unit introductory web design course, or a web authoring course that teaches web design techniques and also covers HTML, creating device- and platform-independent websites using responsive web design techniques, CSS, and SEO. The objectives of this book are to:

- Present a practical approach to web design using a blend of traditional development guidelines with current technologies and trends, including responsive web design

- Give students an in-depth understanding of web design concepts and techniques that are essential to planning, creating, testing, publishing, and maintaining web sites

- Define and describe in detail the six steps in developing a solid web design plan: identify the website's purpose and target audience; determine the website's general content; select the website's structure; specify the website's navigation system; design the look and feel of the website; and test, publish, and maintain the website

- Present the material in a full-color, visually appealing and exciting, easy-to-read manner with a format that invites students to learn

- Provide students with Toolkit marginal elements that indicate related content available in the appendices

- Direct students to the web to do additional research and allow them to evaluate and assess the design techniques and technologies discussed in the book by providing them with search terms in the Q&A marginal elements, Your Turn exercises, and end-of-chapter exercises

- Provide an ongoing case study and assignments that promote student participation in learning about web design

Distinguishing Features

The distinguishing features of *Web Design: Introductory, Fifth Edition* include the following:

Responsive Web Design

This text focuses on the basic concepts of responsive web design that teach considerations for creating websites that are device- and platform-independent.

A Blend of Traditional Development with Current Technologies

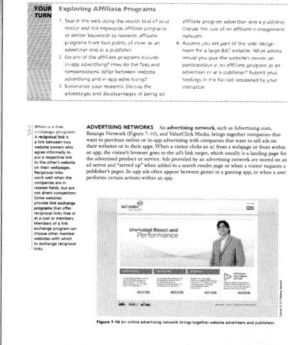

This book goes beyond a theoretical view of web design; every effort has been made to use procedures, tools, and solutions that parallel those used by web designers in today's business world.

Realistic examples support definitions, concepts, and techniques, enabling students to learn in the context of solving realistic problems, much like the ones they will encounter while working in the web design field. In this textbook, students learn to apply best practices while avoiding common pitfalls. In addition, the numerous Design Tips summarize and highlight important topics.

Visually Appealing

The design of this textbook combines screen shots, drawings, marginal elements, boxes, tables, and text into a full-color, visually appealing, and easy-to-read book. The many figures in the book clarify the narrative, reinforce important points, and show screen shots that reflect the latest trends in web design. The marginal elements and boxes highlight features such as exploratory exercises, design topics, common questions and answers, and search terms for students to do additional research on the web.

Introductory Presentation of Web Design

No previous web design experience is assumed, and no prior programming experience is required. This book is written specifically for students for whom continuity, simplicity, and practicality are essential.

DESIGN TIP — More than 80 Design Tips are boxed throughout the book. The function of the Design Tips is to emphasize important web design concepts of which students should be aware as they design websites.

Toolkit Feature

The new Toolkit elements in the margins throughout the book indicate relevant, additional coverage in one of the Appendices on HTML, CSS, RWD, and SEO so students can learn more.

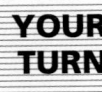

YOUR TURN — Your Turn Exercises

Multiple Your Turn exercises within each chapter provide hands-on activities that allow students to put concepts and skills learned in the chapter to practical, real-world use. Your Turn exercises call for critical thinking and often require online research.

Q&A Boxes

These marginal annotations provide answers to common questions that complement the topics covered, adding depth and perspective to the learning process.

Organization of This Textbook

Web Design: Introductory, Fifth Edition provides basic instruction on how to plan and design a successful website that achieves the website's intended purpose. The material comprises seven chapters, four appendices, and a glossary/index.

CHAPTER 1 — THE ENVIRONMENT AND THE TOOLS   In Chapter 1, students are introduced to the Internet, World Wide Web, websites, and web pages. Topics include domain names; how the Internet and the web influence society; methods and devices users use to connect to the Internet and the web; types of websites; tools for creating websites; and web design roles.

CHAPTER 2 — WEB PUBLISHING FUNDAMENTALS   In Chapter 2, students are introduced to the advantages of web publishing, basic design principles, and writing techniques for the web. Topics include publishing advantages related to connectivity, timeliness, interactivity, reduced production costs, and economical, rapid distribution; responsive web design issues; balance and proximity; contrast and focus; unity; scannable text; using color as a design tool; and technical, privacy, accessibility, and usability issues.

CHAPTER 3 — PLANNING A SUCCESSFUL WEBSITE: PART 1   In Chapter 3, students are introduced to the initial three steps in the six-step planning process for developing a solid website design plan: (1) identify the website's purpose and target audience, (2) determine the website's general content, and (3) select the website's structure. Topics include identifying a specific topic for a website; defining target audience wants, needs, and expectations; choosing content; adding value-added content; and using an outline, storyboard, or flowchart to plan the site's structure.

CHAPTER 4 — PLANNING A SUCCESSFUL WEBSITE: PART 2   In Chapter 4, students are introduced to the remaining three steps in the planning process for developing a design plan: (4) specify the website's structure, (5) design the look and feel of the website, and (6) test, publish, and maintain the website. Topics include the relationship between page length, content placement, and usability; maintaining visual consistency across all pages at the site using color and page layout; and creating both a user-based and a user-controlled navigation and search system that works with touch screens and all device types. A final design plan checklist is provided.

CHAPTER 5 — TYPOGRAPHY AND IMAGES   In Chapter 5, students are introduced to typography and images for the web environment. Topics include typographic principles, guidelines, and tips; web image file formats and sources; and optimization techniques for creating web-ready images.

CHAPTER 6 — MULTIMEDIA AND INTERACTIVITY ELEMENTS   In Chapter 6, students are introduced to the basics of web multimedia and interactivity and methods to add these elements to web pages. Topics include guidelines and sources for using multimedia; types of web page animation; adding and editing web page audio and video; and web-based forms, avatars, live chat, and other interactive web page elements.

CHAPTER 7 — PROMOTING AND MAINTAINING A WEBSITE   In Chapter 7, students learn how to implement a plan to test, publish, promote, and maintain a website successfully. Topics include prepublishing testing of webpages; acquiring server space and uploading a website's files to a server; promoting a published website using search tools, social media, and online advertising networks; the importance of regular website maintenance; and using web analytics to evaluate website performance.

APPENDIX A — HTML 5   This Appendix is a reference for HTML, a markup language used to create webpages. Knowing the basics of HTML syntax and learning about the latest version, HTML 5, allows students to troubleshoot and/or optimize the sometimes-problematic code generated by WYSIWYG editors. Additionally, a fundamental knowledge of HTML 5 tools helps interpret the source code of features and functions found on other websites that students might want to include on their own sites.

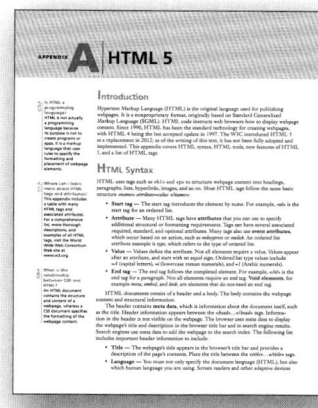

APPENDIX B — CASCADING STYLE SHEETS (CSS)   The CSS Appendix is a brief introduction to Cascading Style Sheets in support of the discussion of CSS in various chapters in this book.

APPENDIX C — RESPONSIVE WEB DESIGN   This new Appendix provides a brief introduction to the decision-making process and the technologies and considerations involved when creating a site for multiple devices, platforms, and screen sizes.

APPENDIX D — SEARCH ENGINE OPTIMIZATION (SEO)   This new Appendix introduces students to how search engines rank and evaluate websites to include in search results, as well as techniques for and careers in SEO.

End-of-Chapter Student Activities

A notable strength of the Shelly Cashman Series textbooks is the extensive student activities at the end of each chapter. Well-structured student activities can make the difference between students merely participating in a class and students retaining the information they learn. The activities in this book include the following:

- **CHAPTER REVIEW**   A review of chapter highlights is presented at the end of each chapter.
- **TERMS TO KNOW**   This list of key terms found in the chapter together with the page numbers on which the terms are defined helps students master the chapter material.
- **TEST YOUR KNOWLEDGE**   Two pencil-and-paper activities are designed to test students' understanding of the material in the chapter: matching terms and short-answer questions.

- **LEARN IT ONLINE**   Reinforce what you learned in this chapter with games, exercises, training, and many other online activities and resources. Reinforcement activities and resources are available at no additional cost on www.cengagebrain.com.

- **TRENDS**   The Trends exercises encourage students to explore the latest developments in the web design technologies and concepts introduced in the chapter.

- **@ ISSUE**   Web design is not without its controversial issues. At the end of each chapter, two topics are presented that challenge students to examine critically their perspective of web design concepts and technologies.

- **HANDS ON**   To complete their introduction to web design, these exercises require that students use the web to gather and evaluate additional information about the concepts and techniques discussed in the chapter.

- **TEAM APPROACH**   Two Team Approach assignments engage students, getting them to work collaboratively to reinforce the concepts in the chapter.

- **CASE STUDY**   The Case Study is an ongoing development process in web design using the concepts, techniques, and Design Tips presented in each section. The Case Study requires students to apply their knowledge starting in Chapter 1 and continuing through Chapter 7 as they prepare, plan, create, and then publish their own websites.

Instructor Resources

The Instructor Resources include both teaching and testing aids and can be accessed online at www.cengage.com/login.

- **INSTRUCTOR'S MANUAL**   Includes lecture notes summarizing the chapter sections, figures and boxed elements found in every chapter, teacher tips, classroom activities, lab activities, and quick quizzes in Microsoft Word files.

- **SYLLABUS**   Contains easily customizable sample syllabi that cover policies, assignments, exams, and other course information.

- **FIGURE FILES**   Illustrations for every figure in the textbook are available in electronic form. Figures are provided both with and without callouts.

- **POWERPOINT PRESENTATIONS**   A one-click-per-slide presentation system provides PowerPoint slides for every subject in each chapter. Presentations are based on chapter objectives.

- **TEST BANK AND TEST ENGINE**   Test Banks include questions for every chapter, feature objective-based and critical-thinking question types, and include page number references and figure references, when appropriate.

- **ADDITIONAL ACTIVITIES FOR STUDENTS**   Consists of Chapter Reinforcement Exercises, which are true/false, multiple-choice, and short answer questions that help students gain confidence in the material learned.

CourseNotes

Cengage Learning's CourseNotes are six-panel quick reference cards that reinforce the most important and widely used features of a software application or technology concept in a visual and user-friendly format. CourseNotes serve as a great reference tool for students, both during and after the course. CourseNotes are available for Adobe Dreamweaver CS6, HTML 5, Web 2.0, Buyer's Guide: Tips for Purchasing a New Computer, Best Practices in Social Networking, Hot Topics in Technology, and many more. Visit **www.cengagebrain.com** to learn more!

About Our Covers

The Shelly Cashman Series is continually updating our approach and content to reflect the way today's students learn and experience new technology. This focus on student success is reflected on our covers, which feature real students from The University of Rhode Island using the Shelly Cashman Series in their courses, and reflect the varied ages and backgrounds of the students learning with our books. When you use the Shelly Cashman Series, you can be assured that you are learning computer skills using the most effective courseware available.

1 | The Environment and the Tools

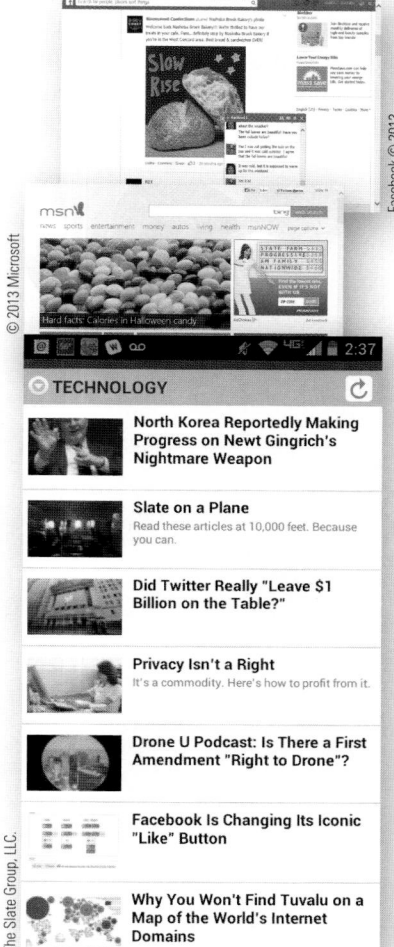

© 2013 Microsoft

Facebook © 2013

The Slate Group, LLC.

Introduction

Designing and building a website is no longer a difficult, intimidating undertaking; evolving web technologies have simplified the job. Applying web technologies is only part of what is required to produce a successful website that is viewable on multiple devices and screen sizes. A website that effectively communicates, educates, entertains, or provides a venue for conducting business transactions also requires good web design. This book explains the basic elements of good web design and shows you how to develop compelling websites and webpages for specific purposes or audiences. Chapter 1 begins the process by describing the Internet and the World Wide Web. Next, you learn about the various ways users connect to the Internet. The chapter then describes different types of websites and the tools for creating them. Finally, the chapter discusses the various roles, responsibilities, and skills essential to successful web design.

Objectives

After completing this chapter, you will be able to:

1. Describe the Internet and the World Wide Web

2. Discuss ways to access the Internet and the web

3. Categorize types of websites

4. Identify web design tools

5. Explain web design principles, roles, and required skills

The Internet and the World Wide Web

A computer **network** consists of connected computers, mobile devices, printers, and data storage devices that share computing resources and data. Computer networks are everywhere — in home offices, in student computer labs, in public places such as coffee shops and libraries, and in the offices of organizations and businesses around the world. The **Internet** is a worldwide public network (Figure 1-1) that connects millions of these private networks. For example, on a college campus, the student lab network, the faculty computer network, and the administration network can all connect to the Internet.

What is Web 2.0?
Web 2.0 technologies and practices are designed to make users' web experiences interactive by incorporating social media and user-driven content into webpages.

Figure 1-1 The Internet is a worldwide public network that connects private networks.

© Cengage Learning; © Mmaxer/Shutterstock.com; © Alfonso de Tomas/Shutterstock.com; © SSSCCC/Shutterstock. com; © iStockphoto.com/Petar Chernaev/Pixelfit; © amfoto/Shutterstock.com; © iStockphoto.com/scanrail; ©iStockphoto.com/scanrail; © iStockphoto.com/sweetym; Source: Microsoft; © Oleksiy Mark/Shutterstock.com; Source: Cengage Learning; © iStockphoto.com/SKrow; © Cengage Learning; © iStockphoto.com/skodonnell; Source: Apple Inc; © iStockphoto.com/skodonnell; Source: Nutrition Blog Network; © iStockphoto.com/arattansi; Source: Microsoft; © Oleksiy Mark/Shutterstock.com; Source: Microsoft; © Cengage Learning

What is Internet2?
Internet2 is a major cooperative initiative among academia, industry, and government agencies to increase the Internet's capabilities and solve some of its challenges. The nonprofit initiative has more than 300 university, corporate, government, and international members and sponsors devoted to developing and using new and emerging network technologies that facilitate research and education.

World Wide Web

The **World Wide Web (web)** is a part of the Internet that consists of connected computers called **web servers** that store electronic documents called webpages. A **webpage** is a specially formatted document that can contain images, text, interactive elements, and hyperlinks, which are links to other pages. A **website** is a group of related webpages. A website's primary page, or **home page**, typically provides information about the website's purpose and content. Figure 1-2 shows the home page of Jive Software. Jive's home page includes standard home page elements, including a company logo, navigation elements, a search feature, and links to additional content.

A **hyperlink**, or simply a **link**, is a word, phrase, or image that connects webpages. Figure 1-3 shows the Gourmet.com home page and the webpage that appears when you click a link on the home page. You often can identify a text link by its appearance. Text links usually are bold, underlined, or differ in color from the rest of the text. An image link might be more difficult to visually identify; however, if you are using a desktop or

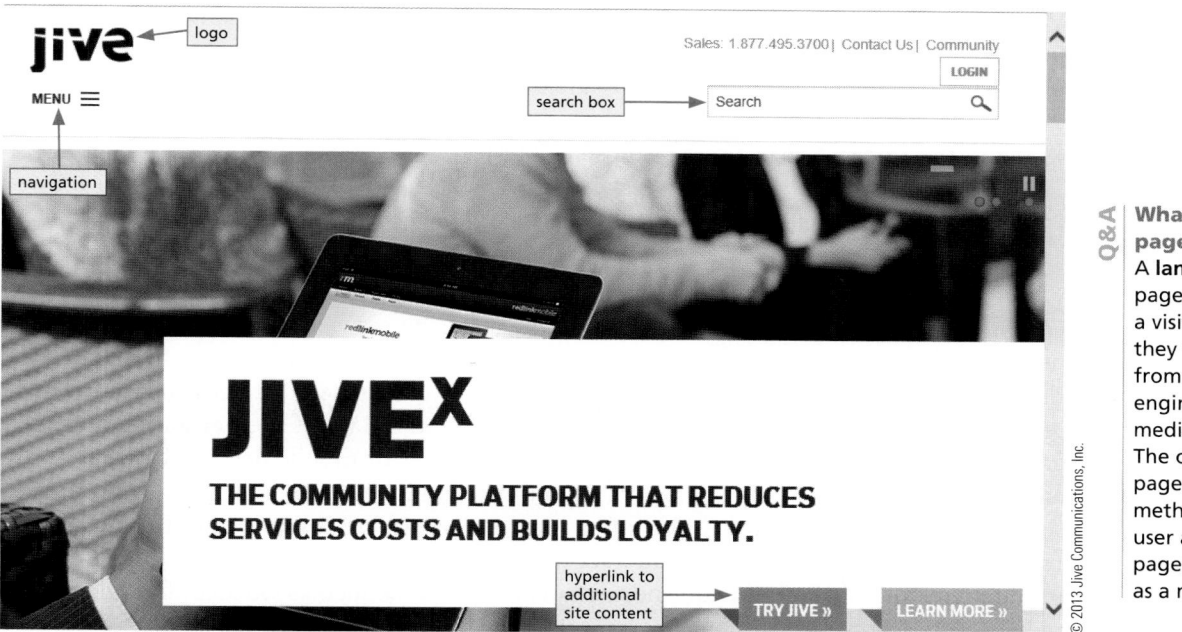

Figure 1-2 A website's primary page is its home page.

Q&A

What is a landing page?
A **landing page** is the page on a website that a visitor sees when they tap or click a link from an ad, search engine result, or social media promotion. The copy on a landing page is specific to the method by which the user arrived at the page, and is often used as a marketing tool.

Figure 1-3 Webpages at the same website or across different websites are connected by links.

laptop computer, pointing to either a text or image link with the mouse pointer changes the pointer from an arrow to a hand pointer. When you tap or click a link, you might view a picture or video, listen to a song, jump to a different webpage at the same website, or move to a webpage at a different website. Exploring the web by moving from one webpage to another is sometimes called **browsing** or **surfing the web**. To visually indicate that you have previously tapped or clicked a text link, the color of a tapped or clicked text link might change. You can see this change in color when you return to the webpage containing the tapped or clicked link.

Q&A

Who originally created the World Wide Web?
Tim Berners-Lee, a programmer at CERN in Switzerland, is credited with the early vision and technological developments that led to today's World Wide Web.

Whether you choose to indicate hyperlinks in text by color, bold, or underline, be consistent throughout your website.

DESIGN TIP

Although some use the terms *Internet* and *web* interchangeably, remember that the Internet and the web are not one and the same. As stated previously, the Internet is a worldwide public network that links private networks. The Internet gives users access to a variety of resources for communication, research, file sharing, and commerce. The web, a subset of the Internet, is just one of those resources.

Influence on Society

The Internet and the web have significantly influenced the way the world communicates, educates, entertains, and conducts business. Friends, families, and business colleagues exchange electronic messages using email, chat, and texting. Students use the web for research, to access podcasts or transcripts of lectures, or to collaborate on a group project. People of all ages access the Internet and the web for entertainment using gaming, music, video, and other apps on their computers or mobile devices. Consumers who shop online save time, gas, and sometimes money by taking advantage of online shopping websites and websites that offer reviews and pricing comparisons. Businesses use Internet and web technologies to interact with their suppliers and customers for increased productivity and profitability. Businesses can also use tools such as videoconferencing to reduce costs associated with business travel or to allow employees to telecommute.

COMMUNICATION   Individuals and organizations of all types use websites to communicate ideas and information. By effectively designing webpages and selectively choosing content, you can ensure that your website's webpages deliver the website's message successfully and persuasively. When a webpage's design is consistent, balanced, and focused, and the content communicates trustworthiness, timeliness, and value, such as the MSN home page shown in Figure 1-4, you are more likely to save a link to the webpage, called a **bookmark** or **favorite** when using a browser, or create a **shortcut** to it on your desktop or mobile device's home screen so you can revisit the website. On the other hand, you quickly will move on from a poorly designed website or if the content appears unreliable, outdated, or trivial. You will learn more about design values in Chapter 2.

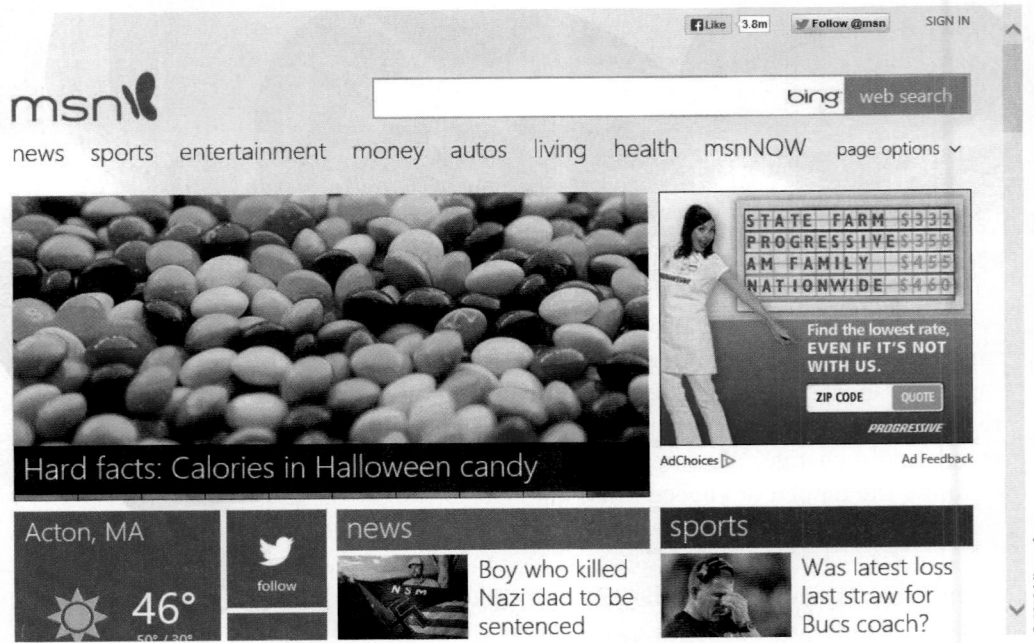

Figure 1-4 The MSN home page communicates up-to-date, accurate information.

Design your website so that it communicates trustworthiness, timeliness, and value.

Other communication options that rely on Internet and web technologies include email, blogging, social networking, social bookmarking, chat, instant messaging, virtual meetings and collaborative workspaces, video sharing, VoIP, interactive gaming, and 3D virtual worlds.

Businesses and individuals heavily rely on electronic messages called **email**. Popular email software, such as Mozilla® Thunderbird®, Microsoft Outlook®, Google Gmail™, or Windows Live Mail®, allows users to attach graphics, video, sound, and other computer files to email messages. Email is a fast, inexpensive, and widely used online communication tool.

Internet Relay Chat (IRC) and **web-based chat** are communication technologies that provide a venue, such as a chat room or discussion forum, where people with common interests can exchange text, video, files, or multimedia messages in real time. **Instant messaging**, also called **IM chat**, is another popular way individuals can exchange one-to-one messages in real time using a chat window that is only visible to those participating in the chat. Examples of IM chat programs are AOL Instant Messenger® (AIM), Yahoo! Messenger, Windows Live Messenger®, ICQ®, and Trillian™. The difference between IRC and IM is that IRC chats are public exchanges between two or more people in a chat room who do not necessarily know each other. With an IM program, you chat privately with people you know. Social networking platforms such as Facebook (Figure 1-5) and Twitter include IM technology. **Mobile IM (MIM)** enables users to chat using mobile devices.

Figure 1-5 IM chat programs allow users to exchange private messages in real time.

chat window

Facebook © 2013

Technology vendors, such as Microsoft, WebEx, and GoToMeeting (Figure 1-6 on the next page), provide access to **collaborative workspaces** or **virtual meeting spaces**, which are websites that allow users to communicate with each other using text, audio, video, whiteboard, and shared files without leaving their own desks. Businesses that use collaborative workspaces and virtual meeting spaces can improve employee productivity and reduce expenses.

Q&A

Is the Internet's societal influence all good?
Being constantly connected has its price. In the past, employees' workdays were done when they physically left the office, but now they can be expected to keep on top of work-related communication during what used to be personal, family, or leisure time. The need to constantly check social media, sports scores, or text messages can have a negative effect on human relationships. To learn more, use a search engine to search for *the Internet's negative effects*.

Q&A

What is text speak?
Text speak describes abbreviations and shortcuts for common phrases commonly used by text and chat users, such as LOL (laugh out loud) or gr8 (great). For more information, use a search engine to search for *text speak*.

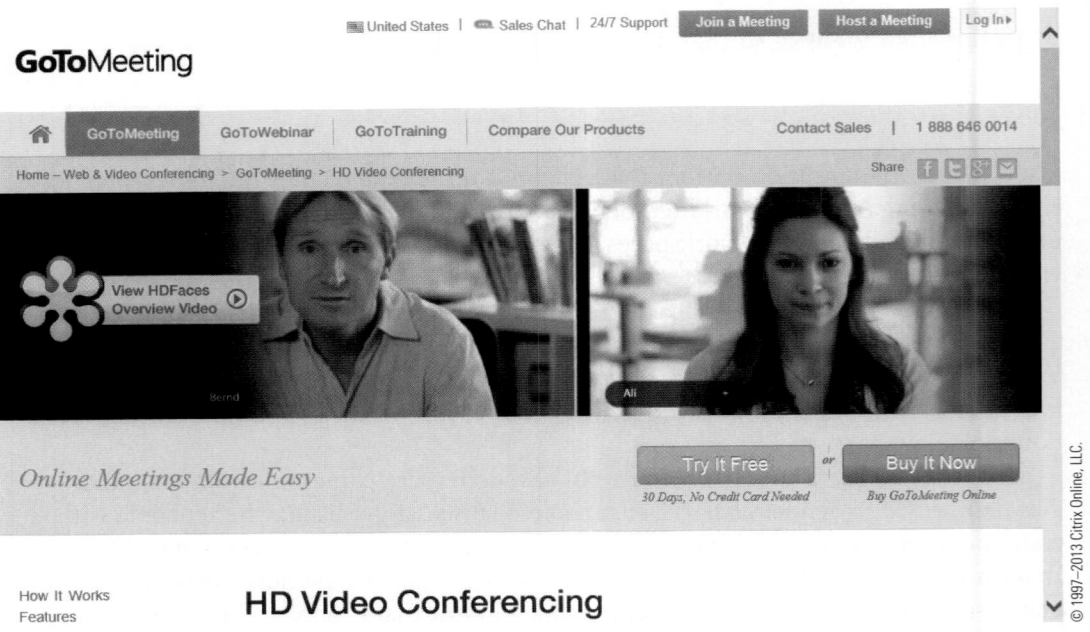

Figure 1-6 Collaborative workspaces support teamwork from remote locations.

A **blog** (short for weblog), such as What's Your Brave? (Figure 1-7), is an online journal or diary. Millions of people go online to share ideas and information by hosting and participating in blogs — a process called **blogging**. Many blogs enable and encourage users to add comments to posts. **Video sharing** websites, sometimes called **video blogging** websites, such as YouTube and Vimeo (Figure 1-7), allow users to share and comment on personal and professional videos.

Figure 1-7 Text and video blogging websites allow web users to share ideas, information, and video files.

Social networking is the term used to describe websites and apps, such as Twitter, Instagram, Facebook, and LinkedIn (Figure 1-8), that allow participants to create a personal network of friends or business contacts. Users then use communication tools provided by the website to interact with those in their personal network by sharing text, comments, pictures, contacts, and more. **Social bookmarking**, provided by websites such as Delicious, Newsvine, FARK, StumbleUpon, and Digg (Figure 1-8), allows users to share their webpage favorites, bookmarks, and **tags** — keywords that reference specific images or documents — with others.

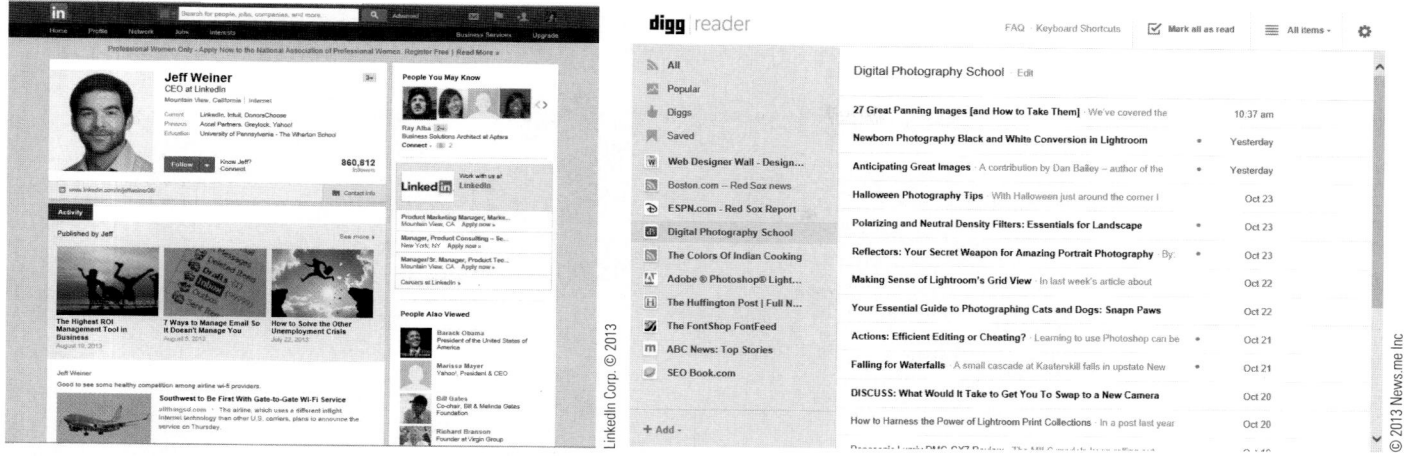

Figure 1-8 Social networking websites and social bookmarking websites allow users to share information with one another.

Gamers by the millions interact with each other by playing **massively multiplayer online games (MMOGs),** such as Minecraft™ and World of Warcraft®. Others create alternative personas that live their lives in **3D virtual worlds,** such as Second Life® or Entropia Universe®.

A **wiki** is a group of related webpages to which users add, edit, or delete content by using a web browser. A well-known example of a wiki is Wikipedia, an online encyclopedia. Figure 1-9 shows a Wikipedia webpage that displays information about mobile web browsers.

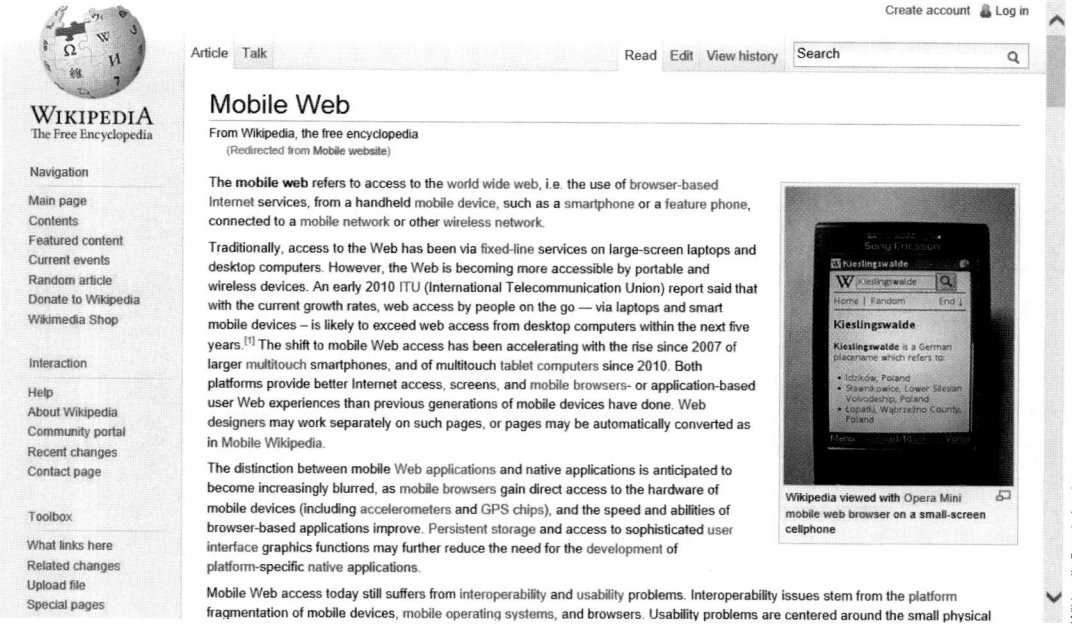

Figure 1-9 Wikipedia and other wiki websites enable users to catalog and manage content collaboratively.

EDUCATION   There are very few topics you cannot learn about by turning to the web. You can take an online course from an academic institution to earn a degree or certificate, or watch a video or read a blog post by an amateur expert. Several universities and academic institutions, such as MIT, publish some or all of their educational materials online, including homework and video lectures, so that they are free and open to everyone

(Figure 1-10). Instructors often use the web to publish podcasts or videos of lectures, webpage links for research, syllabi and grades, and more for their students.

© 2001–2013 Massachusetts Institute of Technology

What is flipped classroom?
Flipped classroom is a teaching model where students learn the concepts at home, often using web technologies such as ebooks and instructor-created videos of lectures. Classroom time is spent employing the practices learned at home.

Figure 1-10 The web offers formal and informal teaching and learning opportunities.

DESIGN TIP Any formal or informal educational website should contain content that is timely, accurate, and appealing. Such websites also should include elements to provide feedback, maintain records, and assess learning. Educational websites should also include information about the authority or experience of the website's content providers.

ENTERTAINMENT AND NEWS   Interactive multimedia experiences and continually updated content lure millions of people to the web for entertainment and news. Popular entertainment websites offer music, videos, sports, games, and more. For example, you can use the web to watch last night's episode of your favorite television program, check out entertainment news at IMDb (Figure 1-11), or play fantasy baseball at mlb.com. At sophisticated entertainment and news websites such as NBCNews.com (Figure 1-11), you can read news stories or watch news clips or video clips from programs. Additionally, the NBCNews website provides interactive elements, such as the ability to add comments or share an article on your social media profile.

DESIGN TIP Include methods to share your website's content by providing links to send content using email, or post to the user's Facebook page, RSS feed, or account on Pinterest or Twitter. Also provide links to related content that website users would find interesting and relevant.

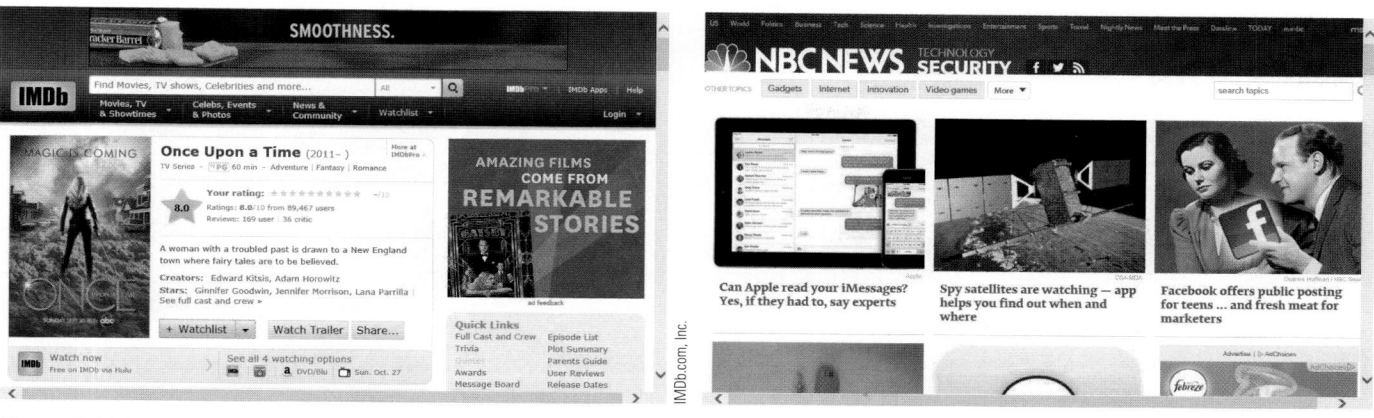

Figure 1-11 Entertainment and news websites provide continually updated multimedia content.

E-COMMERCE **Electronic commerce** or **e-commerce** encompasses a wide variety of online business activities, including consumer shopping and investing and the exchange of business data and transactions within a company or among multiple companies (Figure 1-12). For example, a pet groomer might offer his or her services using an e-commerce website where a pet owner could find valuable information, such as the groomer's telephone number, location, list of services, and rates charged; the pet owner could then schedule an appointment online. At the other end of the e-commerce spectrum, a large manufacturing company could use the Internet and the web to communicate policies and procedures to its employees, exchange business information with its vendors and other business partners, process sales transactions, and provide online support to its customers.

E-commerce websites can be categorized by the participants involved in the transactions (Figure 1-13), such as businesses and consumers.

E-Commerce Transaction Types

Category	Description
Business-to-consumer (B2C) e-commerce	B2C e-commerce involves the sale of an endless assortment of products and services directly to consumers. Transactions take place between an online business and an individual consumer.
Business-to-business (B2B) e-commerce	B2B e-commerce involves the sale of products and services and the exchange of data between businesses, and accounts for the majority of e-commerce transactions in the corporate world.
Consumer-to-consumer (C2C) e-commerce	In C2C e-commerce, business transactions occur between consumers. Examples of C2C e-commerce include online auctions and person-to-person classified ads.

© 2015 Cengage Learning

Figure 1-12 B2C, B2B, and C2C are types of e-commerce transactions.

To develop an e-commerce website, you must determine the potential customers for your products or services. If appropriate to do so, associate your e-commerce website with a database that supplies up-to-date product information such as available inventory, sizes, colors, and more. Provide a search feature so customers can easily find what they need, and electronic payment services, such as direct purchase or a third-party payment service such as PayPal.

DESIGN TIP

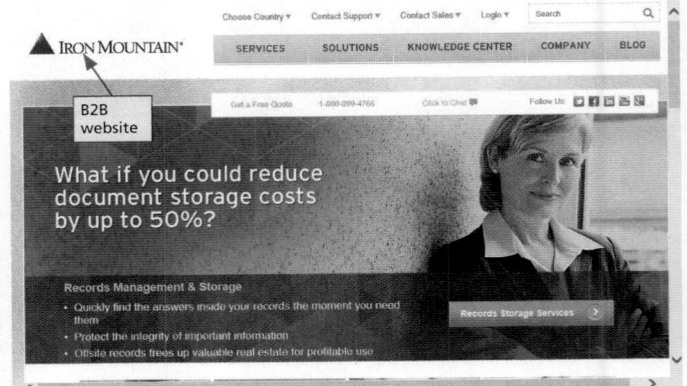
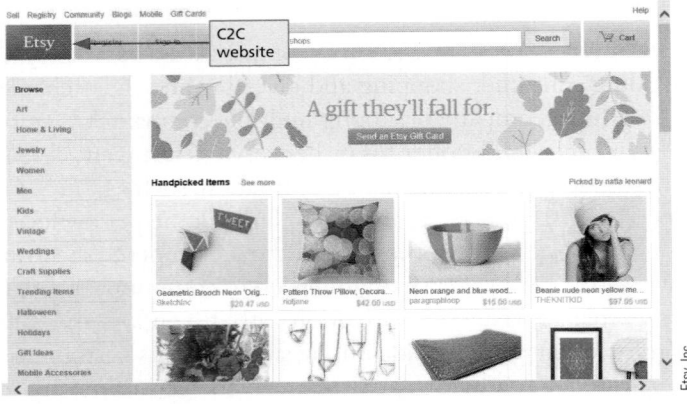

Figure 1-13 E-commerce involves all business transactions that use the Internet.

Ways to Access the Internet and the Web

Users access the Internet and web using a variety of means. In the earliest days of the web, the most common way to access the Internet was using a dial-up telephone line. Today, faster access methods, including digital dedicated lines, cable broadband, and wireless transmissions, are used by both individuals and organizations.

The speed at which data travels from one device to another is the **transfer rate**. Transfer rates measure the number of bits the line can transmit in one second (expressed as bits per second, or bps). Transfer rates range from thousands of bits per second (called kilobits per second or **Kbps**) to millions of bits per second (called megabits per second or **Mbps**). A faster transfer rate translates into more expensive Internet access. Transfer rate has a direct impact on the user's experience with a website; Chapter 2 discusses the effect of Internet access speeds on web design considerations.

Cable Internet Access

Cable television (CATV) lines enable home or business users to connect to the Internet over the same coaxial cable that delivers television transmissions (Figure 1-14). Data can travel very rapidly through a cable modem connected to a CATV line, typically moving at speeds from 5 Mbps to 7 Mbps (download). Then, using a splitter, the line from the cable company connects to both the television and computer. Cable Internet access typically is available only in urban and suburban areas.

Q&A

What is broadband?
The term, broadband, defines high-speed data transmissions over a communication channel that can transmit multiple signals at one time. ISDN, ADSL, and CATV Internet access are all examples of broadband Internet access.

Q&A

What is Bluetooth?
Bluetooth is a popular, short-range wireless connection that uses a radio frequency to transmit data between two electronic devices, such as a smartphone and an earpiece.

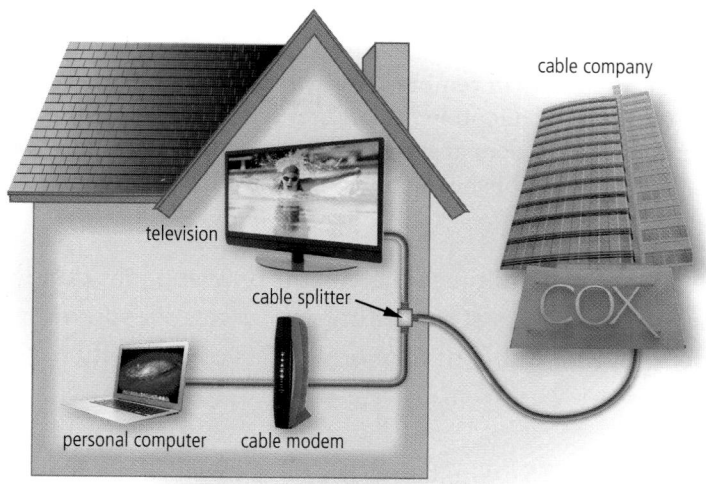

Figure 1-14 Cable Internet access requires a line splitter and cable modem.
© iStockphoto.com/tiridifilm; image100/Alamy; ERIK S. LESSER/Landov; © iStockphoto.com/SKrow; © Pablo Eder/Shutterstock.com; © Cengage Learning

Fixed and Mobile Wireless Access

Fixed wireless is Internet connectivity service that uses satellite technology. Radio signals transferred between a transmitting tower and an antenna on a house or business provide a high-speed connection. People not physically connected to a network can use their computer or mobile device to access the Internet and web using **mobile wireless** technologies, which include radio signals, **wireless fidelity (Wi-Fi)** technologies, cellular telephones, and wireless providers' broadband networks. Wi-Fi provides wireless connectivity to devices within a certain range. A Wi-Fi network may be password protected or open to the public.

Standards for mobile communications, including voice, mobile Internet access, video calls, and mobile TV, are classified by generation. **3G**, the third generation, provides mobile broadband access to devices such as laptop computers and smartphones. 3G devices support speech and data services, as well as data rates of at least 200 kbps (kilobits per second). **4G** systems improve on 3G standards by supporting services such as gaming and streamed multimedia.

Mobile devices that provide Internet access include laptop computers, smartphones, tablets, ebook readers, and other handheld devices. These devices use an internal antenna or wireless card to connect to the Internet either at a **hot spot**, a location that provides public Internet access, or directly to a wireless provider's network. Some mobile devices enable you to set them up as a mobile hot spot. You can pay for mobile access on a per-Kb basis, or buy a flat-rate monthly plan with unlimited text and data usage.

Telephone Line Access

The **Public Switched Telephone Network (PSTN)** used to be the main way all users connected to the Internet; PSTN still uses high-speed telephone access, despite developments in mobile and broadband systems. Although initially built to handle voice communications, the telephone network is also an integral part of computer communications. Data, instructions, and information can travel over the telephone network over dial-up lines or dedicated lines, which are described in the following sections.

Q&A **Should I use Wi-Fi with my mobile devices?**
You should check your mobile provider's recommendations and your data plan to decide which method is best for you. Typically, mobile devices use significantly less cellular data when you are connected to Wi-Fi than when you are using cellular service.

Q&A **Are there risks to using Wi-Fi?**
Security experts recommend when using a public Wi-Fi network that you avoid accessing personal information, such as financial transactions. If you have a Wi-Fi network in your home or business, use passwords and encryption to avoid unauthorized and potentially damaging access by others. For more information, use a search engine to search for *Wi-Fi safety tips*.

DIAL-UP LINES   A **dial-up line** is a temporary connection that uses analog telephone lines. Because of its slow access speed, dial-up access is the least popular Internet access method, and today is used only in remote areas where cable and other methods are not available. Similar to using the telephone to make a call, a modem at the sending end dials the telephone number of a modem at the receiving end. When the modem at the receiving end answers the call, it establishes a connection enabling data to transmit.

DESIGN TIP   Although large images and multimedia elements on webpages can degrade the audience's viewing experiences at slower Internet access speeds, most websites now assume users have broadband cable or wireless connectivity.

DIGITAL DEDICATED LINES   Unlike a dial-up line in which the connection is reestablished each time it is used, a **dedicated line** is a constant connection between two communications devices that uses the local telephone network. A dedicated line provides a higher-quality connection than a dial-up line, better suited for viewing or listening to **streaming media** — video or sound that downloads to a computer continuously to be watched or listened to in real time, such as watching TV programs, web conferencing, and gaming. Businesses sometimes use dedicated lines to connect geographically distant offices. Three types of digital dedicated lines are Integrated Services Digital Network (ISDN) lines, digital subscriber lines (DSL), and T-carrier lines.

Integrated Services Digital Network (ISDN) is a set of standards for digital transmission of data over standard copper telephone lines. With ISDN, the same telephone line that could carry only one computer signal now can carry three or more signals at once, through the same line, using a technique called **multiplexing**. Multiplexing allows for more data to transmit at the same time over the same line.

DSL is another digital line alternative for the small business or home user.

- A **digital subscriber line (DSL)** transmits at fast speeds on existing standard copper telephone wiring. Some DSL installations can provide a dial tone, so you can use the line for both voice and data.
- An **asymmetrical digital subscriber line (ADSL)** is a type of DSL that supports faster transmissions when receiving data than when sending data. ADSL is ideal for Internet access because users generally download more data from the Internet than they upload.

A **T-carrier line** is any of several types of digital lines that carry multiple signals over a single communications line. Whereas a standard dial-up telephone line carries only one signal, digital T-carrier lines use multiplexing so that multiple signals can share the telephone line. T-carrier lines provide extremely fast data transfer rates.

- The most popular T-carrier line is the **T-1 line**. Businesses often use T-1 lines to connect to the Internet.
- A **fractional T-1** line is a less-expensive, slower connection option for home owners and small businesses. Instead of a single owner, multiple users share a fractional T-1.
- A **T-3 line** is equal in speed to 28 T-1 lines. T-3 lines are the most expensive connection method. Main users of T-3 lines include large companies, telephone companies, and service providers connecting to the Internet backbone.

Internet Service Providers

An **Internet service provider (ISP)** is a business that has a permanent Internet connection and provides temporary Internet connections to individuals and companies. ISPs are either regional or national.

- A **regional ISP**, such as Windstream (Figure 1-15), provides Internet access for customers (individuals or businesses) in a specific geographic area.

- A **national ISP** provides Internet access in most major cities and towns nationwide. National ISPs may offer more services and generally have larger technical support staffs than regional ISPs. An example of a national ISP is EarthLink (Figure 1-16).

A cable company, such as Verizon, can be an ISP as well as provide cable television and telephone access. Negotiating one price for all of those services can save you money and hassle, but can provide limited options if you are tied into one provider for all three because you can only choose from within the plans for each service offered by that provider.

Q&A How can I keep safe while using the Internet?
Using the Internet is not without risks, including exposure to computer viruses, accidentally sharing personal information, and more. Be aware that others could share anything you type and any video or photo you post, even if you consider the exchange to be private. For more information, use a search engine to search for *Internet safety tips*.

Figure 1-15 A regional ISP provides Internet access for homes and businesses in a specific geographical area.

Figure 1-16 A national ISP provides Internet access for homes and businesses across the United States.

Web Browsers

To view webpages, you need a **web browser**, also called a **browser**, which is a software program that requests, downloads, and displays webpages stored on a web server. Most browsers share common features, such as an Address bar, a Favorites list, a History list, tabs that open multiple pages in one browser window, and Back and Forward buttons for navigating. The Google Chrome browser (Figure 1-17) is the most widely used browser software on desktop and laptop computers, with about 40 percent of the market. Microsoft Internet Explorer (Figure 1-17) is the second-most popular web browser software with approximately 29 percent of the browser market. Mozilla Firefox ranks third, with approximately 18 percent of the browser market. Opera, Safari, and other browsers make up the remaining share of the browser market for desktops and laptops.

The size of a smartphone or tablet screen is much smaller than that of a desktop or laptop computer. Browsers for mobile devices take into consideration the size of your screen when displaying webpage content. Many mobile devices also include a touch screen, which enables you to interact with the device by tapping, dragging, and other touch gestures. Mobile web browsers are capable of resizing and reordering the content and navigation on a webpage, making browsing easier for mobile users. Some companies create mobile versions

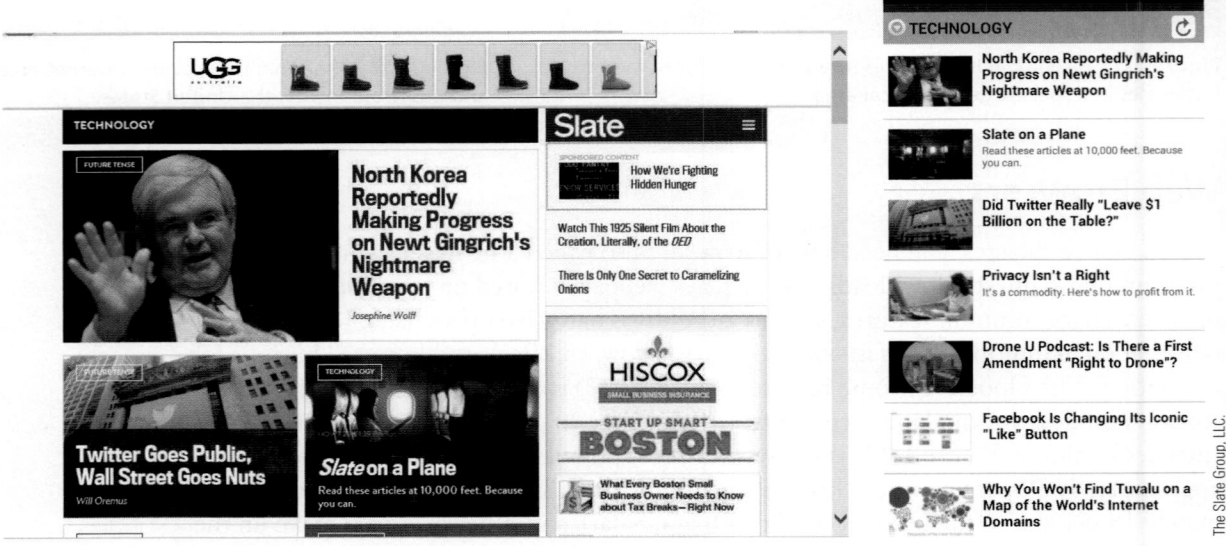

Figure 1-17 Google Chrome and Microsoft Internet Explorer are examples of web browsers.

of their websites; in other cases, websites use a design strategy called **responsive web design (RWD)**. The goal of RWD is to create websites that adjust layout and, in some cases, content, to the device and screen displaying the webpages. You will learn more about RWD in later chapters. Mobile web browsers are available for tablets, smartphones, ebook readers, and other devices. Some mobile web browsers are scaled-down versions of browsers used for desktop or laptop computers. Others, such as Android, are specific to the device on which they are located. The website for Slate uses RWD; Figure 1-18 shows how the Slate home page appears when viewed on a desktop or laptop (left) and using a smartphone (right).

Figure 1-18 Mobile web browsers are available for tablets and smartphones.

DESIGN TIP Some web designers who follow the RWD approach recommend using a 'mobile first' strategy. Developers who follow this strategy assume their websites will be used with mobile devices, and prioritize design considerations, navigation, and layout strategies that work best with mobile devices and browsers.

You can access a webpage by entering its unique address, called the **Uniform Resource Locator (URL)**, in a browser's Address bar. At a minimum, a URL consists of a domain name and a top-level domain designation. Many URLs also include folder and file designations indicating the path to a specific webpage. If a URL includes folder and file names, a forward slash character follows the top-level domain designation. Mobile versions of websites often use the 'm.' designation before the domain name. Figure 1-19 illustrates the URL or path to the news page on boston.com.

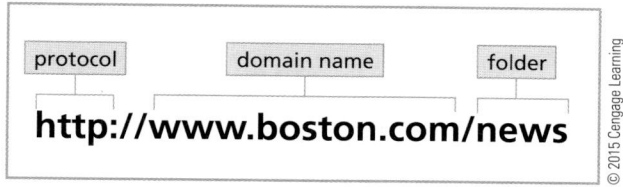

Figure 1-19 A URL identifies a computer on the Internet.

An **IP address** is the numeric address for a computer connected to the Internet. Every device in a computer network has an IP address. The Internet Assigned Numbers Authority (IANA) works with regional and local entities to assign IP addresses. A **domain name** is the text version of a computer's numeric IP address. Companies known as domain name registrars are responsible for assigning domain names. A **top-level domain (TLD)** designation (Figure 1-20) indicates the type of organization or general domain — commercial, nonprofit, network, military, and so forth — of the domain name. Some countries have their own TLDs, such as Australia (.au), France (.fr), and Canada (.ca).

Top-Level Domains

Top-Level Domain	Domain Type	Top-Level Domain	Domain Type
.aero	Air-transportation industry	.jobs	Human resources managers
.asia	Asia Pacific community	.mil	U.S. military
.biz	Businesses	.mobi	Consumers and providers of mobile products and services
.cat	Catalan linguistic community	.museum	Museums
.com	Commercial, personal	.name	Individuals
.coop	Cooperative associations	.net	Network providers
.edu	Postsecondary institutions	.org	Noncommercial community
.gov	U.S. government	.pro	Credentialed professionals
.info	General information	.tel	Business and individual contact data
.int	International treaty organization	.travel	Travel industry

Figure 1-20 Top-level domains identify the type of organization or general domain for which a domain name is registered.

Q&A

Who controls the registration of domain names?
The Internet Corporation for Assigned Names and Numbers (ICANN) controls the Domain Name System (DNS) and the registration of domain names through its accredited registrars, such as Network Solutions or register.com.

© 2015 Cengage Learning

In a URL, a **protocol**, or rule, precedes the domain name and top-level domain designation. The protocol specifies the format used for transmitting data. For webpages, that protocol is the **Hypertext Transfer Protocol (HTTP)**, which is the communications standard for transmitting webpages over the Internet. You can type the protocol when you enter the webpage domain name and top-level domain designation in the browser's Address bar; however, it is generally not necessary to do so. Most web browsers will insert the HTTP protocol automatically when the requested webpage downloads into the browser.

DESIGN TIP
Select a short, easy-to-remember domain name that ties directly to a website's purpose or publisher's name. Examples of effective domain names include slate.com (commentary and articles about current affairs), business.com (business-oriented search directory), and ask.com (search tool).

YOUR TURN

Exploring Domain Name Registration

1. Identify three to five possible domain names for a computer repair business.
2. Use a search engine to search for domain registry services.
3. Tap or click one of the domain registry services to open it in your browser.
4. Follow the steps on the domain registry website to search existing domain names and determine if your possible domain names are available.
5. Submit the results of your domain name search as requested by your instructor.

Types of Websites

Types of websites include personal, organizational/topical, and commercial. A website's type differs from its purpose. The type, determined by the company or individual responsible for the website's creation, is the category of website. The purpose of a website is its reason for existence — such as to sell products, share information, or collect feedback. Chapter 3 provides detailed discussion about defining purpose. An overview of personal, organizational/topical, and commercial websites follows, along with the individual design challenges they present.

Personal Websites

Individuals create their own **personal websites** for a range of communication purposes. You might use a personal website to promote your employment credentials, share news and photos with friends and family, or share a common interest or hobby with fellow enthusiasts. Depending on your website's purpose, you might include your résumé, blog, photo gallery, biography, email address, or a description of whatever you are passionate about — from Thai food to NASCAR racing.

Creating a personal website typically is less complex than creating other types of websites, with fewer resources available than when creating a commercial website. Working independently means you must assume all the roles necessary to build the website. Web roles are discussed later in this chapter. Despite these challenges, you can publish a successful website to promote yourself and your services, or simply tell the world what you are all about. You can also use a content management system, discussed later in the chapter, to allow you to focus on the content of your website and not its structure. The web offers a range of tools for creating personal websites. As free alternatives to creating a personal website to communicate and share information with your friends and acquaintances, you can turn to blogging or social networking tools, such as Facebook. Rather than create a website to showcase your résumé, references, and business connections to potential employers, LinkedIn provides a platform for showcasing your experience, education, and skills, and also enables you to network with colleagues and others in your industry.

DESIGN TIP

Be careful what you put online, whether it is on a personal website or a social networking website. Employers and college recruiters can find information, posts, or photos quite easily, even with privacy settings enabled. Unscrupulous users scan the web for personal information, which they use for malicious purposes, such as identity theft. Assume that anything you put online has the potential to stay there forever, even if you attempt to delete or hide it.

Organizational and Topical Websites

A website owned by a group, association, or organization, whether it is a professional or amateur group, is an **organizational website**. For example, if you belong to the Advertising Photographers Association of North America, you might volunteer to create an organizational website to promote member accomplishments or to encourage support and participation. Conversely, as a photographer, you might choose to design a website devoted to black-and-white photography to share your knowledge with others, including tips for amateurs, photo galleries, and online resources. A **topical website** focuses on a specific subject. The purpose of both types of websites is to provide a resource about a subject.

Professional, nonprofit, international, social, volunteer, and various other types of organizations abound on the web. An organization that lacks funding might encounter the same challenges creating its website as an individual creating a website — specifically, limited resources, including people to create and maintain the website. Figure 1-21 shows the World Health Organization organizational website.

Figure 1-21 Organizational websites are owned by a group, association, or organization.

Q&A

How can I evaluate web content? As you browse the web, you will find that some organizational and topical websites lack accurate, timely, objective, and authoritative content. You must always carefully evaluate a website's content for these four elements. For more information, use a search engine to search for *critical evaluation of webpage content*.

DESIGN TIP Take care to ensure that your webpages contain accurate, current, objective, and authoritative content.

Commercial Websites

The goal of many **commercial websites** is to promote and sell products or services of a business, from the smallest home-based business to the largest international enterprise. The design and content of a large enterprise's website might be much more sophisticated and complex than that of a small business's website. Figure 1-22 contrasts the home page for a large B2B enterprise, SAP, which sells and supports software, with that of a small B2C business, Paul Mitchell Design, which is a construction and design firm.

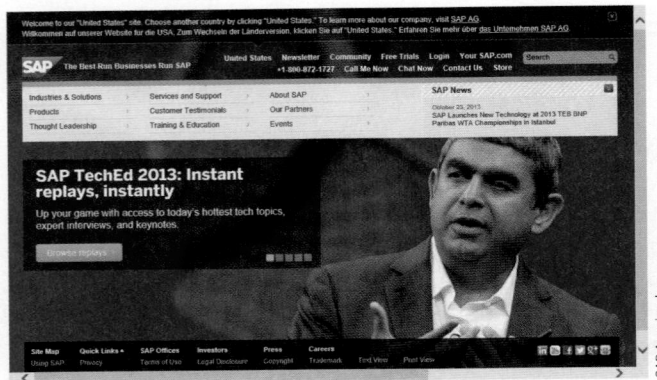

Figure 1-22 Commercial websites promote and sell products and services.

In addition to websites that promote and sell products or services, commercial websites also include websites that generate their revenue largely from online services like advertising, such as search tool websites and portal websites.

SEARCH TOOLS Search tools are websites that locate specific information on the web based on a user's search requirements. Such tools include search engines, metasearch engines, and search directories.

A **search engine** is a web-based search tool that locates a webpage using a word or phrase found in the page. To find webpages on particular topics using a popular search engine, such as Google, Bing, or ask.com, you enter terms or phrases, called **keywords**, in the search engine's text box and tap or click a button usually labeled Search or Go. The search engine compares your search keywords or phrases with the contents of its database of webpages and then displays a list of relevant pages. A match between a keyword search and the resulting occurrence is a **hit**.

A search engine might use a variety of methods to create its website database, called its **index**. For example, most search engines use software **spiders** or **robots**, which are programs that browse the web for new pages and then add the webpages' URLs and other information to their indexes. Some search engines might also use meta tags to build their indexes. **Meta tags**, which are special codes added to webpages, contain information such as keywords and descriptive data regarding a webpage. Other search engines might also use the information in a webpage title — the text that appears in the browser title bar when a webpage downloads — or keywords in the page text to index a webpage.

A **metasearch engine** is a search engine, such as Mamma or Dogpile, that performs a keyword search using multiple search engines' indexes. Figure 1-23 shows an example of a keyword search using the popular search engine Google. Figure 1-24 illustrates the same keyword search using the Dogpile metasearch engine.

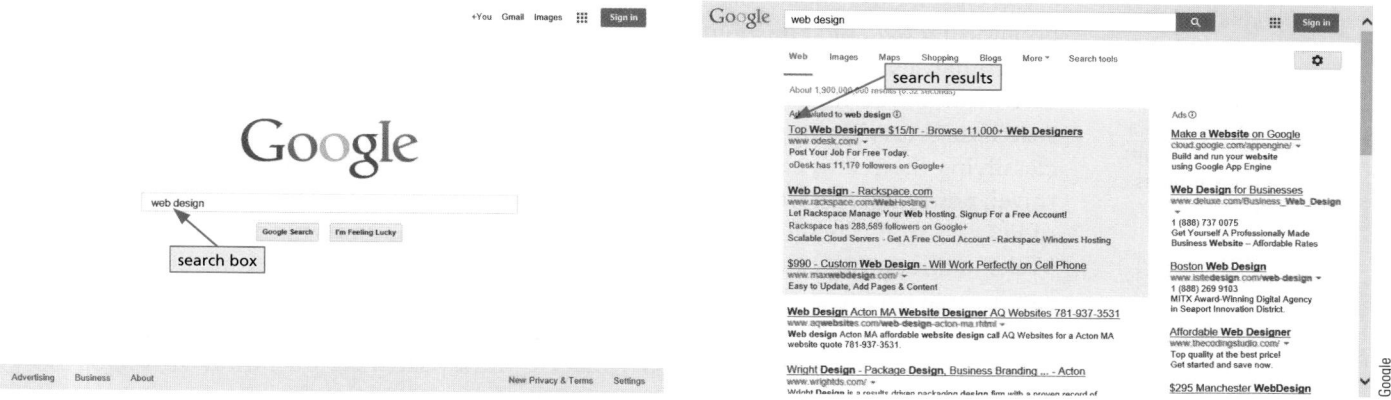

Figure 1-23 A keyword search using a search engine returns a list of webpages related to the keyword or phrase.

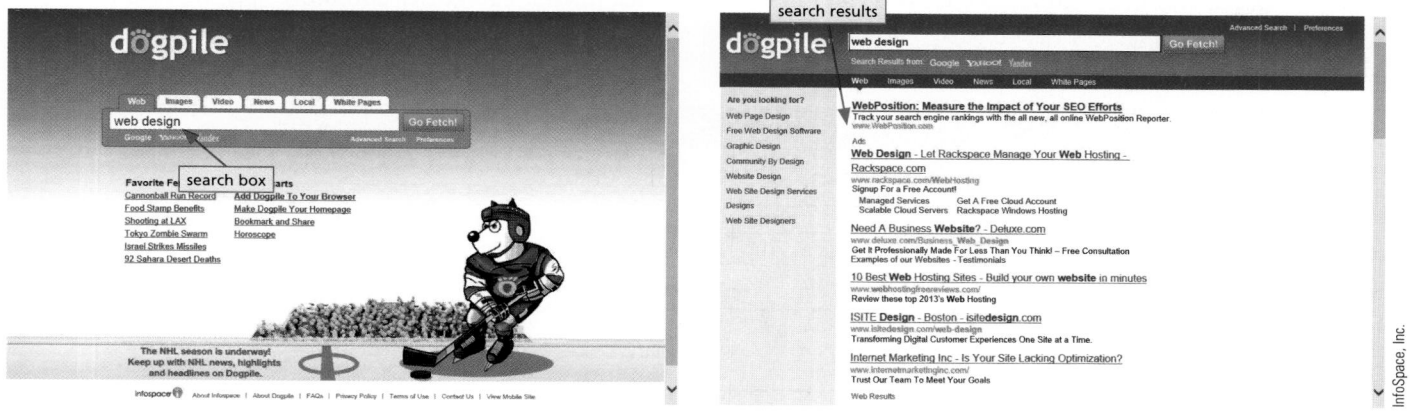

Figure 1-24 A metasearch engine searches the indexes of multiple search engines.

Search engine optimization (SEO) is the process of designing a webpage to increase the likelihood that the webpage will appear high in a search engine's search results list, and increase the likelihood of the webpage being visited. Search engine optimization tools include meta tags, descriptive page titles, relevant inbound links from other websites, and clearly written text.

TOOLKIT
SEO Tools
To learn more about meta tags and other SEO tools, see Appendix D.

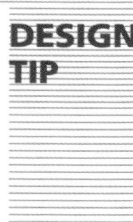

DESIGN TIP

Adding meta tags to your webpages and carefully wording each webpage title can increase the probability that your webpages will be included in many search engines' indexes and that your pages will appear in search results lists for important keywords and phrases. Only include meta tags that directly relate to your website content and purpose.

Q&A

When should I use a search directory or search engine? Humans review and categorize the entries in a search directory, so if you are looking for information on a specific topic, a directory is a good place to start. Search engines will return a wider array of results, but might not be as accurate.

In addition to designing and writing your content for SEO, you can include paid or sponsored placements in your website marketing plan. In a paid or sponsored placement, the website publisher pays the search engine a fee to list their webpages at or near the top of the search results list when a visitor uses specific keywords. Figure 1-23 illustrates a Google search results list for the phrase, web design; paid placements are sponsored search results and appear prominently above and to the right of the list. You learn more about using paid or sponsored placement as a marketing tool in Chapter 7.

Unlike a search engine, a **search directory** builds its webpage index using human interaction. Website owners can submit website information to a search directory. The search directory's editors review webpages they find or that are submitted to them, classifying them into categories such as arts and entertainment, jobs, health and fitness, travel, news, and so forth. The search directory's own webpages present a hierarchy of links — from the most general to the most specific to the owner-submitted webpages. Website directories can be general, or cover only specific topics. Website directories also can include paid links within their results.

To use a search directory, such as the Open Directory Project (Figure 1-25), you can tap or click category and subcategory links to work your way down from the top of the hierarchy to eventually find webpages with useful information about a specific topic. For example, tapping or clicking the Food link in the search directory's general Recreation category link leads to a webpage with additional links to Food subcategories, such as Spicy, which you can tap or click to see further categories and more specific results.

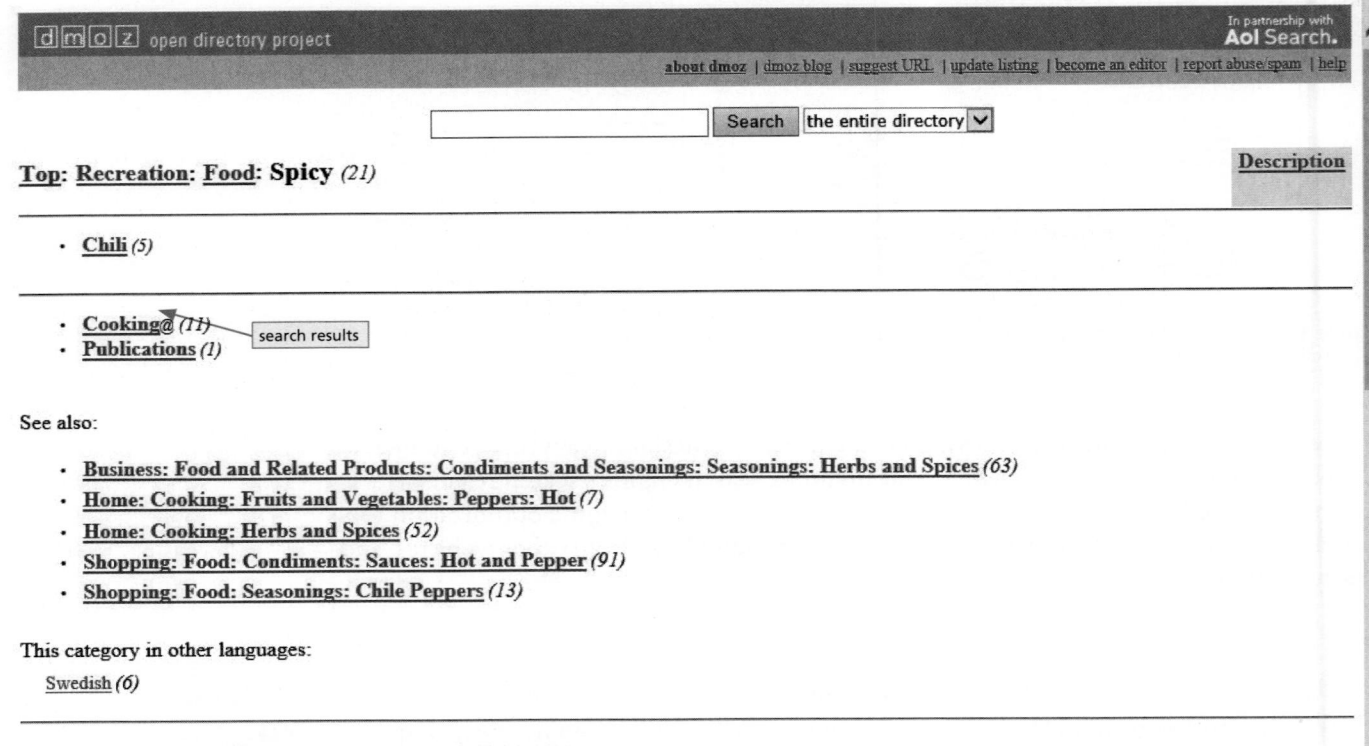

Figure 1-25 A search directory provides a hierarchy of linked categories and subcategories.

Exploring a Search Directory

1. Use a search engine to search for the Open Directory Project (dmoz).
2. Tap or click the home page listed in the search results to open the home page.
3. Tap or click the Computers link and then follow the subcategory links as necessary to locate pages on basic web design. Return to the home page and tap or click the suggest URL link at the top of the page. Review the requirements for submitting webpage information to the directory.
4. Consider how you would submit a new website's pages to the Open Directory Project.
5. Submit your plan in the format requested by your instructor.

Today, many popular search tools are hybrids that combine a search engine with a search directory. Additionally, some search tools actually provide the webpage indexes used by other search tools. Because search tools' webpage indexes are created in a variety of ways, the indexes can vary substantially from search tool to search tool. For best results, you should become comfortable searching the web for specific information using more than one search tool.

PORTALS   **Portals** — websites that offer a starting point for accessing information — can be general consumer portals, personal portals, vertical or industry portals, corporate portals, or hyperlocal portals.

- A **general consumer portal** website offers a variety of features, including search services, email, chat rooms, news and sports, maps, and online shopping. Many web users begin their web-based activities, including searching for specific information, from a portal, often setting a portal as a personal home page. Two early ISPs — AOL and MSN — and some of the web's original search tools, such as Excite and Yahoo!, have evolved into general consumer portals.

- A **personal portal** is a version of a general consumer portal, such as MyYahoo!, which a user can customize for personal preferences.

- A **vertical portal**, such as usa.gov or farms.com (Figure 1-26), provides a starting point for finding information about specific areas of interest — in these two examples, U.S. government agency websites and farming topics, respectively.

- A **corporate portal**, run on a company's intranet, provides an entry point for a company's employees and business partners into its private network.

- A **hyperlocal portal** provides information about and is written by someone living in a specific geographical area. Figure 1-26 shows the Patch.com hyperlocal portal for the area of Oak Forest, Illinois.

Figure 1-26 Hyperlocal and vertical portals offer a variety of services, links, media, and information.

YOUR TURN

Exploring Consumer Portals

1. Use multiple tabs in a search engine to search for Excite, AOL, MSN, and Patch. Open each portal website in a different browser tab.

2. In each tab, tap or click the portal in the search results to display the portal page.

3. Review the features offered by each of the portals. Identify the five features you believe are common to most portals.

4. Consider how analyzing the features of existing portal websites can help you plan the content for a new consumer portal website.

5. Determine how you might design a hyperlocal portal for your area. Include details such as the geographical area it will encompass, the intended audience (for example, parents, foodies, or outdoor enthusiasts), and sample content.

6. Submit your findings in the format requested by your instructor.

OTHER TYPES OF WEBSITES   Many other types of websites exist (Figure 1-27). Users visit travel and mapping websites to book flights or rent automobiles, get driving directions to a restaurant, or plan a bike ride. Financial websites enable users to pay bills, transfer funds between bank accounts, and make investments. Career websites provide searchable job databases, online resumes, and networking opportunities. Almost anything you would like to learn about can be found on the web: recipes, language translations, home décor, pet care, and much, much more.

Types of Websites

Category	Purpose	Examples
Travel	Book a flight or hotel	Travelocity, Expedia
Mapping	Get driving directions or plan a bike ride or run	Mapquest, MapMyRoute
Financial	Pay bills, transfer funds between bank accounts, and make investments	Citizens Bank, eTrade
Career	Provide searchable job databases, online resumes, and networking opportunities	Monster.com, CareerBuilder
Web publishing	Enable users to publish web content in a blog or website	Wordpress, Joomla

© 2015 Cengage Learning

Figure 1-27 Diverse websites exist for a variety of purposes.

Web Design Tools

Web technology is constantly changing — a new browser feature, scripting language, or mobile platform seemingly revolutionizes the way the world accesses the Internet. As soon as these new technologies surface, some web designers charge ahead to implement these latest advances on their websites. Websites should undoubtedly implement web technology that represents true improvement; however, it is important first to determine the merit of new technologies. As a web designer, you should ask the following questions:

- Does the new technology meet currently accepted standards for web development and design?
- What specifically can the new technology do to further the purpose of my website?
- How will implementation of the new technology affect my website's visual appeal, accessibility, and usability?
- What impact will adding this technology have on security and other website elements?
- What are the direct and indirect costs of implementing the new technology?
- How soon will I see a return on investing in this new technology?

After evaluating the impact a new technology will have on your website, you can then make an informed decision about implementing the technology.

Make sure to integrate any new technologies with the design, features, and content of your website. Only add the new technology if it will enhance the experience for website visitors.

TOOLKIT

HTML Tags
See Appendix A for more information on HTML tags and tag modifiers, called **attributes**, and how they are used.

Various tools exist to help you to create webpages and add dynamic content, animation, and interactivity. Successfully using these tools requires varying levels of skill and knowledge. Webpage creation tools include markup languages, Cascading Style Sheets (CSS), scripting languages, text editors, HTML editors, WYSIWYG editors, web templates, and content management systems (CMS).

Markup Languages

A **markup language** is a coding system that uses tags to provide instructions about the appearance, structure, and formatting of a document. The markup languages used to create webpages are HTML, XML, XHTML, and WML.

Q&A

How will HTML 5 differ?
HTML 5 includes tags for creating webpage sections and easily adding video and audio. For more information, use a search engine to search for *HTML 5 new features*.

HTML The **Hypertext Markup Language (HTML)** is a markup language used to create webpages. The most current HTML standard is HTML 4.01, which specifies, among other things, that HTML tags must be in lowercase, surrounded by brackets, and inserted in pairs. HTML 5 is in draft format and has yet to be finalized. A tag defines the target, such as <font>....</font>, and the attribute defines the aspect of the target, such as the color, point size, or weight of a font. Technology standards for the web are set by the World Wide Web Consortium (W3C). The W3C, through an HTML working group, continues to pursue advancements in the HTML standard.

The HTML markup language uses predefined codes called **HTML tags** to define the format and organization of webpage elements. For example, the <html> ....</html> tag pair indicates the beginning and the end of a webpage, respectively. The <b> ....</b> HTML tag pair indicates the text between the tags is set in bold. When a webpage downloads into a browser, the browser reads and interprets the HTML tags to display the webpage with organized and formatted text, images, and links. Figure 1-28 shows the home page of a small online boutique, Flirty Finds, and the underlying HTML code for the page.

Figure 1-28 HTML tags define webpage elements.

DESIGN TIP Even if you are designing a website using a content management system or WYSIWYG editor (both described later in this chapter) that does not require the use of markup codes, it is important to understand the basic principles of markup languages to understand how webpages are coded.

XML   **Extensible Markup Language (XML)** is a markup language that uses both predefined and customized tags to facilitate the consistent sharing of information, especially within large groups. Whereas HTML defines the appearance and organization of webpage content, XML defines the content itself. For example, using XML, a programmer can define the custom tag <serialnum> to indicate that the information following the tag is a product serial number.

XHTML   **Extensible Hypertext Markup Language (XHTML)** combines the features of both HTML and XML. Webpages created using XHTML look better than HTML-coded webpages when viewed on smartphones and other handheld computers. Another benefit is that webpages created with XHTML avoid user-access issues experienced by many users who view webpages using assistive technologies (including screen reader software).

WML   The **Wireless Markup Language (WML)** is an XML-based markup language used to design webpages specifically for mobile browsers. WML uses Wireless Application Protocol (WAP) to allow Internet access by wireless devices.

Exploring a Webpage's Underlying Markup Language

YOUR TURN

1. Start your browser and type the URL of the webpage of your choice in the Address bar.
2. View the webpage's underlying markup tags in a new window. (*Hint*: if you are using a desktop or laptop, right-click or CTRL+ click the webpage, then click View Source or View Page Source. If you are using a mobile browser, you might not be able to view the HTML code, or you might need to install an app to do so.)
3. Scroll the window to view the markup tags.
4. Refer to Appendix B to identify several of the markup tags.
5. Submit your findings in the format requested by your instructor.

Cascading Style Sheets

TOOLKIT

CSS Benefits
See Appendix B for the benefits and guidelines for using CSS.

A **Cascading Style Sheet (CSS)** is a document that uses rules to standardize the appearance of webpage content by defining styles for elements such as font, margins, positioning, background colors, and more. Web designers store CSS specifications for a website in a separate document, called a **style sheet**. A web designer can attach the style sheet to multiple website pages; any changes made to the style sheet automatically apply to the associated webpages. Cascading refers to the order in which the different styles are applied. Chapter 4 discusses CSS in greater detail.

Apply Cascading Style Sheets (CSS) to all pages in a website to ensure that all the pages have the same look.

DESIGN TIP

Scripting Languages

Scripting languages are programming languages used to write short programs, called scripts, that execute in real time at the server or in the web browser when a webpage downloads. **Scripts** make webpages dynamic and interactive by adding such features as multimedia, animation, and forms or by connecting webpages to underlying databases. JavaScript, Active Server Pages (ASP), PHP: Hypertext Preprocessor (commonly abbreviated as PHP), and MySQL are examples of scripting languages.

DESIGN TIP   A web designer might choose to purchase ready-made scripts to perform routine or common functions, such as e-commerce shopping carts, FAQs (frequently asked questions) lists, and banner ad management.

Active content is webpage content created using a scripting language such as JavaScript and ASP. Unfortunately, hackers can use active content to transmit malware. **Malware** is malicious software, including computer viruses and Internet worms, which can infect a single computer or an entire network. Some visitors' web browsers might block active content by default, requiring visitors to instruct their browsers to display the content.

Text and HTML Editors

You can create a simple webpage by typing HTML tags and related text into a document created in a plain text editor, such as Notepad (Figure 1-29), the text editor available with the Windows operating system. A **text editor** is software used to create plain (ASCII) text files. Some web designers or programmers prefer to use an HTML editor to create webpages. An **HTML editor** is a text editor enhanced with special features that easily insert HTML tags and their attributes. HTML-Kit, CoffeeCup (Figure 1-29), BBEdit, and NoteTab are examples of HTML editors.

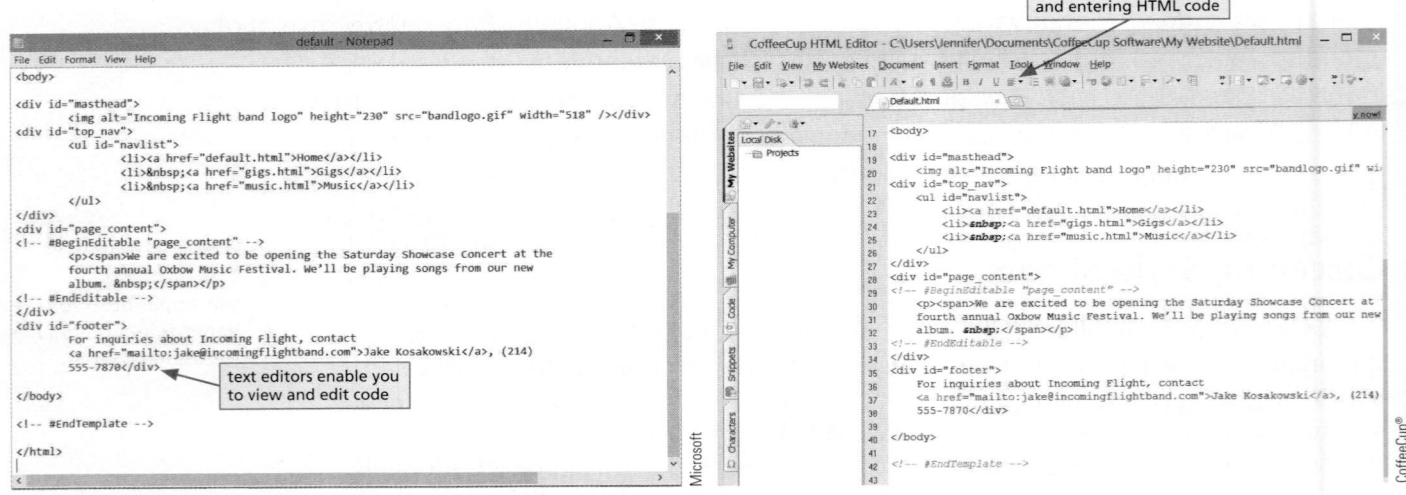

Figure 1-29 Web designers can use text and HTML editors to create webpages.

WYSIWYG Editors

Many web designers use **WYSIWYG editors**, such as Adobe® Dreamweaver®, InnovaStudio® WYSIWYG Editor©, Ephox® EditLive!®, and Microsoft® Expression Web®, to create webpages. WYSIWYG stands for "what you see is what you get." Inserting and formatting text and inserting images or links in a webpage using a WYSIWYG editor is similar to creating a document in a word processor, such as Microsoft Word. Additionally, using a WYSIWYG editor to create webpages eliminates the need to learn a markup language, which can involve complex coding procedures, because the WYSIWYG editor automatically generates the underlying markup language tags as you insert and format text, images, and links. Most WYSIWYG editors also allow you to view and manipulate the underlying HTML code, if desired. Additional benefits of using WYSIWYG editors include the capability to create webpages rapidly.

If you are looking for a professional-strength WYSIWYG editor to create and manage complex, interactive, and animated webpages, either Microsoft® Expression® Web (Figure 1-30) or Adobe® Dreamweaver® would be a good choice. Expression Web and Dreamweaver offer sophisticated website design, publishing, and management capabilities. Software vendors who create WYSIWYG editors often provide additional support and resources at their websites, such as clip art and multimedia, training seminars, user forums, and newsletter subscriptions.

Figure 1-30 Web designers use WYSIWYG editors to create and manage complex, interactive webpages.

Using a WYSIWYG editor presents some challenges.

- Although most WYSIWYG editors have a preview option to simulate how a webpage looks in a browser, in fact, the webpage might look quite different when viewed with various versions of different browsers. Proprietary, nonstandard code generated by some WYSIWYG editors contributes to the inconsistent display. Some critics claim WYSIWYG editors are really WYSINWYG editors — "what you see is *not* what you get."

- A second challenge is that some WYSIWYG editors insert unnecessary code, creating larger, slower-loading webpages.

- Finally, some WYSIWYG editors — especially older versions — might not adhere to the latest markup language standards.

Chapter 2 discusses inconsistent display between web browsers and browser versions in more detail. Even if your WYSIWYG editor includes tools for previewing, accessibility checking, and compatibility checking, you should still perform additional testing using multiple browsers and devices before launching your website.

Web Templates and Content Management Systems

With little or no knowledge of HTML or other web design tools, users can quickly create a website and its webpages using a web template or a content management system.

A **web template** is a predesigned model webpage that you can customize for fast website or webpage creation or updating. Some B2B web hosting websites, such as Yahoo! Small Business and Homestead, provide web templates (in addition to hosting services) that make it quick and easy for a small business owner to create his or her e-commerce website, focusing on the webpage's content rather than on the design details.

Other websites, such as DreamTemplate, TemplateWorld, and TemplateMonster, sell an enormous variety of predesigned web templates for creating personal, organizational/ topical, and commercial websites. Additionally, a number of websites, such as PixelMill or Expression Graphics, sell web templates for a specific WYSIWYG editor, such as Dreamweaver. Finally, many WYSIWYG editors, such as Expression Web (Figure 1-31), also provide web templates for fast website and webpage creation.

Figure 1-31 Web templates are customizable model webpages.

A **content management system (CMS)** is a software system that provides authoring and administrative tools that enable the management of web content development, including authoring, reviewing, editing, and publishing. Content providers working within a CMS use web templates and style sheets to efficiently add or update webpage content. The templates, style sheets, and other frequently used content elements, such as a logo graphic, are stored in a database called a **content repository**. HP Autonomy and Typo3 are two examples of robust content management system software applications.

In addition to creating public webpages with templates or a CMS, website designers can use these technologies to control the look and function of all the pages at internal websites on a company's intranet. An **intranet** is a private network within a large organization or commercial entity that uses Internet and web technologies to share information among only its members, employees, or business partners. Employees who have no web design experience or programming expertise can add webpages or update content on existing webpages on the intranet.

Other web design technologies support communication and collaboration among web users; these include technologies for incorporating blogs, wikis, social networking, social bookmarking, and collaborative workspaces. For example, Microsoft® SharePoint Designer® 2013 is a professional WYSIWYG editor designed for the SharePoint® services environment. You can use SharePoint Designer to create interactive websites that allow employees to collaborate over the web from any location. Employees can use tools such as shared workspaces, blogs, and wikis and manage and share document libraries. Many other technology companies, such as IBM, Cisco, and Jive, also offer technologies designed to provide web-based communication and collaboration.

Web Design Roles

People plan and develop websites of all sizes working independently, in small groups, or as part of a large team. Ongoing communication between web development team members is crucial to the success of any website design project that involves multiple participants. Depending on the circumstances and the complexity of the web development project, you might take on one or more of the following web design roles.

Creative Roles

If you assume a creative role, your focus primarily will be on how the website looks and feels. Jobs in the creative role category include content writer/editor, SEO expert, web designer, artist/graphic designer, and multimedia producer.

As a **content writer/editor** or **SEO expert**, you create and revise the text that visitors read when they visit a website, and choose the links, images, video, or other media that enhances your text content. To achieve your website's purpose, you must write specifically for the web environment and a targeted web audience and take into consideration current SEO practices. An employer frequently looks for a highly creative applicant with demonstrated print and Internet writing experience, including SEO and social media.

As a **web designer**, your primary role is to create webpages that combine text, images, and links using tools such as markup languages; CSS; and text, HTML, and WYSIWYG editors. Your responsibilities also might include graphic design and website setup and maintenance. To be a marketable webpage designer, you must communicate effectively, have a thorough knowledge of webpage design technologies, be familiar with RWD and other techniques for designing for multiple devices, have graphic design talent, and possess some programming skills.

The role of a **web artist/graphic designer** is to create original art such as logos, stylized typefaces, and avatars or props for 3D virtual worlds. This highly creative role demands experience with high-end illustration and image-editing software, such as Adobe Creative Suite, as well as specialty hardware, such as scanners and digital cameras.

As a **multimedia producer,** you design and produce animation, digital video and audio, 2D and 3D models, and other media elements to include in a website. This role demands experience with sophisticated hardware and software, as well as familiarity with art theory and graphic design principles.

Q&A

What is a software developer kit?
A **software development kit (SDK)**, sometimes called a devkit, contains the technology and tools needed to create apps or software to be used on a certain platform or device. SDKs often contain guidelines and rules about the type and format of programs; developers must license the SDK and abide by all guidelines.

Q&A

How can I find a career in web design?
Many entry level positions exist for web designers who have basic skills or interests. Certifications in web design show potential employers you possess some knowledge about web design. For more information about certifications that can help you train for a career in web design, use a search engine to search for web design certifications.

TOOLKIT

Careers in SEO
For more information about SEO careers, see Appendix D.

Technical Roles

If you play a technical role, your focus will be primarily on a website's functionality and security. Examples of types of jobs in the technical role category include web programmer, database developer, and network/security administrator.

A **web programmer** must be highly skilled in scripting languages, such as JavaScript, Active Server Pages (ASP), PHP: Hypertext Preprocessor, and MySQL. These languages are used to create interactive and dynamic webpages. Scripted webpages also handle data from web-based forms, such as those you complete when registering for an account on a website.

A **database developer** must possess the technical skills to plan, create, secure, and maintain databases of varying complexity. A large percentage of website content derives from databases, including storage of customer data and products on e-commerce websites. Database developers need to know how to integrate databases successfully with webpages, and to protect the data from unauthorized access.

A **network/security administrator** ensures the day-to-day functionality of the network and protects it from internal and external threats. Duties and responsibilities include ongoing network inspection, maintenance, and upgrades. An administrator must be aware of security alerts and advisories, protect the network with intrusion-detection software, and have a fully developed plan of action if the security of the network is compromised.

Oversight Roles

If you assume an oversight role, your focus is either on managerial and administrative issues or marketing/customer service. Examples of types of jobs in the oversight role category include tester and web administrator/webmaster.

All websites need to go through a testing process. **Testers** examine the website for usability across different browsers and devices.

The responsibilities of **web administrator** or **webmaster** vary. If he or she is working alone, the web administrator assumes all the roles, including creative, high-tech, and oversight. In an organizational or business setting, the web administrator might oversee a web development team that includes creative and technical roles. A web administrator must have familiarity with databases, markup and scripting languages, content development, creative design, marketing, and hardware.

Sometimes the web administrator takes on the role of the system architect. A **system architect** determines the structure and technical needs required to build, maintain, and expand the website.

Other Web Roles

As technology changes and develops, new roles are created to incorporate these trends. Some jobs that have emerged in recent years include social media expert, e-commerce director, cloud architect, mobile app developer, mobile strategy expert, and user experience (UX) designer.

Exploring Web Design Roles

1. Use a search engine to search for job search websites, such as monster.com.
2. Tap or click one of the job search websites to open it in your browser.
3. Follow the steps on the job search website to search for jobs related to three of the web design roles discussed in this chapter, including one of the newer roles.
4. Summarize your research by listing the job description, skill requirements, salary information, and job location for at least two job postings for each of the three web design roles you would be interested in.
5. Compare the skills needed for the job with your own skill set; what additional training will you need?
6. Submit the results of your domain name search in the format requested by your instructor.

Chapter Review

The Internet is a worldwide public network that links millions of private networks. The highly visual, dynamic, and interactive World Wide Web is a subset of the Internet. The Internet and the web have dramatically changed the communication, education, entertainment, and business practices of millions of people worldwide.

Users can access the Internet and the web over cable television lines or through the Public Switched Telephone Network (PSTN) over dial-up or dedicated lines. Fixed wireless connections are used where DSL or cable access is not available. Laptops and mobile devices, such as tablets and smartphones, access the Internet using mobile wireless connectivity methods. Internet service providers (ISPs) provide Internet connections to individuals, businesses, and other organizations.

A web browser, or browser, is a software program that requests, downloads, and displays webpages. To view a webpage, enter its unique address, called a Uniform Resource Locator (URL), in the browser's Address bar. The two most popular web browsers for desktop and laptop computers are Google Chrome and Microsoft Internet Explorer. Mobile web browsers take into consideration the size of the screen to optimize websites for the device.

Websites can be categorized as personal, organizational/topical, or commercial. Commercial websites include B2C, B2B, and C2C e-commerce; entertainment/news; search tool; and portal websites.

Web design technologies include markup languages, Cascading Style Sheets (CSS), scripting languages, text and HTML editors, WYSIWYG editors, and predesigned web templates and content management systems. Responsive web design techniques enable websites to adapt layout and content for different screen sizes and resolutions.

Depending on resources, developing a website might be the job of an individual person, two or three people, or a large web development team. Although actual titles vary and responsibilities can overlap, web design roles include creative, technical, and oversight, as well as those dealing with new technologies and strategies.

TERMS TO KNOW

After reading the chapter, you should know each of these key terms.

3D virtual world (7)
3G (11)
4G (11)
active content (26)
app (4)
asymmetrical digital subscriber line
   (ADSL) (12)
attributes (24)
blog (6)
blogging (6)
bookmark (4)
browser (13)
browsing the web (3)
business-to-business (B2B) e-commerce (9)
business-to-consumer (B2C) e-commerce (9)
cable television (CATV) line (10)
Cascading Style Sheet (CSS) (25)
cloud computing (4)
collaborative workspace (5)
commercial website (18)
consumer-to-consumer (C2C) e-commerce (9)
content management system (CMS) (28)
content repository (28)
content writer/editor (29)
corporate portal (21)
database developer (30)
dedicated line (12)
dial-up line (12)
digital subscriber line (DSL) (12)
domain name (15)
e-commerce (9)
electronic commerce (9)
email (5)
Extensible Hypertext Markup Language
   (XHTML) (25)
Extensible Markup Language (XML) (25)
favorite (4)
fixed wireless (11)
fractional T-1 line (12)
general consumer portal (21)
hashtag (7)
hit (18)
home page (2)
hot spot (11)
HTML editor (26)
HTML tag (24)
hyperlink (2)
hyperlocal portal (21)
Hypertext Markup Language (HTML) (24)

Hypertext Transfer Protocol (HTTP) (16)
IM chat (5)
index (18)
instant messaging (5)
Integrated Services Digital Network
   (ISDN) (12)
Internet (2)
Internet Relay Chat (IRC) (5)
Internet service provider (ISP) (13)
Internet2 (2)
intranet (28)
IP address (15)
Kbps (10)
keyword (18)
landing page (3)
link (2)
malware (26)
markup language (24)
massively multiplayer online game
   (MMOG) (7)
Mbps (10)
meta tag (18)
metasearch engine (19)
mobile IM (MIM) (5)
mobile wireless (11)
multimedia producer (29)
multiplexing (12)
national ISP (13)
network (2)
network/security administrator (30)
organizational website (17)
personal portal (21)
personal website (16)
portal (21)
protocol (16)
Public Switched Telephone Network
   (PSTN) (11)
regional ISP (13)
responsive web design (RWD) (14)
robot (18)
script (25)
scripting languages (25)
search directory (20)
search engine (18)
search engine optimization (SEO) (19)
SEO expert (29)
shortcut (4)
social bookmarking (6)
social networking (6)

software development kit SDK (29)
spider (18)
streaming media (12)
style sheet (25)
surfing the web (3)
system architect (30)
T-1 line (12)
T-3 line (12)
tag (6)
T-carrier line (12)
tester (30)
text editor (26)
text speak (5)
topical website (17)
top-level domain (TLD) (15)
transfer rate (10)
Uniform Resource Locator (URL) (15)
vertical portal (21)
video blogging (6)

video sharing (6)
virtual meeting space (5)
Web 2.0 (2)
web administrator (30)
web artist/graphic designer (29)
web browser (13)
web programmer (30)
web server (2)
web template (28)
web-based chat (5)
webmaster (30)
webpage (2)
web designer (29)
website (2)
wiki (7)
wireless fidelity (Wi-Fi) (11)
Wireless Markup Language (WML) (25)
World Wide Web (web) (2)
WYSIWYG editor (26)

Complete the **Test Your Knowledge** exercises to solidify what you have learned in the chapter.

TEST YOUR KNOWLEDGE

Matching Terms

Match each term with the best description.

_____ 1. app

_____ 2. browser

_____ 3. webpage

_____ 4. hyperlink

_____ 5. e-commerce

_____ 6. robot

_____ 7. landing page

_____ 8. Search engine optimization (SEO)

_____ 9. content management system (CMS)

a. The page on a website that a visitor sees when they tap or click a link from an ad, search engine result, or social media promotion.

b. A webpage's unique text address.

c. A software program.

d. A business that has a permanent Internet connection and provides temporary connections to individuals and companies for a fee.

e. A web content writing technique that includes using meta tags, descriptive page titles, relevant inbound links from other websites, and clearly written text to increase the likelihood that the webpage will appear high in a search engine's search results list.

_____ 10. Internet service provider (ISP)

_____ 11. Uniform Resource Locator (URL)

_____ 12. style sheet

f. A specifically formatted electronic document that contains text, graphics, and other information and is linked to similar, related documents.

g. A document that a web designer can attach to multiple website pages to ensure design continuity.

h. A word, phrase, or graphical image that connects pages at the same website or pages across different websites.

i. The conducting of a variety of business activities online, including shopping, investing, and the exchange of data and services between business partners.

j. A software program used to request, download, and display webpages.

k. A program that searches the web for new webpages in order to create or update a search index.

l. A software program that provides website authoring and administrative tools.

Short Answer Questions

Write a brief answer to each question.

1. Describe the relationship between the Internet and the World Wide Web.

2. Describe the difference between a search engine and a search directory.

3. Define the following terms: CATV lines, fixed wireless, mobile wireless, dedicated lines, and dial-up Internet access.

4. List and explain SEO techniques and tools.

5. Describe briefly the following tools for creating websites and webpages: HTML, XHTML, text and HTML editors, WYSIWYG editors, web templates, and content management systems (CMS).

6. Identify the primary responsibilities associated with each of the following web design roles: content writer/editor, artist/graphic designer, web designer, web programmer/database developer, and web administrator.

7. Define the following terms: Internet Relay Chat (IRC), instant messaging (IM), blog, wiki, and collaborative workspace.

8. Define the following terms: Uniform Resource Locator (URL), IP address, domain name, top-level domain, and Hypertext Transfer Protocol (HTTP).

Investigate current web design developments with the Trends exercises.

TRENDS

Write a brief essay about each of the following trends, using the web as your research tool. For each trend, identify at least one webpage URL used as a research source. Be prepared to discuss your findings in class.

1 | Responsive Web Design

Responsive web design (RWD) strategies optimize websites to be viewable on multiple device types and screen sizes. Research guidelines and techniques for responsive web design. Submit your findings in the format requested by your instructor.

2 | Social Networking and Bookmarking

How do social networking and bookmarking websites such as Facebook and Digg affect Internet users' personal interactions with the Internet? As a web designer, how can you take advantage of these trends? Visit at least one social networking and social bookmarking website to see how users share information. Identify at least one website that encourages and provides opportunities for users to share content using these technologies.

Challenge your perspective of the web and web design technology with the @Issue exercises.

AT ISSUE

Write a brief essay in response to the following issues, using the web as your research tool. For each issue, identify at least one webpage URL used as a research source. Be prepared to discuss your findings in class.

1 | Impact on Lifestyle

With developments in technology such as smartphones, people are constantly able to stay connected. Whether by phone calls, text messages, alerts from websites about new content, or social networking websites such as Facebook and Twitter, technology provides many distractions. How do these developments enhance daily life? How have they changed daily life from five or ten years ago? What is a negative impact? Discuss the impact of technology on your lifestyle and that of those around you.

2 | Meta Tag Abuse

Web designers use meta tags to enable search engines to easily categorize webpage content. Some web designers use meta tags that reflect popular search trends, but have nothing to do with their webpage content. Use a search engine to search for meta tag abuse. Is including unrelated meta tags unethical? How should search engines deal with websites that misuse meta tags? If possible, find examples of commonly misused meta tags. Discuss your conclusions regarding the ethical use of meta tags.

Use the World Wide Web to obtain more information about the concepts in the chapter with the Hands On exercises.

1 | Explore and Evaluate: A Portal

Browse the web to locate a portal. Follow links from the home page to view at least three related pages at the website. Then answer the following questions; be prepared to discuss your answers in class.

  a. Who owns the website and what is its URL?

  b. Is it a general consumer portal, a vertical portal, or a corporate portal?

  c. Were the home page and related pages visually appealing? If yes, why? If no, why not?

  d. Does the portal have an overall focus?

  e. How easy was it to navigate to related pages using the home page links?

  f. Identify the type of pages you were led to; were they related to the portal website or were they separate websites?

  g. Were you able to identify any advertisements or paid promotional placements?

  h. How long did it take for you to find useful information at the website?

2 | Search and Discover: Mobile Web Browsers

Using a search engine, perform a keyword search to identify popular types of mobile browsers. Read industry expert and user reviews of one mobile browser. Answer the following questions and submit the answers the format requested by your instructor.

  a. Which device(s) can use the mobile browser?

  b. Are the reviews positive? What features do the experts and users like or dislike?

  c. Are there any typical browser features that are missing? If so, what are they?

  d. Does the browser come embedded on a device or can users download it? If it is available for download, is it free?

  e. Is the browser's interface visually appealing? Why or why not?

  f. Are there any identified security risks to the browser?

  g. Do you have any experience using this browser? If so, describe your experience.

  h. Would you use or recommend this mobile browser? Why or why not?

Work collaboratively to reinforce the concepts in the chapter with the Team Approach exercises.

1 | Compare WYSIWYG and HTML Editors

Pair up with one or more classmates and work as a team to determine the benefits of using WYSIWYG editors and HTML editors. One team member or group should research the benefits of WYSIWYG editors; the remaining team member(s) should investigate advantages of HTML editors.

a. Using a search engine, find at least three sources listing advantages or disadvantages of your chosen editor type.

b. Answer the following questions:

- What qualifications are necessary to use the editor?
- What are the two main advantages to using the editor?
- What are two disadvantages to using the editor?

c. Find three examples of your chosen type of editor.

d. Present your findings to your other team member(s). As a group, determine which you would choose.

e. Submit your findings in the format requested by your instructor.

2 | Team and Client Communication Challenges

Join with four or five classmates to establish a mock web development team. Assume the web development team has been hired by a client to plan and create a B2C e-commerce website. Each team member should choose one or more of the creative, high-tech, or oversight roles discussed in this chapter. Then use the web to research current challenges that individuals in each role might face, and identify potential resolutions to those challenges. Next, as a team, brainstorm communication issues that might arise among team members and between the team members and the client. Identify ways to resolve any potential communication issues. Finally, prepare a detailed report describing potential design and communication challenges and the team's approach to handling them. Submit the report to your instructor and be prepared to present your report to the class.

CASE STUDY

Apply the chapter concepts to the ongoing development process in web design with the Case Study.

The Case Study is an ongoing development process using the concepts, techniques, and Design Tips presented in each chapter.

Background Information

You now will begin the process of designing your own personal, organizational/topical, or commercial website. As you progress through the chapters in this book, you will learn how to use design as a tool to create effective webpages and websites. At each chapter's conclusion, you will receive instructions for completing another segment of the ongoing design process.

The following are suggestions for website topics. Choose one of these topics or determine your own. Select a topic that you find interesting, feel knowledgeable about, or are excited about researching.

1. Personal website
   * Share a hobby or special interest: music, remote control cars, mountain biking, fantasy sports, or other
2. Organizational/topical website
   * Increase support and membership for: Habitat for Humanity, Red Cross, or a campus organization
   * Promote awareness of: health and fitness, endangered species, or financial assistance for college
3. Commercial website
   * Start a new business: childcare or dog walking, or expand an existing business with a web presence
   * Sell a service: tutoring, web design, graphic design, or home maintenance
   * Sell a product: DVD labels, workout programs or gear, or beauty/boutique products

The evaluation of your completed website, which will consist of 5 to 10 webpages, will be based primarily on the application of good web design concepts.

Chapter 1 Assignment

Follow Steps 1–6 to complete a plan for developing your website.

1. Identify which type of website you will design — personal, organizational/topical, or commercial. Write a brief paragraph describing the website's overall purpose and its targeted audience. Create a name for your website.
2. List at least three general goals for your website. You will fine-tune these goals into a mission statement in a subsequent chapter.
3. List elements in addition to text — photos, music, animation, and so forth — that you could include on your website to support your general goals.
4. Identify the design tools you expect to use to develop your website.
5. Identify an available domain name and URL for your website. Research to make sure it is available.
6. Submit your findings in the format requested by your instructor. Be prepared to discuss your plan with the class.

2 | Web Publishing Fundamentals

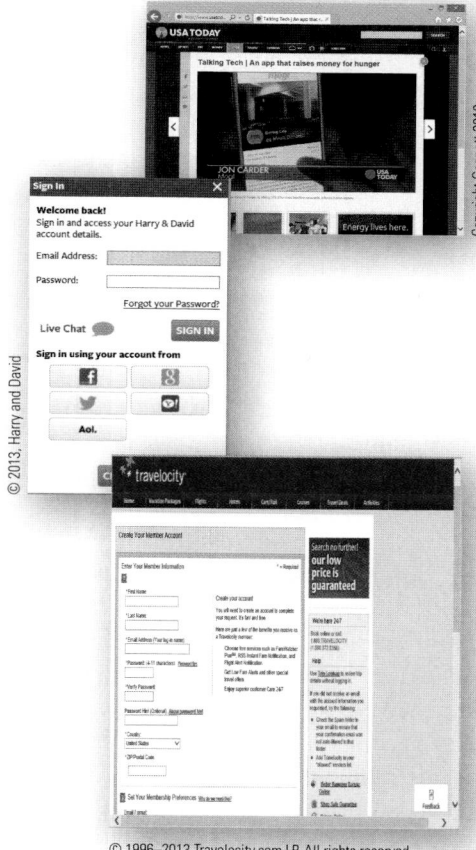

Introduction

Chapter 1 introduced you to the Internet and the web and design tools used to create webpages. In this chapter, you learn about the advantages of web publishing and discover the basic design principles behind publishing a successful website. The chapter discusses responsive web design, adding interactivity to your website, writing for the web, and effective uses of color and layout. Finally, you learn about the technical, legal, privacy, accessibility, and usability issues surrounding web publishing.

Objectives

After completing this chapter, you will be able to:

1. Describe the advantages of web publishing

2. Discuss basic web design principles

3. Define the requirements for writing for the web

4. Explain the use of color as a web design tool

5. Identify web publishing issues

Advantages of Web Publishing

"Is print dead?" Content publishers have been debating this question for years, without a clear consensus. No one can argue that today many people are turning to electronic delivery of information over printed books, magazines, and newspapers. As more and more people purchase ebook readers, tablets, and smartphones, web designers must embrace responsive web design to make content accessible on multiple device types and screen sizes. Print publishing has its benefits. It enables you to share and distribute publications without relying on access to technology. Additionally, some people prefer the feel of the weight of a book, magazine, or newspaper in their hands. Despite these benefits, web publishing has many advantages over print including currency, connectivity, interactivity, cost, and delivery.

The Currency Advantage

Whether you are planning your next semester's classes on your laptop, researching movie times and locations using a tablet, or checking the weather from your smartphone, you expect that the web content you are accessing is current. A print publication cannot reflect more current information without being reprinted and distributed, whereas web publishers can update content instantaneously and continually.

The web's **currency advantage** lies in the ability to quickly and inexpensively update webpages. For example, suppose the chief executive officer (CEO) of a company suddenly leaves the company and the company's board of directors wants to assure customers of a smooth transition to new management. In just a few minutes and at a very low cost, the company's web administrator could update or create a new webpage that includes a press release explaining the change in management, along with a photograph and biography of the new CEO. The designer then could publish or republish the webpage to the company's website, and submit the content through its Twitter feed, Facebook page, RSS (Really Simple Syndication), or other apps or services, where it appears in users' inboxes or news feeds. Using its website and connectivity tools, the company can communicate with customers instantly, and by initiating the exchange of information, the company increases its reputation for trustworthiness.

Many websites provide updates on an hourly or daily basis. News websites and blogs often post updates on a real-time basis as stories develop. For example, a news website may have several reporters using web tools to post updates, stories, videos, photos, or interviews of a swiftly unfolding news event. As noted in Chapter 1, news organizations exploit the web's currency advantage by hosting popular, high-traffic websites, such as washingtonpost .com or USATODAY.com (Figure 2-1), to provide continually updated weather, stock market quotes, and stories about newsworthy events — seconds after the events occur.

Website visitors expect that websites providing sports, news, and weather information or e-commerce opportunities offer timely content presented in a fresh, appealing manner. If visitors do not find timely content at these types of websites, they are likely to leave, perhaps finding what they need on a competitor's website. Since these websites rely on high traffic to sell advertisements or the company's products, currency is one of the more important goals of web publishing.

DESIGN TIP Although your website might not need as frequent updating as a news-oriented or B2C website, you still must take care to keep the website's content up to date, and take advantage of connectivity tools to communicate and interact with website visitors.

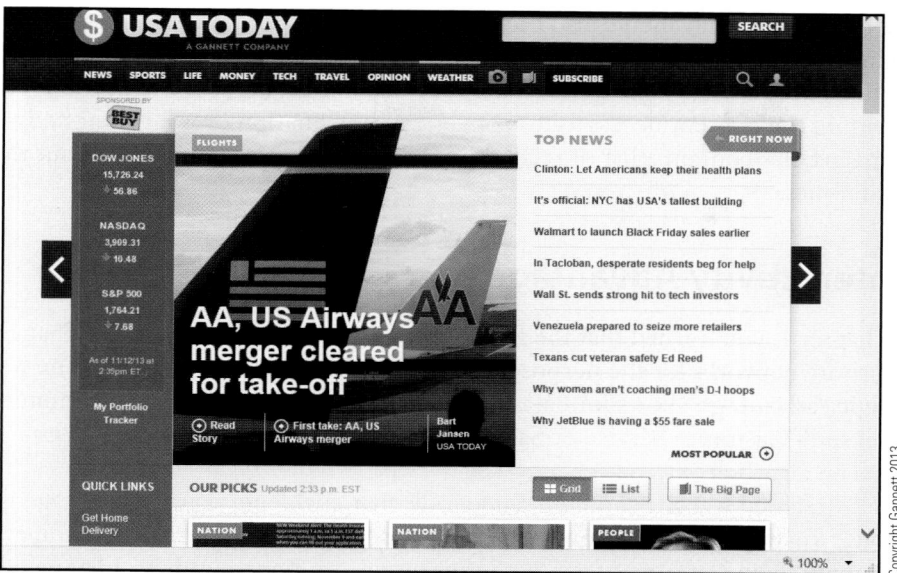

Figure 2-1 High-traffic news-oriented websites exploit the web's currency advantage.

The Connectivity Advantage

Sharing a story, press release, article, or blog post from a website is an instantaneous process. Using content **aggregators** that display preferred content from several sources such as RSS feeds, social networking tools such as Facebook pages and Twitter feeds, and social news websites such as Digg or StumbleUpon, a website's administrators instantly can alert followers to new content. In addition, the same tools can allow those users to share links to the content with their friends and followers, spreading the news quickly, as the article from USA Today shown in Figure 2-2 illustrates. Unlike photocopying a news article or book content, sharing a link to the original source does not violate copyright laws. The web's **connectivity advantage** is the ability to instantaneously distribute and share content.

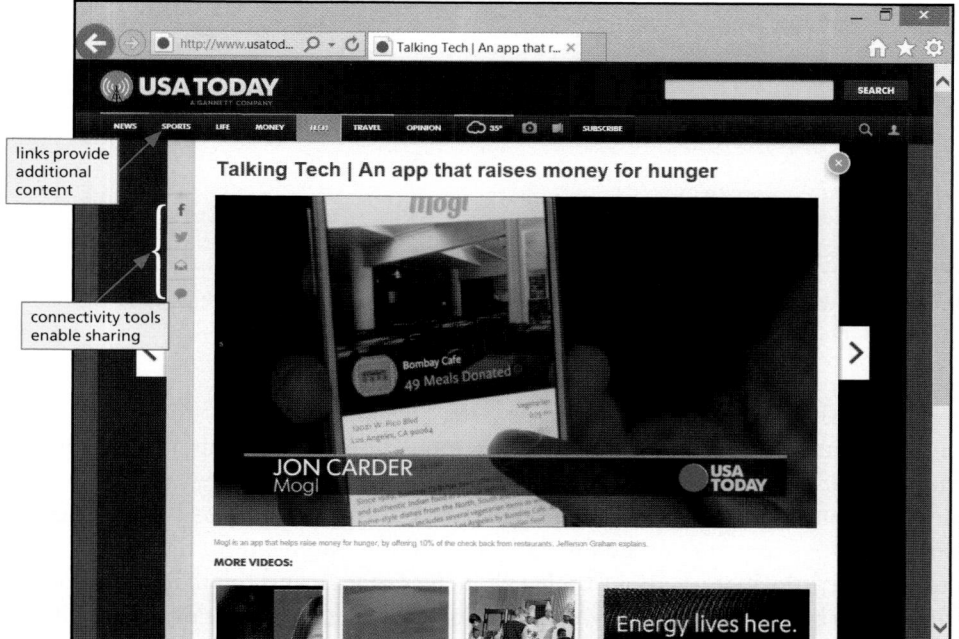

links provide additional content

connectivity tools enable sharing

Figure 2-2 Web articles can include tools for sharing the content and links to supplemental information.

Do all websites contain continually updated content?
No. Some websites focus on content that might not change over time, for example websites that publish biographies or content based on research papers. The primary concerns of visitors to these types of websites are author credibility and content accuracy.

The connectivity advantage also can streamline the writing process. A web article can include links directly in the content to additional resources or background. This enables the author to keep articles short, which helps to make them more attractive to read, while still providing the content necessary to convey the information or tell the story. In addition, many articles contain a list of related links to other stories or articles about the same or related topics.

The Interactivity Advantage

In Chapter 1, you learned that the Internet is a worldwide public network that connects smaller private networks for the purpose of sharing data and other resources. The web's **interactivity advantage** allows for data and resource sharing that enables communication with a website's Customer Service or Sales Department or that allows users to post comments on an article.

A well-designed website should include tools that enable its visitors to engage in interactive, two-way communication with the website's publisher. At a minimum, every website should include a page of contact information — phone numbers, mailing addresses, physical location addresses, and email addresses. To encourage interactivity and communication, a website should include links to its blog, Twitter feed, or Facebook page, and enable users to share website content with others. Figure 2-3 shows the contact page for Nike's website, which includes several methods by which a user could contact Nike.

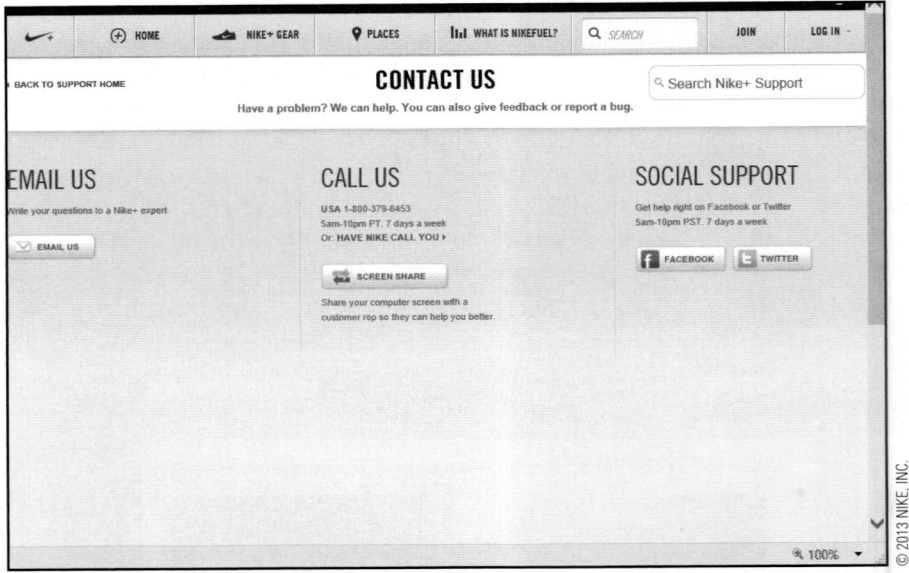

© 2013 NIKE, INC.

Figure 2-3 A website's contact page encourages communication between the website and its visitors.

Depending on the purpose of its website, a company could use other tools to promote interactivity and communication. For example, blogs are an important internal and external tool for promoting interactivity and communication between companies and their vendors, customers, and other business partners. Companies such as Ballard Designs (Figure 2-4) host blogs that encourage interactivity and communication. Blogs help a company to provide information about their products, services, and related news topics that may be of interest to customers. By encouraging customers to reply or comment to blog posts or share with others, a company can help build a community of customers.

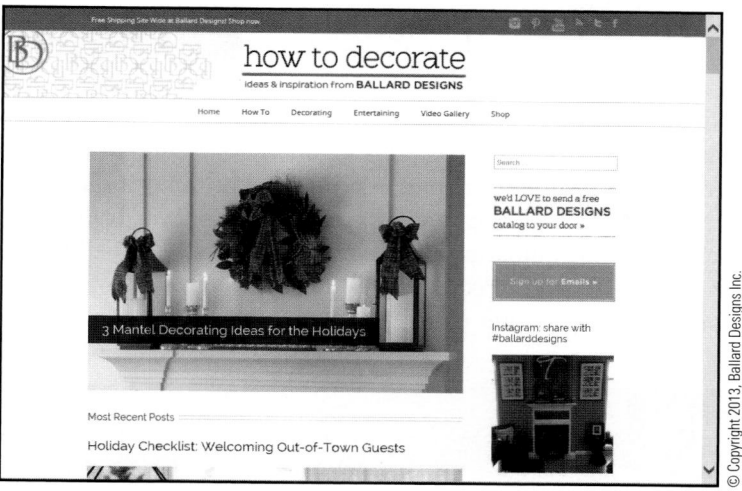

Figure 2-4 Blogs are an important communication tool for businesses.

Many websites, such as e-commerce websites, encourage website visitors to create accounts. Visitors create website accounts so they can order products quickly and easily, participate in surveys, sign up for newsletters, request sales or customer support, register for events, or return products. Many websites enable users to sign in by providing the website with access to the user's personal Facebook or other social networking profile, as illustrated in Figure 2-5, which shows a window from the Harry and David website. The advantage of using your social networking profile to sign in is that you can save time by not having to retype the information. Other benefits can include the ability to share posts about your purchases or receive information about sales promotions. You should always read the fine print when agreeing to share your social networking profile with a business. Often the terms enable the company to access your posts, friends list, and profile information, which could violate your privacy.

Q&A

Do other advantages exist to using social networking and other interactivity tools?
Yes. Website administrators rely on data such as the number of users who commented on, shared, viewed, or "liked" webpage content to gauge success. This type of data is called analytics. To learn more, use a search engine to search for *web analytics*.

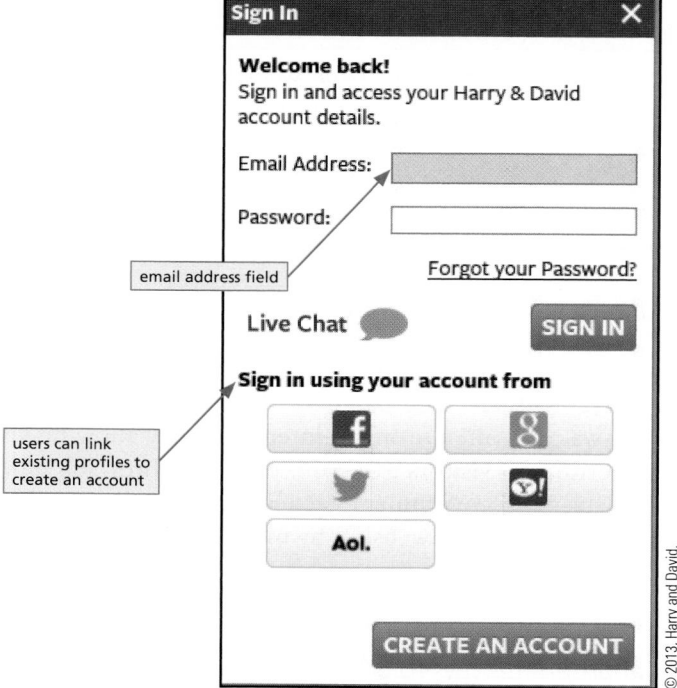

Figure 2-5 Setting up an account on a website can streamline shopping and give the user access to sales and coupons.

Companies also use **web-based forms** to gather contact information and preferences from website visitors. Figure 2-6 shows an example of a form from the Travelocity website. Common web-based form elements include text boxes, check boxes, option buttons, drop-down list boxes, and a Submit or Send button. To use a web-based form, a visitor simply types information, clicks a check box, selects an option button, or selects an item from a drop-down list and then clicks the Send or Submit button to send the information to the website. Forms can be just a few questions, or broken out into several pages to make entering and validating the data easier. WYSIWYG editors and web hosting services provide tools to create forms efficiently. Working with web-based forms is discussed in more detail in Chapter 6.

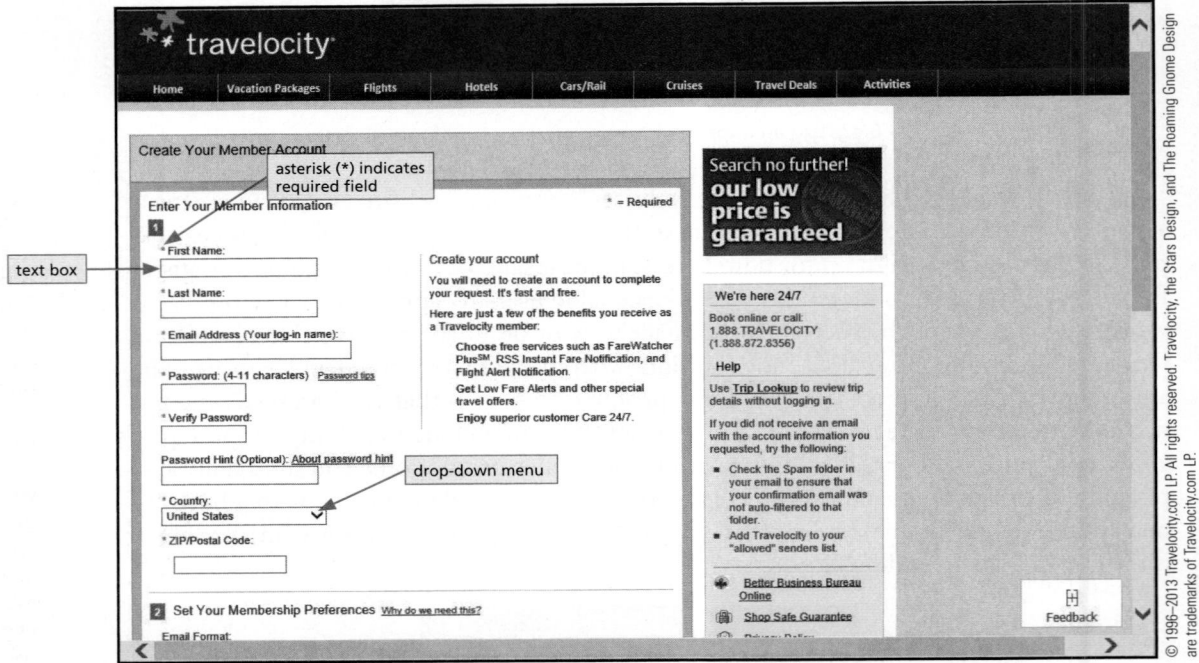

Figure 2-6 Web-based forms are used to gather information from website visitors.

DESIGN TIP After you publish your website, plan to review the website's content for credibility, accuracy, and timeliness on a regular basis and update the content as necessary.

Websites of all types promote interactivity and communication using methods beyond traditional contact pages, blogs, and web-based forms. News-oriented websites, such as CNN.com and FOXNews.com, often promote interactivity by allowing visitors to comment on articles or by permitting visitors to submit their own breaking news stories and images. Some businesses and government agencies, such as the Small Business Administration, promote interactivity at their websites by offering chat rooms visitors can join to discuss topics in real time.

DESIGN TIP Build into your website appropriate ways to promote interactivity, such as a contact page, web-based form, or blog.

Exploring Currency and Interactivity

1. Use a search engine to search for examples of the following websites: news, e-commerce, and blog.
2. Open each website in a different tab.
3. Explore each website and answer the following questions:
   a. Is the website's content current, or does it appear to be outdated? Give examples to support your answer.
   b. What tools, such as forms or comments, does the website use to promote interactivity and communication?
   c. What social media tools are included in the website to promote connectivity?
4. Submit your results in the format requested by your instructor.

The Cost Advantage

Compared with print, updating web content is more cost effective. However, the costs associated with developing and maintaining a website can be quite expensive. A website budget may include the following costs:

- Web design
- Multimedia development
- Website hosting
- Domain name registration
- Promotional services

Publishing web content has some **cost advantages** over print. Print costs include purchasing paper and ink, printing, and distribution. Unlike print, the cost of publishing web content does not vary based on its length, color composition, or design complexity. Whereas each printed piece incurs an individual cost, a website's expenses are not affected by the number of visitors. To add interest to your webpages and break up text, you will want to add images or other multimedia. You may be able to find free downloads for photos, animations, video, and sound clips for use at your website; however, you might incur some additional cost to prepare these types of content elements for the best display and quality. You also can purchase reasonably priced photos and multimedia elements.

As with print, the complexity of the colors and layout of your web content may increase the design costs. The technological specifications of the web mean that it does not matter whether your design is a simple one-color text piece or a sophisticated piece with hundreds of colors — the cost to publish on the web is the same. Note, however, that whenever you incorporate multimedia in your webpages, the pages generally are larger and your website might require more storage space. You also might be limited by the amount of web server space your website hosting service provides or by budget constraints if you must lease extra web server space to support your website's multimedia elements. For example, a website hosting service might limit server space for website files to 5 MB for a flat monthly fee; if you need more space, you might incur additional cost. Chapter 6 discusses adding multimedia to a website in more detail.

Q&A

Where can I find free photographs? Using professional photographs can enhance your webpage content. Websites such as www.flickr.com and www.morguefile.com allow photographers to post photos for use, for little or no cost. No matter where you get your photos, remember always to give credit to the artist. Cost-free does not mean copyright free — the artist still owns the rights to the images, even if you do not have to pay for them.

The Delivery Advantage

The web's **delivery advantage** enables the fast and inexpensive distribution of published information over the Internet and the web. For instance, imagine that as a volunteer for your community hospital, you need to publicize the upcoming health fair. Because you want to get the information out quickly to as many people as possible, you use your website and connectivity tools to reach current and former patients, community members, and medical professionals. You can use the web and the Internet to promote the webpage containing information about the health fair in many ways, including:

- Adding a link to the event to the hospital website's calendar.
- Sending email messages with a link to the health fair brochure at your website to last year's participants or other potentially interested individuals or organizations.
- Posting links to the website on your Twitter feed and Facebook page and creating ads or promotions using social media.
- Creating a landing page specifically for the health fair.
- Querying related websites, such as the community Chamber of Commerce or local health and fitness clubs, to ask them to include a link to the health fair webpage on their website, or to email their database of contacts.

These methods cost very little, and the news about the event would be available almost immediately. Distributing the same content using print takes more time because the content must go through a printing process, then be distributed using the mail or by hanging posters.

DESIGN TIP Use your website to expand upon your printed content. For example, if you have a large event to promote, mail a postcard directing users to the landing page for the event. Postcards cost less than letters to print and mail. Provide minimal details on the postcard, and have participants sign up for the event online to save the costs of printing and sending registration materials.

Basic Web Design Principles

Q&A

Do web design principles change? Yes. As new web technologies, programming languages, apps, and tools develop, so do the current principles of web design. For more information about the most updated web design principles, use a search engine to search for *web design principles* and filter or sort the results to show only the most recent articles.

Webpages should be visually attractive, convey a powerful message, and leave a distinct impression. Responsive web design ensures the content is viewable on multiple devices and screen sizes. Successful web publications that accomplish these objectives combine creativity with the basic design principles of balance and proximity, contrast and focus, and unity and visual identity.

Balance and Proximity

In design, **balance** is the harmonious arrangement of elements. Balance, or the absence of balance, can significantly impact the effectiveness of a webpage to express its message. Web elements in a **symmetrical** arrangement appear centered or even; symmetry suggests a conservative, safe, and peaceful atmosphere. The Art Institute of Chicago home page (Figure 2-7) illustrates a symmetrical arrangement of web elements. **Asymmetrical**, or off balance, design creates an energetic mood. Asymmetrical designs typically do not adapt well to mobile devices. Responsive web design guidelines recommend using grids to lay out content so that you can easily move, resize, and reorder it to fit the device.

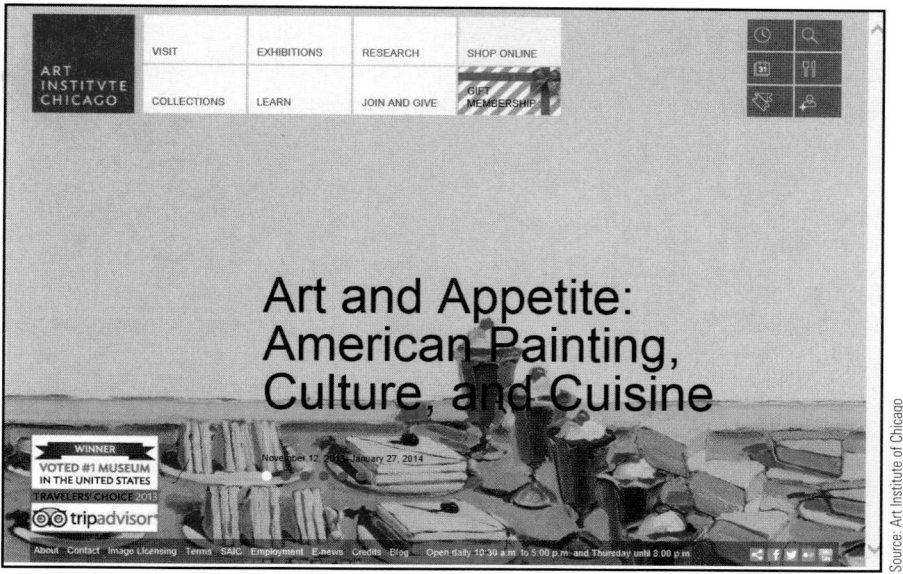

Source: Art Institute of Chicago

Figure 2-7 Responsive web design techniques recommend symmetrical, or balanced, layout.

Proximity, or closeness, is strongly associated with balance. Proximity, as applied to webpages, means that you place related elements close to each other. For example, position a caption near an image, an organization's name near its logo, and headings and subheadings near related body copy. Doing so visually connects elements that have a logical relationship, making your webpages more organized. Elements on the Martha Stewart home page (Figure 2-8) illustrate proximity: images appear above or to the left of explanatory text or captions, and headings and subheadings appear above related links.

The empty space surrounding text and images, called **white space** in design, also can define proximity and help organize webpage elements, eliminate clutter, and make content more readable, as illustrated in the Martha Stewart home page.

© 2013 Martha Stewart Living Omnimedia, Inc.

Figure 2-8 Place related webpage elements in proximity to each other and allow sufficient white space.

 **DESIGN TIP**

You can create white space by adding line breaks, paragraph returns, paragraph indents, and space around tables and images. Responsive web design principles allow for minimal white space for websites viewed on smartphones and other devices with small screens.

Contrast and Focus

Contrast is a mix of elements to stimulate attention. Contrast also establishes a **focal point**, which is a dominating segment of the webpage that directs visitors' attention to a center of interest or activity. What do you want your website's visitors to focus on and to remember — a company name, a tag line or logo, a powerful photo, or some combination of these? Determine first what element on your webpage is the most important, and then use contrast to establish that dominance visually.

 **DESIGN TIP**

Using a slide show or gallery enables you to have one central focal point with content that changes automatically or as a result of user intervention. You can feature several articles at once in a small amount of space.

Pages that lack contrast, such as those with a solid block of text or a jumble of competing elements, are uninteresting or confusing. You can create contrast by using text styles, color choices, element size, and more. For example, setting a company name in a larger typeface distinguishes it from subheads and body text, which typically are a smaller typeface. Similarly, a dark background with light, brightly colored text might draw more attention than a cream background with black text. By varying the size of webpage elements, you can establish a visual hierarchy of information that will show your visitors which elements are most important. Element size and typeface on The University of Virginia home page (Figure 2-9) create contrast and establish a focal point for the page.

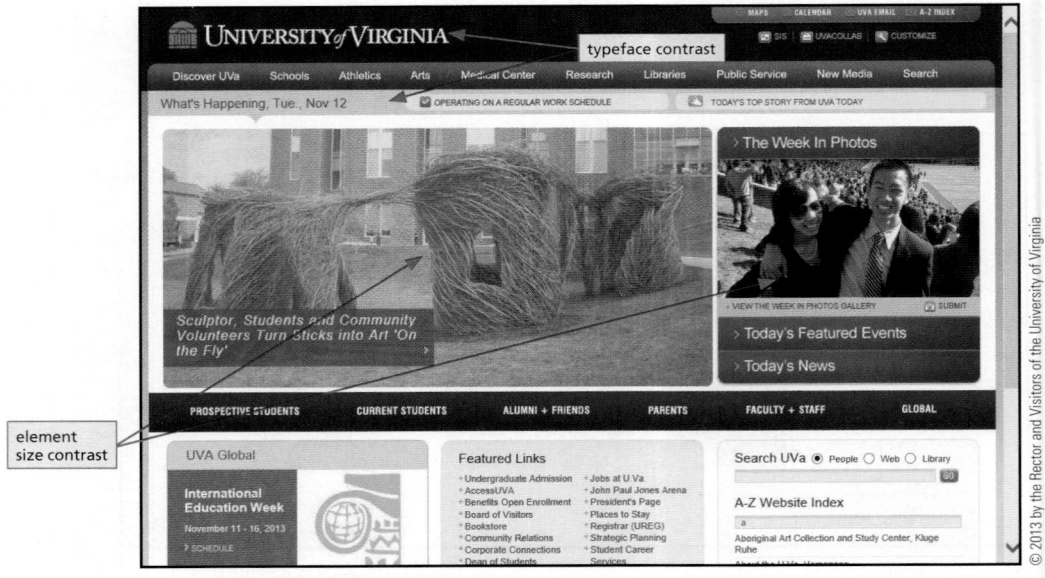

Figure 2-9 Use contrast on a webpage to stimulate attention and establish the page's focal point.

Unity and Visual Identity

All the pages at a website must have **unity**, or a sense of oneness or belonging, to create and maintain the website's **visual identity** — the combination of design elements identified with the website and its publisher. Especially important to businesses, visual identity must be consistent, not only throughout a website, but also with the business's TV or radio ads, or print publications, such as brochures, business cards, and letterheads.

Creating and maintaining a visual identity is an important aspect of branding a business or organization. A general definition of the term **brand** is the assurance or guarantee that a business or organization offers to its customers. Businesses and other large organizations take care to develop and reinforce their own brand over time, generally with the guidance of marketing professionals. Some brands, such as Ford Motor Company (assurance of quality vehicles), are decades old; others, such as Starbucks (guarantee of upscale coffee products) are relatively new.

The consistent application of **branding specifications** for color, images, and text applied to all of the entity's media strengthens and promotes the brand. Examples of design elements that promote unity, create a visual identity, and contribute to branding an entity both in print media and on webpages include logos, fonts, colors, and tag lines. A **tag line** is a concise statement that a consumer readily associates with a business, organization, or product. An example of a tag line is Southwest Airlines' "You are now free to move about the country."

To help promote unity, visual identity and branding, web designers use consistent placement and repetition of elements, such as the company name, logo, and tag line, and application of the same color scheme across all pages at a website, as shown at the Subway website (Figure 2-10). Chapter 4 discusses unity, visual identity, and branding in more detail.

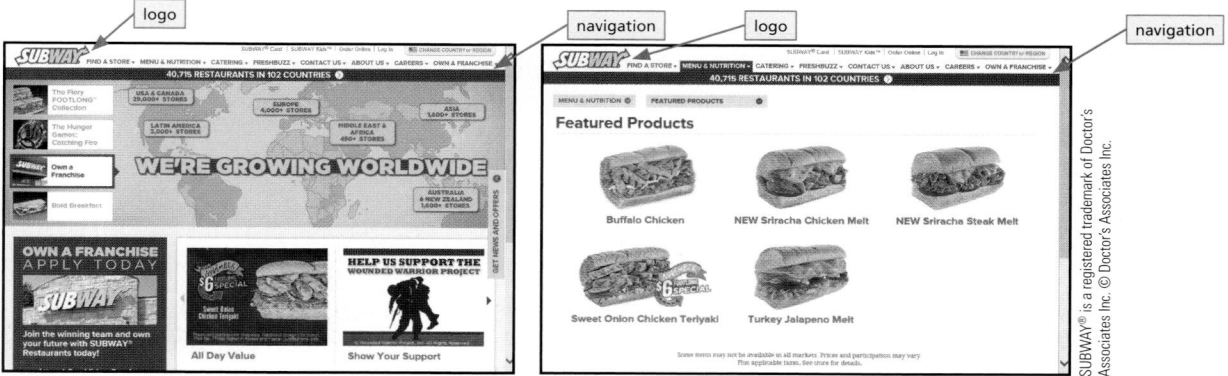

Figure 2-10 Consistent placement and repetition of elements and application of a color scheme across all pages at a website promotes unity and visual identity.

Alignment is the placement of objects in fixed or predetermined positions, rows, or columns. Applying consistent alignment will ensure that your webpages have a coherent, structured presentation. Visitors to a webpage expect page elements to line up; for example, the text in a photo caption should line up with the left edge of the photo beneath which it appears. If elements on a webpage do not align, the page will look jumbled and be perceived as inconsistent and unprofessional. When the elements on a webpage align horizontally, they appear consistently to the left, right, or centered. When webpage elements align vertically, they are also top-justified, assisting in readability and ensuring an organized appearance, as shown on the Office Depot home page (Figure 2-11). As previously mentioned, the use of grids for responsive web design layout ensures pages will adapt to different screen sizes and device types.

Figure 2-11 Horizontal and vertical alignment of webpage elements ensures a consistent presentation and increases readability.

 **DESIGN TIP** Web designers use grids and horizontal layouts, as well as simplified typography, single-page layouts, and an 'app-like' interface as part of responsive web design.

Writing for the Web

In general, when writing for the web, use language that is straightforward, contemporary, and geared toward an educated audience. Avoid overly promotional language that might not appeal to visitors and avoid the use of industry jargon or slang. With responsive web design a visitor might only see a list of headings and article titles on a webpage, which they click to expand articles they wish to read. Use wording in headings that clearly communicates the content of a webpage or section. Avoid misleading or clever headings that might confuse or annoy visitors. Be cautious regarding the use of humor. Small doses of humor correctly interpreted can enliven content and entertain. Remember, though, humor can be taken out of context and might be misunderstood or misinterpreted, especially if your audience includes visitors whose first language is not English.

To help web users more easily find your website, carefully consider the text that you place in headings to use search engine optimization techniques to their best advantage. To learn more about SEO techniques for headings, see Appendix D.

DESIGN TIP

Whatever the particular circumstances of a user's web needs, an interesting webpage competes with distractions such as conversations, ringing phones, and time constraints. Consequently, website visitors generally scan webpage text quickly to find useful information that is accurate and current, easy to read, and well organized.

To keep webpage text succinct, place information that is not crucial, such as historical backgrounds or related topics, on linked subsidiary pages, either within the content as linked text, or as a separate link or list of links at the bottom or side of an article. For example, in a business news article about a company, you can include links to the company's website, the NASDAQ website to show the company's current stock price, and a related story from a previous day.

DESIGN TIP

Accuracy and Currency

When writing or curating content for your website, confirm its accuracy using reliable sources. Refer to respected subject experts, professional organizations, trade journals, and other resources with a proven track record. Typographical and spelling errors can embarrass you and diminish your website's credibility. If you publish your webpages with such errors, your visitors might question how closely you checked your content and how committed you are to your purpose. To avoid these types of errors, perform spelling and grammar checks by writing the text content for your webpages in a word processor, content management system, or WYSIWYG editor that includes proofing tools. Proofread your content, and then ask at least one other person to review it before you add the text to a webpage.

As noted earlier in this chapter, after you publish your website, you must keep the content on your webpages current. To demonstrate the currency and freshness of your website's content, you can add the last updated date and/or time to your webpages.

Establish credibility for your website by providing accurate, verifiable content. Show content currency by including the date the content was last updated.

DESIGN TIP

Scannability

Most website visitors, especially those using mobile devices, prefer to quickly scan webpages for useful information, not read long passages of onscreen text. Using the **chunked text** technique, break webpage text into small sections with headings, subheadings, and bulleted lists that adequately but concisely cover the topic. For example, consider the same information presented in Figure 2-12 as dense paragraph text and then as chunked text. The chunked text is much easier to scan, and will adapt better to devices with smaller screens, as the content under the headings and subheadings can be hidden until a website visitor clicks on it.

Dense Paragraph Text Example

When writing or curating content for your website, confirm its accuracy using reliable sources. Refer to respected subjec[t]... professional organizations, trade journals, and other reso[urces]... proven track record.

Typographical and spelling errors can embarrass you[r]... ish your website's credibility. If you publish your webpag[e]... errors, your visitors might question how closely you che[ck]... content and how committed you are to your purpose.

To avoid these types of errors, perform spelling and [grammar]... checks by writing the text content for your webpages in [a word]... processor, content management system, or WYSIWYG [editor]... that includes proofing tools. Proofread your content, an[d ask]... at least one other person to review it before you add the [content to your]... webpage.

Chunked Text Example

To ensure accurate and credible webpages:

- Confirm content accuracy with reliable sources.
- Refer to respected subject experts and others with a proven track record.
- Use proofing tools to check for spelling and grammatical errors
- Ask at least one person to proofread content

© 2015 Cengage Learning

Figure 2-12 Chunked text is much easier for readers to scan online than dense paragraph text.

DESIGN TIP

Website visitors typically scan online text looking for useful information instead of reading the text word for word. Chunking text allows your website visitors to quickly scan your webpages. This improves usability and also makes your page content more easily readable on a mobile device.

Q&A

Is chunked text appropriate for all webpage text?
In some situations, a webpage might contain lengthy text articles that are intended to be printed and read offline. In these situations, you should present the text in its entirety and not chunked.

Q&A

How can you ensure your web content will be well-received and not offend readers?
Netiquette is a list of guidelines that help web users and developers to interact and create content. Netiquette rules govern the use of certain words, phrases, and formatting. For more information, use a search engine to search for *netiquette*.

Remember that visitors to your website will likely scan your webpages rather than taking the time to read every word. Also, be aware that many website users assume that colored or underlined text represents a hyperlink. To ensure **scannability**, you should write your webpage content with the following guidelines in mind:

- Use chunked text, where appropriate, to create short paragraphs and bulleted lists.
- When it is necessary to write longer paragraphs, begin each paragraph with a topic sentence that summarizes the general idea of the whole paragraph. A visitor who scans only the first sentences of each paragraph will still get the overall picture of your webpage's purpose.
- Avoid using colored text or underlines for emphasis because they are associated with links. Be consistent with how you format links so website visitors can identify links easily.
- Use uppercase characters carefully because they can reduce scannability. Some visitors might also consider text in uppercase characters to be the equivalent of shouting.

Scannability is also affected by the choice of navigational elements, color scheme choices, and fonts. You learn more about these topics in Chapters 4 and 5.

Organization

The **inverted pyramid style** is a classic news writing style that places a summary (or conclusion) first, followed by details, and then any background information. Web content writers use the inverted pyramid style by placing summary chunked text on the home page and adding links to subsidiary pages containing related details and background information.

Sometimes using chunked text for scannability is inappropriate; for example, for a press release, where it is necessary to retain the press release's dense text paragraphs. Writing the press release text in the inverted pyramid style is particularly useful in helping visitors quickly understand the text's general idea. Figure 2-13 illustrates the format of the inverted pyramid.

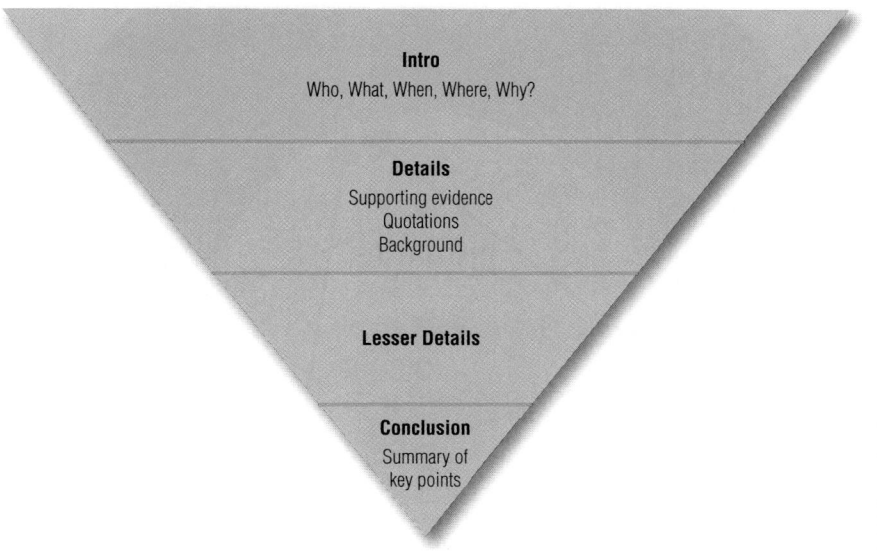

Figure 2-13 The inverted pyramid style is a classic newswriting style.

When writing in the inverted pyramid style, summary text should include the "who, what, when, where, and why" of the topic. Avoid transitional words or phrases, such as "similarly," "as a result," or "as stated previously."

DESIGN TIP

Color as Web Design Tool

Color can be a powerful design tool for creating attractive, effective websites. The use of color helps to set a website's mood as well as provide contrast between page elements. To use color as a design tool effectively, you must understand color basics: the color wheel, how monitors display colors, and visitors' expectations for color on the web.

The Color Wheel

A basic tool for understanding color as a design tool is the **color wheel**, shown in Figure 2-14, which can help you choose effective and appealing color combinations. The basis of the color wheel is the set of **primary colors** — red, yellow, and blue. The **secondary colors** — orange, green, and purple — result from combining two primary colors. The green, blue, and purple colors are **cool colors**, which suggest tranquility and detachment. The yellow, orange, and red colors are **warm colors**, which are associated with activity and power. **Complementary colors** are those directly opposite each other on the wheel. A combination of complementary colors creates a significant amount of contrast. Conversely, a combination of colors adjacent to each other generates significantly less contrast.

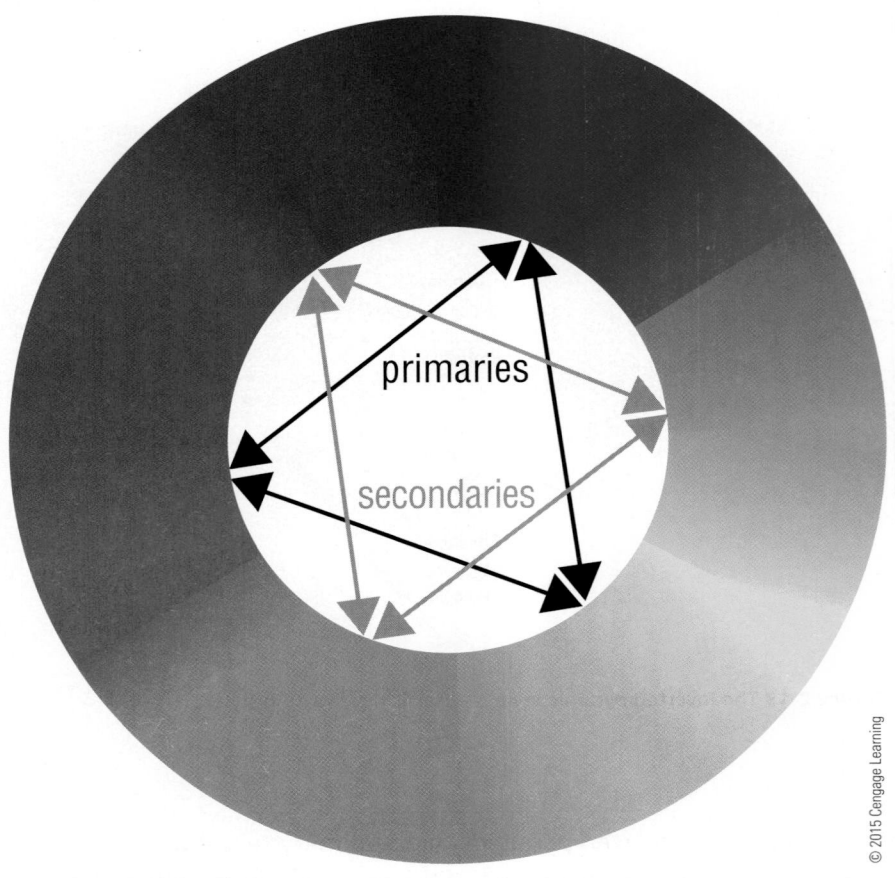

© 2015 Cengage Learning

Figure 2-14 The color wheel consists of primary and secondary colors.

The RGB Color System

Computer monitors project color using the **RGB color system**, which combines channels of red, green, and blue light. The light from each channel is emitted in various levels of intensity. These levels are **values** and measure from 0 to 255. To create colors, specify different values from the channels. For example, combining values 255 (red), 102 (green), and 153 (blue) produces a dusty rose color.

Because each light channel can emit 256 levels of intensity, an RGB system can produce more than 16.7 million possible colors (256 red x 256 green x 256 blue = 16,777,216). A monitor's **color depth** is the actual number of colors that a monitor displays, stated in bits. For example, an 8-bit monitor can display 256 colors, a 16-bit monitor can display 65,536 colors, and a 24- or 32-bit monitor can display 16.7 million colors.

If you are using a text editor to create a webpage by manually entering markup tags, you specify a color for a webpage element by entering the color's hexadecimal code, which is the equivalent of the color's RGB values. The **hexadecimal system** uses 16 symbols, the letters A–F and digits 0–9, to signify values. For example, the hexadecimal code for the light green color with the RGB values of 153:255:153 is 99FF99. If you are using a WYSIWYG editor, you do not need to understand the hexadecimal system in detail; simply select a color and the editor will determine and enter the appropriate hexadecimal code for you (Figure 2-15).

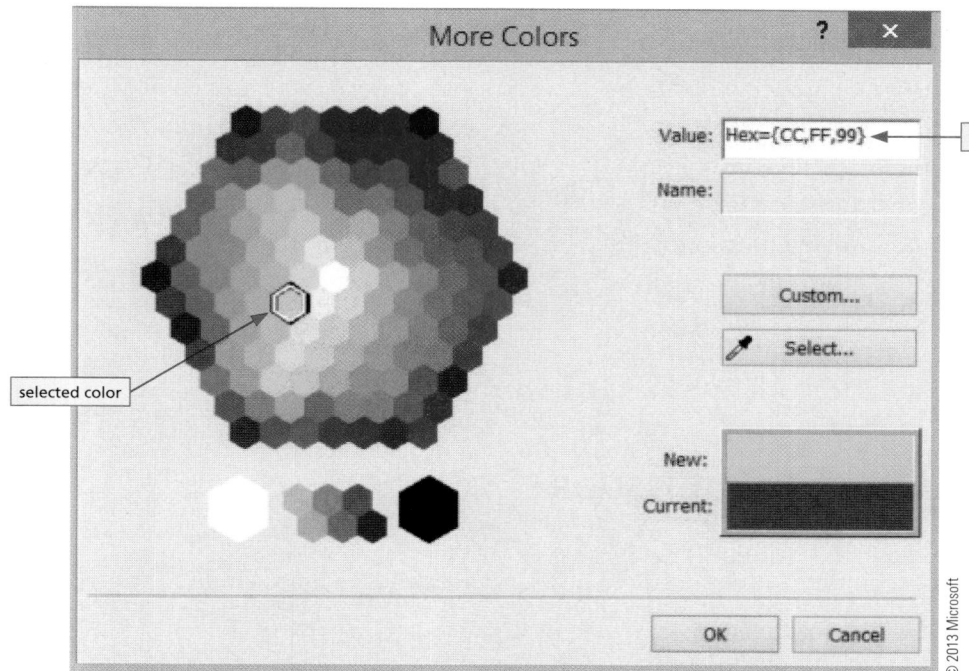

Figure 2-15 WYSIWYG editors such as Expression Web enable you to pick colors without knowing their hexadecimal value.

Target Audience Expectations

Over time, certain colors have come to symbolize particular qualities. Also, color symbolization differs across various cultures. For example, in some cultures white represents good or purity, black represents negativity, red represents passion, and purple represents royalty. Keep in mind the qualities generally associated with different colors when selecting colors for your website. If your website's target audience is global, research color associations in various countries to ensure that you are not creating a connotation that you do not intend.

Q&A

What is the browser- or web-safe palette?
The web-safe palette is a set of 216 of the available 256 colors displayed by an 8-bit monitor. Fewer and fewer web visitors today have 8-bit monitors; therefore, many web designers no longer restrict their color choices to the web-safe palette.

Q&A

Does color matter?
Yes. For example, although white represents purity in the United States, it can mean death or mourning in some Asian countries and might be offensive to those visitors. For more information about using color as a design tool, use a search engine to search for *website color palettes*.

DESIGN TIP

Before making color choices for your website, visit several commercial and noncommercial websites to find examples of color schemes you like that fit with your website's branding. Consider using a color scheme generator to find compatible colors.

When selecting colors for your website, allow yourself some leeway in making color decisions. Certain combinations produce different results and responses. Consider the intended purpose of your website, the experience you desire for your targeted audience, and their expectations. Then choose an attractive color scheme and apply colors from this scheme to webpage elements, such as the background, text headings and subheadings, and links. When designing webpages for a commercial entity or other large organization, be sure to follow the entity's branding specifications for the use of color.

Exploring Webpage Color Schemes

1. Use a search engine to search for examples of the following websites: news, e-commerce, and B2B.
2. Open each website in a different tab.
3. Analyze the color scheme at each website by answering the following questions:
   a. Is the color scheme attractive, visually appealing, and consistent across pages?
   b. Is the color scheme effective in supporting the website's overall message and main purpose? If yes, how? If no, why?

   c. How do you personally respond to the website's color scheme?
4. Explain how each of these websites uses color as a design tool. Discuss your personal response to each website's color scheme and how your response might guide you when planning a color scheme for a B2C website.
5. Submit your findings in the format requested by your instructor.

Web Publishing Issues

Successful web publishing further includes recognizing certain technical, legal and ethical, accessibility, and usability issues, as well as the design techniques that can effectively manage them.

Technical Issues

Before creating your website, you should understand a few technical issues related to good design. These issues include bandwidth, differences among browsers, and monitor resolution.

BANDWIDTH   Bandwidth is the quantity of data transmitted in a specific time frame, measured in bits per second (bps). You learned about transmitting data over a network and the data's transfer rate in Chapter 1. A larger bandwidth indicates a higher data transfer rate. In Chapter 1, you also learned that visitors can access the Internet using a variety of low transfer rate or high transfer rate methods, and that device types can affect transfer rates. The bandwidth or transfer rate of the Internet connection, the amount of traffic on the Internet at a specific time, and a webpage's file size all affect how quickly the webpage downloads in a visitor's browser.

As a web designer, you have no control over how your target audience members access the Internet and web or the amount of traffic across the Internet. You do have control over the file size of the webpage, which includes all its elements such as text, images, and multimedia. A visitor to your website generally will wait no longer than 5 to 10 seconds for a webpage to download before moving on to another website; therefore, you must take bandwidth into consideration when you choose elements to include on your webpages. Even with the increased usage of high-speed Internet access methods, the file size of your pages should always be a consideration when designing effective websites.

Use images sparingly, and consider using **thumbnail** images, which are miniature versions that link to larger images. In addition to careful image choices, you can take steps to optimize images for quick download time by reducing image file sizes using image-editing programs such as Corel® PaintShop Pro X6® or Adobe Photoshop® CS6. Chapter 5 discusses optimizing graphics in more detail.

BROWSER DIFFERENCES   In Chapter 1, you learned that Google Chrome, Microsoft Internet Explorer, and Mozilla Firefox are today's most widely used browsers for desktop and laptop computers. These popular browsers, along with most mobile browsers, are **graphical display browsers**. Along with text, graphical display browsers can display elements such as photographs, clip art, animations, and video. Most visitors will view your website with a graphical display browser. Browsers can vary as to the support levels they offer for HTML or XHTML tags, CSS, and scripting languages. Because of these varying support levels, webpages might appear differently when viewed with different browsers or with different versions of the same browser. You should test your webpages with different browsers and browser versions before publishing your website.

A visually impaired visitor using adaptive software to convert webpage text into audio might choose to turn images off in his or her graphical display browser. When adding images to a webpage, you should specify an alternative text description for each image. **Alternative text**, also called *alt text*, is language that briefly describes each image that loads in a webpage; such information appears in place of turned-off images and helps visitors better understand a page's content. If you are using a text or HTML editor, you can add the HTML <img> </img> tag attribute alt=text to add alternative text to the image. If you are using a WYSIWYG editor, you can use an option provided by the editor to specify an alternative text description for each image.

SCREEN RESOLUTION   **Resolution** is the measure of a display device's sharpness and clarity, related directly to the number of pixels it can display. A **pixel**, short for picture element, is a single point in an electronic image. The pixels on a display device are so close together that they appear connected. Resolution is expressed as two numbers — the number of columns of pixels and the number of rows of pixels that a display device can display. At higher resolutions, the number of pixels increases while their size decreases. Page elements appear large at low resolutions and decrease in size as resolution settings increase.

A webpage viewed on a desktop or laptop will appear differently depending on the resolution setting of the user's monitor. If you design webpages for a lower resolution, such as 1024 x 768, a visitor viewing the webpage at a higher resolution will see a blank area on one or both sides of the page. However, a visitor viewing the page at a lower resolution must scroll the page horizontally to see all its content. Scrolling a webpage horizontally hampers readability and is likely to frustrate visitors.

When designing websites for mobile devices, you must account for a smaller screen size and the auto-rotate feature included in many smartphones and tablets. **Auto-rotate** enables the user to change the angle of a rectangular screen in order to change the screen orientation from landscape (wider) or portrait (higher). Figure 2-16 shows the same webpage viewed on a smartphone in both orientations. In addition, by using finger gestures such as pinching, many mobile devices enable users to zoom in and out to better view images or text.

TOOLKIT

Responsive Web Design
For more information about designing webpages that accommodate mobile devices' rotation and zoom features, see Appendix C.

Figure 2-16 Mobile devices use auto-rotate to change from portrait to landscape orientation.

DESIGN TIP   When designing a webpage, use techniques that adapt to multiple resolutions. For example, design for a lower resolution and then add an attractive background that appears on either side of the page when viewed at a higher resolution.

Q&A

Should I design a separate mobile website?
The current trend is to use responsive web design techniques so that websites can be viewed on multiple devices and screen sizes. For more information about web design expert recommendations regarding creating websites for mobile devices, use a search engine to search for *creating mobile websites*.

MOBILE VERSIONS   Creating a mobile version of your website is another way to ensure your website can be viewed on mobile devices. The most important consideration when modifying a website for access by mobile devices is to simplify the navigation and content to accommodate a smaller screen size and the use of a stylus or touch screen. You can address the bandwidth differences by reducing the number of images, replacing paragraphs with lists, and removing unnecessary or duplicate HTML code. Ensure that interactive website experiences, such as shopping or commenting, are easy to do on a mobile device.

Web design experts discourage the creation of mobile website versions, and recommend responsive web design techniques to create device-independent websites. When working with an older website design, or one that is complex, you can create a mobile version of your website as a temporary, or easier choice, until you can complete a major redesign of the website.

Viewing Websites on Mobile Devices

1. Using a desktop or laptop computer, view the webpage of your choice in your browser.
2. If you have a mobile device, view the website using your mobile device. If you do not have a mobile device, use a search engine to search for mobi.ready, and follow the instructions to view the website as it might appear in a mobile device.
3. Document the differences in how each page appears when viewed in a browser compared with mobile view.
4. Discuss differences in navigation, content, and number of images and animations.
5. Submit your findings in the format requested by your instructor.

Legal and Privacy Issues

You should take the time to familiarize yourself with legal and privacy issues related to publishing a website. Legal issues include copyright infringement and content liability. Criminal activity based on identity theft is a major problem for both businesses and consumers. If you gather visitor information — names, addresses, credit card numbers — at your website, you must take steps to protect the privacy of that information and secure it from unauthorized access or theft.

LEGAL ISSUES   At some time, you might see a great image on a webpage that would be perfect for your website. To get it, all you need to do is download a copy of the image to a storage device on your computer. Although it is relatively easy to copy an image, doing so is potentially illegal and unethical. By downloading and using the image without permission, you could violate the creator's **copyright**, or ownership right to the image. You are responsible for obtaining all permissions for content on your website, and can be subject to fines or prosecution for any violations.

United States laws protect published and unpublished intellectual property, such as webpage text or images, by copyright, regardless of whether the content owner registers the property with the U.S. Copyright Office. In general, the law states that only the owner may print, distribute, or copy the property. To reuse the property, the user must obtain permission from the owner. The owner may also request compensation for the usage or acknowledgment of the source.

A **copyright notice** is text that includes the word, copyright, or the © symbol, the publication year, and the copyright owner's name. Most websites today, especially commercial websites, add a copyright notice at or near the bottom of the home and subsidiary pages. Figure 2-17 illustrates a copyright notice at the bottom of the Chase home page.

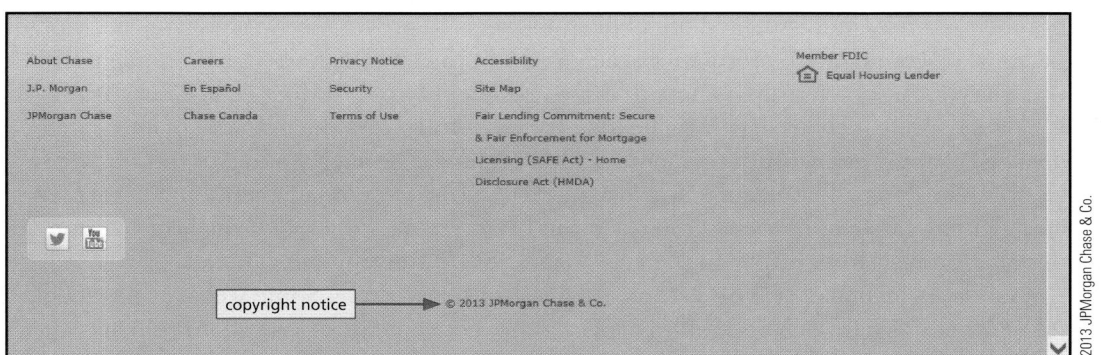

Figure 2-17 Webpages at commercial websites generally include a copyright notice.

DESIGN TIP
Using connectivity tools to allow website visitors to share your content helps to protect you from copyright concerns. These tools direct the visitor back to your website, which allows you to share your content or connect to other websites' content while clearly crediting the source.

Publishing a website might expose you to potential liabilities, such as copyright infringement, defamation, or libel, especially when you use website content from different sources or include links to webpages at other websites. For protection against these potential liabilities, you can post on your website a disclaimer of liability notice prepared by an attorney. Figure 2-18 illustrates the disclaimer of liability notice at the Ohio Department of Health website.

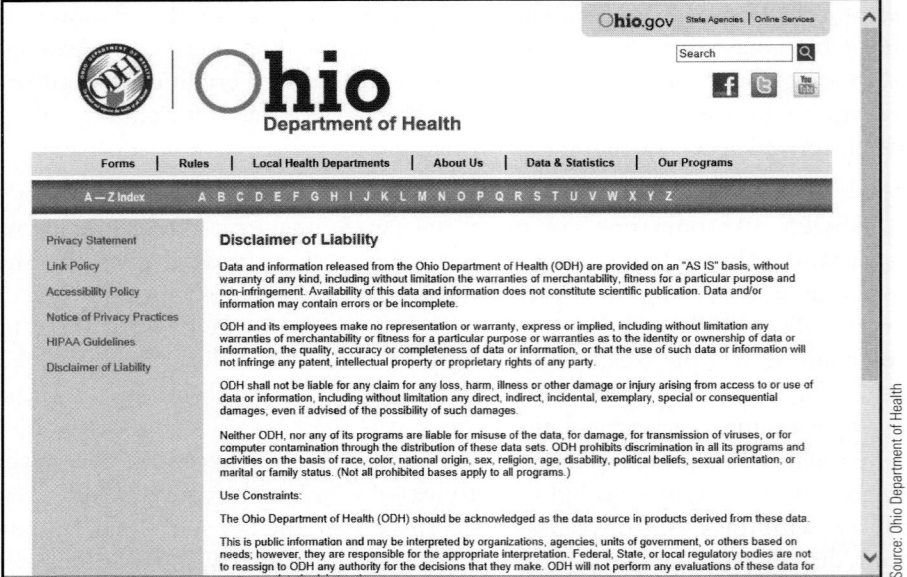

Figure 2-18 A disclaimer of liability notice can help protect website owners against potential liabilities.

Q&A

What are digital certificates and signatures?
Digital certificates and signatures are methods for verifying a content's source. For more information about these tools, use a search engine to search for *digital certificates and signatures*.

PRIVACY ISSUES Many websites, especially e-commerce websites, collect sensitive **personally identifiable information (PII)**, such as Social Security numbers, credit card numbers, names, addresses, and telephone numbers. To provide security for transmission of personal or confidential information, such as credit card transactions, e-commerce websites use encryption, which prevents unauthorized recipients from reading data. **Encryption** is a process that encodes data into illegible content. To restore the usability of encrypted data, users apply **decryption** techniques, which remove the encryption and return data to its original format. The **Secure Sockets Layer (SSL)** protocol safeguards and encrypts confidential information as it travels over the Internet. Webpages with the https:// protocol designation instead of http:// in their URL use SSL to transmit customers' data.

Cookies are small text files stored on a visitor's hard drive. Some websites post cookies to a visitor's hard drive. Cookies make it more convenient for visitors to return to their favorite websites by storing their login data or webpage customization preferences.

Cookies can also reveal a user's information when they track pages visited and other visitor statistics. Most of the time, a visitor is not aware that a website has installed a cookie on his or her computer. Chapter 7 discusses tracking visitor statistics using server logs and cookies in more detail.

Protecting sensitive information a user provides voluntarily is only part of the privacy issue. The server's transaction log records every request for a page from a web browser to a web server. Many websites automatically collect certain information from visitors, such as domain names, browser types, and operating systems from these server transaction logs. Although the content of this information is not sensitive, websites collect it without a visitor's approval or control, violating the privacy of users without their knowledge.

Website visitors have legitimate concerns about how all their information, whether willfully submitted or automatically gathered, is being used. Additionally, visitors are concerned about the steps being taken by website publishers to ensure that their information remains secure and out of the hands of unauthorized parties. Privacy advocates have been working to come up with guidelines and practices for website owners and visitors to protect personal data from being misused. The term, **big data**, refers to large and complex collections of information from a variety of sources, including website statistics, e-commerce transactions, social media profiles, databases, and other personally identifiable information about a person available through public records and other sources.

To ease visitors' concerns, many websites, especially e-commerce websites, include a **privacy policy statement** that explains the use of information submitted by a visitor or gathered automatically through server logs and cookies. For example, such a statement might explain that the website owners use the information only to gather demographic data about website visitors and will not release data to any third party. Figure 2-19 illustrates a portion of the privacy policy statement on the Privacy and Security webpage at the J.P. Morgan website.

Q&A

Should I be worried about big data? While privacy advocates use the term, big data, to refer to large collections of personal data collected and used without permission, some corporations use it to refer to data sets and collection tools used for legitimate business purposes, such as record keeping or targeted marketing. For more information about big data, use a search engine to search for *big data concerns*.

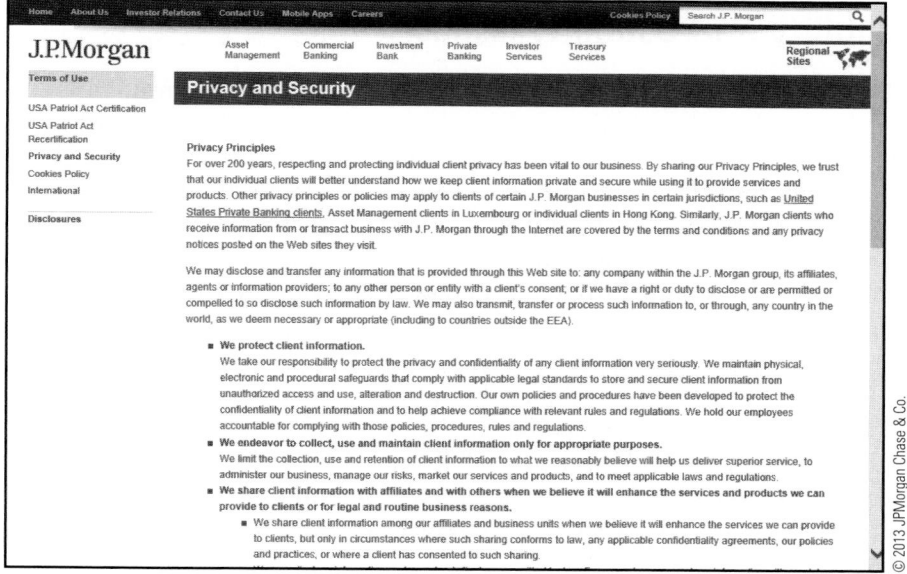

Figure 2-19 A privacy policy statement posted at a website explains how visitor information is used.

Establish privacy and data security policies for your website operations. Make sure that everyone associated with designing, maintaining, and operating the website is aware of the policies. Explain your policies to website visitors by publishing a privacy and security policy statement.

In addition to posted privacy and security statements, many commercial and organizational websites also participate in the privacy and security standards certification programs offered by entities such as TRUSTe and BBBOnline. Members in good standing of these certification programs may indicate compliance with the program's privacy and security standards by displaying program seals, or graphic symbols, on their webpages.

YOUR TURN

Exploring Website Privacy and Data Security Issues

1. Use a search engine to search for websites for the following organizations: BBBOnline, TRUSTe, Online Privacy Alliance, and National Consumers League.
2. Open each website in a different tab.
3. Review the privacy and data security issues and tools discussed at each website.

4. Explain how you would use this information to ensure the privacy of visitors' information and the security of visitors' data at your website.
5. Submit your findings in the format requested by your instructor.

Accessibility and Usability Issues

Q&A

What are some accessibility guideline examples? For more information about web accessibility guidelines, use a search engine to search for *WAI* and *Section 508*.

Web designers incorporate features called web **accessibility** to ensure their websites are usable by people with various types of special needs, such as lost or impaired vision or color blindness. Web accessibility is an important issue for the World Wide Web Consortium (W3C), which sets web standards. To advance web accessibility, the W3C sponsors the web Accessibility Initiative (WAI), a consortium of government agencies, IT industry representatives, and nonprofit organizations representing people with special needs. The WAI encourages accessibility through technology, guidelines, and research. Currently, the WAI guidelines are specifications, not regulations, which many organizations choose to adopt for their websites.

To further support web accessibility, the U.S. Congress instituted Section 508 of the U.S. Rehabilitation Act. Section 508 requires that all U.S. government agencies use accessibility technologies and follow accessibility guidelines to ensure that people with special needs can acquire the public information posted to the agencies' websites. Many e-commerce and educational websites and most U.S. government websites now provide a statement of commitment to web accessibility, including information describing how accessibility issues are handled at the website. Figure 2-20 illustrates the web accessibility statement at the Consumer Product Safety Commission (CPSC) website.

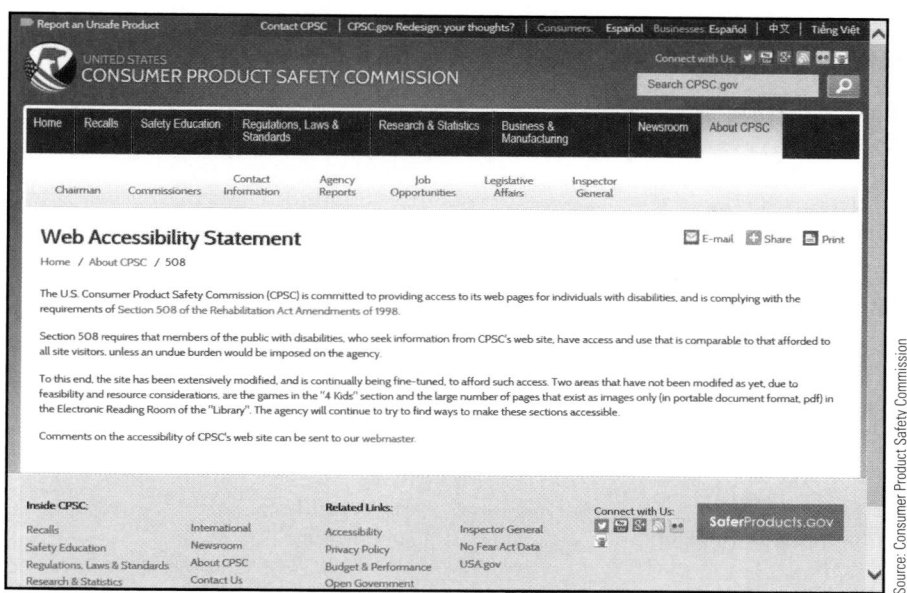

Figure 2-20 Many e-commerce and educational websites and most U.S. government websites affirm their web accessibility compliance.

Source: Consumer Product Safety Commission

Although some people use the terms web *accessibility* and web *usability* interchangeably, they are related, but different, concepts. Whereas web accessibility deals with ensuring access to web-based information, web **usability** involves designing a website and its pages so that all visitors to the website can easily and quickly satisfy their goals. Web designers incorporate **user experience (UX)** practices into webpage design. The goal of UX is to enhance the user's website experience in order to meet the user's needs and make the user feel their visit was worthwhile.

Q&A

What are UX principles?
UX incorporates all elements of good web design, including website structure, the use of text, color, and images, navigational elements, and other design guidelines discussed throughout this text. For more information about UX, use a search engine to search for *user experience guidelines*.

Chapter Review

Print publishing cannot match the benefits of the web for delivering current, interactive content and for efficient, cost-effective distribution of information. The objective of web publications is to deliver a specific message and leave a distinct impression. Achieving these objectives requires combining creativity with the fundamental design principles of balance and proximity, contrast and focus, and visual identity and unity. Website visitors quickly want to find accurate, easy-to-read, well-organized, and concise information that they can use. Writing content with these attributes requires applying specific techniques including chunked text and inverted pyramid-style content. Color can powerfully enhance a website's message and personality. Persuasive, effective color use involves being aware of established color principles and conventions. Using the principles of responsive web design ensures your webpages can be viewed on multiple devices. Successful web publishing further includes recognizing certain technical, legal, privacy, accessibility, and usability issues, and applying the design techniques that can manage them effectively.

TERMS TO KNOW

After reading the chapter, you should know each of these Key Terms.

accessibility (62)
aggregator (41)
alignment (50)
alternative text (57)
asymmetrical (46)
auto-rotate (57)
balance (46)
bandwidth (56)
big data (61)
brand (49)
branding specifications (49)
chunked text (51)
color depth (54)
color wheel (53)
complementary colors (54)
connectivity advantage (41)
contrast (48)
cookies (60)
cool colors (53)
copyright (59)
copyright notice (59)
cost advantage (45)
currency advantage (40)
decryption (60)
delivery advantage (45)
encryption (60)
focal point (48)
graphical display browser (57)

hexadecimal system (54)
interactivity advantage (42)
inverted pyramid style (52)
netiquette (52)
personally identifiable
    information (PII) (60)
phishing (59)
pixel (57)
primary colors (53)
privacy policy statement (61)
proximity (47)
resolution (57)
RGB color system (54)
scannability (52)
secondary colors (53)
Secure Sockets Layer (SSL) (60)
spoofing (59)
symmetrical (46)
tag line (49)
thumbnail (56)
unity (49)
usability (63)
user experience (UX) (63)
values (54)
visual identity (49)
warm colors (53)
web-based form (44)
white space (47)

TEST YOUR KNOWLEDGE

Complete the Test Your Knowledge exercises to solidify what you have learned in the chapter.

Matching Terms

Match each term with the best description.

____ 1. connectivity
____ 2. netiquette
____ 3. symmetrical
____ 4. hexadecimal system
____ 5. cookies
____ 6. color depth
____ 7. UX
____ 8. contrast
____ 9. alignment
____ 10. auto-rotate
____ 11. spoofing
____ 12. accessibility

a. The creation of a fraudulent version of a website and masking its URL.
b. Small text files stored on a website visitor's computer.
c. Focus on enhancing the user's website experience.
d. A feature that changes the screen orientation from landscape to portrait.
e. Instant sharing and distribution of website content.
f. Uses codes for colors using RGB values.
g. The actual number of colors that a monitor displays, stated in bits.
h. A mix of elements to stimulate attention.
i. Web layout where elements appear centered or even.
j. A list of guidelines that help web users and developers to interact and create content.
k. Web design guidelines applied to websites and pages to ensure ease of use by people with special needs.
l. Arrangement of objects in fixed or predetermined positions.

Short Answer Questions

Write a brief answer to each question.

1. List and explain the advantages of web publishing over print.

2. Identify the basic design principles that help webpages deliver a powerful message and leave a distinct impression.

3. Discuss how responsive web design principles influence web design.

4. Discuss the role of branding in promoting unity and maintaining visual identity.

5. Define chunked text and discuss reasons for using chunked text to create scannable web content.

6. Explain the role of color as a web design tool.

7. Describe the color wheel and identify primary colors and secondary colors.

8. Explain the advantages and considerations unique to creating a mobile version of a website.

9. Briefly discuss each of the following web publishing issues:

   a. Bandwidth
   b. Monitor resolution
   c. Legal and privacy concerns
   d. Usability and accessibility

Test your knowledge of chapter content and key terms.

LEARN IT ONLINE

Instructions: Reinforce what you learned in this chapter with games, exercises, training, and many other online activities and resources. Reinforcement activities and resources are available at no additional cost at **www.cengagebrain.com**.

Investigate current web design developments with the Trends exercises.

TRENDS

Write a brief essay about each of the following trends, using the web as your research tool. For each trend, identify at least one webpage URL used as a research source. Be prepared to discuss your findings in class.

1 | Section 508

Research the latest developments in accessibility standards. Make a list of three important accessibility considerations, and note whether they are new or existing issues. Visit two websites to see if these websites meet the considerations.

2 | UX

Research UX guidelines and techniques for enhancing website users' experience. Find at least one web design blog entry that discusses UX. Visit any websites the blog author mentions, and see if your experience at the website matches that of the author. Make a note of anything that you would change about the website.

Challenge your perspective of the web and web design technology with the @Issue exercises.

Write a brief essay in response to the following issues, using the web as your research tool. For each issue, identify at least one webpage URL used as a research source. Be prepared to discuss your findings in class.

1 | Personally Identifiable Information

Make a list of at least three websites into which you have entered personally identifiable information. Think about the information you have entered into each source and whether you feel comfortable knowing that others could access this data. Make a note of anything you might want to change or could do in the future to protect your personally identifiable information.

2 | Target Audience Color Expectations

Explain how target audience expectations and preferences affect the use of color as a web design tool. Give website examples to support your explanation.

Use the World Wide Web to obtain more information about the concepts in the chapter with the Hands On exercises.

1 | Explore and Evaluate: Branding

Browse the web to find an example of a webpage whose branding, in your opinion, is inconsistent or ineffective. Suggest changes to logos, layout, fonts, colors, and other design principles to improve the website's branding.

2 | Search and Discover: Privacy and Accessibility Issues

Search the web to identify at least two websites that address privacy or accessibility issues directly at their websites.

1. Explain how one website addresses privacy and the other website addresses accessibility.

2. How would you address the issues of privacy and accessibility when developing a website?

3. Would your approach be the same as or different from that of the reviewed websites? If the same, why? If different, why not?

Work collaboratively to reinforce the concepts in the chapter with the Team
Approach exercises.

1 | Rate Art Museum Websites

Form a team with three of your classmates. Have each team member visit the home
page plus three subsidiary pages of a different art museum website, such as those for
the Museum of Fine Arts in Boston, The Museum of Modern Art in New York, or the Art
Institute of Chicago. Rate each website on how well the website incorporates the basic
design principles presented in this chapter:

• Balance and proximity

• Contrast and focus

• Unity and visual identity

a. Use a rating scale of 1 through 5, where 5 is the highest rating. Meet as a team and
summarize your ratings; using your summary, rank the four websites from highest to
lowest.

b. Explain how you would use the design principles embodied at the highest-ranking
website to plan the design for your website. Be prepared to discuss your findings
with the class.

2 | Compare Interactivity at E-Commerce Websites

Form a team of three or four classmates to evaluate how the following e-commerce
websites use web design to promote interactivity with their customers, potential
customers, partners, and other interested parties. Which of the e-commerce websites
is the most successful at promoting interactivity? Which is the least successful? Why?
Suggest ways that the least successful website might better promote interactivity.

a. Reuseit

b. Cisco Systems

c. eBay

d. etsy

Write a report of your team's findings and be prepared to discuss your report in class.

Apply the chapter concepts to the ongoing development process in web design
with the Case Study.

**The Case Study is an ongoing development process using the concepts, techniques, and
Design Tips presented in each chapter.**

Background Information

As you progress through the chapters, you will learn how to use design as a tool to
create effective webpages and websites. At each chapter's conclusion, you will receive
instructions for completing each segment of the ongoing design process.

In this chapter's assignment, you are to identify methods and tools to manage currency,
encourage connectivity, and promote interactivity and communication at your website.
Discuss costs associated with development of your website. Create a tag line, describe
how you plan to use color at your website, find resources for your website's topic,
practice writing and editing scannable text, apply responsive web design techniques, and
create a plan for handling accessibility and usability issues.

Chapter 2 Assignment

1. In the format requested by your instructor, do all of the following:

   a. Identify the element(s) that you could include on your website that would convey to its audience that the website's content is current.

   b. Identify the connectivity tools you will use to encourage users to publish or promote your content, and explain how you will use them.

   c. Identify ways you can promote interactivity at your website.

   d. Create an appropriate tag line for your website and describe how you will use it in the website's design.

   e. Describe how you plan to use color at your website.

   f. Write three paragraphs about your website's topic in inverted pyramid style. Then rewrite the paragraphs as chunked text.

   g. Describe how you plan to use basic design principles to enhance your website's usability.

   h. List ways you plan to make your website accessible.

2. Submit your findings in the format requested by your instructor and be prepared to share your plan with the class.

3 | Planning a Successful Website: Part 1

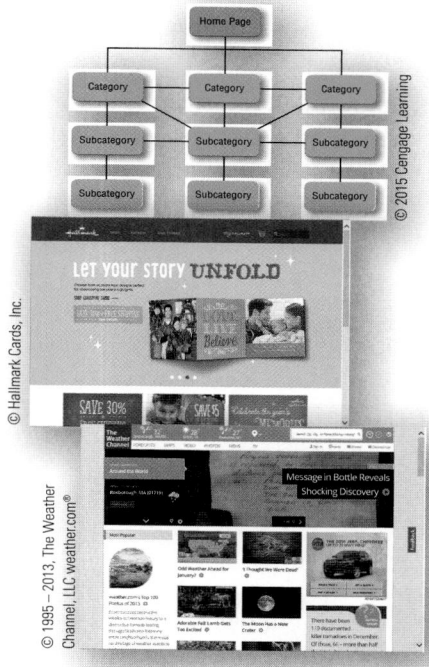

Introduction

Chapters 1 and 2 introduced you to the Internet and the World Wide Web, different types of websites, and basic web design tools and roles. You also learned about important techniques for writing text for webpages and using color as a design tool along with privacy and security considerations.

Chapters 3 and 4 explain important steps in website planning. In this chapter, you explore some of the first steps in the website development process: defining the website's purpose and target audience; determining the website's general content; and specifying the website's structure. Then, using what you have learned about the website planning process, you begin to develop a plan for your own website. You complete your website's plan in Chapter 4. Completing the steps in Chapters 3 and 4 helps you to create a comprehensive website. The order of the steps may overlap or switch depending on the complexity of your website and the number of people involved in its planning. It is important to think of the website as a complete project, where each step and component must complement and align with the plans for other steps. Before finalizing your website plan, you should review all steps to ensure there is no conflict between later steps and decisions made earlier in the project.

Objectives

After completing this chapter, you will be able to:

1. Describe the website development planning process

2. Complete Step 1: Identify the website's purpose and target audience

3. Complete Step 2: Determine the website's general content

4. Complete Step 3: Select the website's structure

The Website Development Planning Process

The best way to ensure the success of any project is to plan it carefully. It takes thorough preparation to develop a website that will achieve its goals and attract and influence its audience. Creating a website requires you to invest significant time and other resources; planning helps ensure the website development process is efficient, cost-effective, and successful. Before you begin to create your first webpage, you must develop a solid, detailed plan for the website, called a **website plan** or **design plan**. This plan determines the purpose, audience, content, structure, navigation system, visual design, and publishing and maintenance strategy. Following the six major steps illustrated in Figure 3-1 is a good way to approach the development of a detailed website plan.

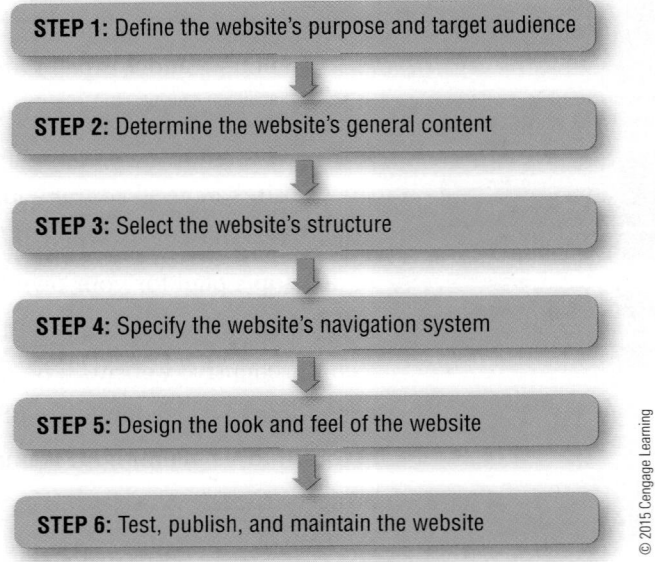

STEP 1: Define the website's purpose and target audience

STEP 2: Determine the website's general content

STEP 3: Select the website's structure

STEP 4: Specify the website's navigation system

STEP 5: Design the look and feel of the website

STEP 6: Test, publish, and maintain the website

© 2015 Cengage Learning

Figure 3-1 Creating a successful website begins with developing a detailed website plan.

DESIGN TIP When creating a design plan, be sure to have colleagues, managers, or other stakeholders review the plan. Although you might think that visual design would be the most important aspect of a website, you need to first determine the purpose, audience, content, and structure to come up with a visual design that meets the needs of your website.

Because planning is critical to the development of a successful website, this book devotes two chapters to a thorough discussion of the six steps illustrated in Figure 3-1. This chapter discusses Steps 1 through 3. Chapter 4 discusses Steps 4 through 6. In this and subsequent chapters, a specific web design example is used to explain the concepts related to developing a detailed design plan. In this scenario, you are the head of the web design department at Regifting, a new B2C e-commerce company that focuses on selling reusable and recycled products and services. You need to work with your team of web designers to develop a website plan for the new company.

Step 1: Define the Website's Purpose and Audience

The first step when developing a solid website design plan involves defining the website's goals, objectives, and audience, and then formulating a written purpose statement for the website. **Goals** are the results you want your website to accomplish within a specific timeframe, which can be weeks, months, or years. **Objectives** are those methods you will choose to accomplish the website's goals. Although anyone around the world who has a computer or mobile device that can access the Internet has the potential to visit your website, you must identify the specific group of visitors you want to reach with your website. Recognizing the website's **target audience**, and knowing their wants, needs, and expectations, enables you to create a website that provides the most value for that audience. A formal, written **purpose statement** summarizes your website's goals and objectives to ensure they meet the audience's expectations and needs.

Website Goals

Although a website has a primary goal, it might also have additional secondary goals. For example, in this chapter's example, your website's primary goal is to sell products or services. You could have a combination of secondary goals that support your website's primary goal, such as providing customer service, educating customers about new products or services, promoting communication between employees and customers, informing shareholders of business developments, keeping customers informed about business changes in your industry, and so forth.

In the example, your team has identified a primary goal and multiple secondary goals for the new website:

- Primary goal:
  - Increase sales of reusable and recycled goods.
- Secondary goals:
  - Promote awareness of the company and its products and mission, and build a community of engaged customers and potential customers.
  - Establish the company's credibility in the field of environmentally sound businesses.
  - Educate website visitors about tips for using, and developments in, environmentally friendly products.
  - Inform shareholders and potential investors of business developments and plans.
  - Encourage visitors to return to the website by providing updated information in the form of a blog with articles by industry experts.

Website Objectives

After identifying the website's goals, your next step is to determine the website's objectives, which are the methods the website developers use to accomplish the goals. For example, if the primary goal is to sell a product or service, the objectives to accomplish that goal might include posting testimonials from customers who have purchased the product or service or offering a 20 percent price discount for customers who purchase the product or service in the next 30 days.

You and your team have defined the following objectives for the Regifting website to accomplish the new website's primary and secondary goals:

- Develop an attractive, informative, and easy-to-use website to promote an online awareness of the company.
- Provide authoritative information and advice at the website to establish credibility.
- Include links to articles and quick tips to educate website visitors about the importance of using reusable and recycled products.
- Employ social media tools to inform and engage current and potential customers and investors.
- Offer online tools to encourage website visitors to make changes to reduce their carbon footprint.

Q&A

Why is a call-to-action important? A call-to-action helps you to measure your website's success by providing methods for visitors to interact with the website. For more information, use a search engine to search for *website call-to-action*.

Every website should include a **call-to-action** in its objectives list. A call-to-action is a suggestion or offer that requires the website visitor to interact with the website by purchasing a product, following the company's social media account(s), making a donation, sharing or commenting on an article, requesting an appointment, signing up for an account, or registering for an event or program.

You and your team identify the following calls-to-action that you will incorporate into the Regifting website in order to help reach its objectives:

- Purchase products
- Sign up for an account profile
- Follow the website's social media profiles

DESIGN TIP　You will refer back to your goals and objectives constantly as you complete the website plan. Before publishing the website, you should evaluate how well the website's content, structure, and design help to meet the website's goals and objectives.

Target Audience Profile

To begin the process of creating a profile of your website's target audience, imagine the ideal visitor for your website. Think of what visitors' website experience will provide them and how their actions may help you reach your website goals. A **target audience profile** is a research-based overview that includes information about potential website visitors' demographic and psychographic characteristics. **Demographic characteristics** include gender, age group, educational level, income, location, and other characteristics that define who your website visitors are. **Psychographic characteristics** include social group affiliations, lifestyle choices, purchasing preferences, political affiliations, and other characteristics that explain why visitors might want to access your website.

DESIGN TIP　Make sure that your target audience profile aligns with your goals and objectives. You might need to revise your website plan to ensure that the target audience will interact with your website in a way that helps your website meet its goals.

Using research and reports prepared by and sold by companies who specialize in demographic and psychographic research, you can ask and answer questions similar to the following to develop a formal target audience profile for your website:

- What is the age range for your likely audience members?
- What are audience members' gender, educational background, and marital status?
- What are the typical careers and income levels of audience members?
- What types of devices do your audience members typically use to access the website?
- What social media profiles do your audience members typically use?
- Where do audience members live?
- What are audience members' social group affiliations, lifestyle choices, interests, and purchasing preferences?

Based on this information, your team has developed the target audience profile for the new website for the Regifting example, as shown in Figure 3-2.

Regifting Website
Target Audience Profile

The typical website visitor:

- Is between 25 and 55 years old
- Is 60% likely to be female, and 40% likely to be male
- Has a minimum of two years of college
- Has an annual income of at least $50,000
- Lives primarily in suburban and urban areas on either coast of North America
- Has children and is active in community and nonprofit organizations
- Is aware of current environmental issues and wants to minimize his or her carbon footprint

© 2015 Cengage Learning

Figure 3-2 A target audience profile identifies potential website visitors by defining *who* they are and *why* they are likely to visit your website.

After you identify the members of your target audience, your next step is to determine the audience members' wants, needs, and expectations.

Target Audience Wants, Needs, and Expectations

Successful websites fulfill their audience's wants, needs, and expectations in both general and specific ways. In general, all audiences expect an attractive, interesting, and well-organized website that conveys useful information and is easy to use. An audience's specific expectations for a website will vary based on the website's purpose. For example, a B2C website must offer the products or services that visitors want to purchase in order to meet its audience's specific expectations. If a website does not meet its target audience's various expectations, visitors will take their business elsewhere.

After you identify your website's target audience, conduct a **needs assessment** by answering questions such as the following to determine your target audience's wants, needs, and expectations:

- What do audience members expect to gain from a visit to your website?
- What usability or accessibility issues are important to audience members?
- Are audience members generally experienced or inexperienced web users?
- Do audience members frequently use social media tools to share and comment on website content?
- Will audience members have any cultural biases, norms, or customs that you must accommodate in the website's design and organization?

Your team has performed a needs assessment and identified the target audience's major wants, needs, and expectations for the new website example, as shown in Figure 3-3.

Regifting Website
Target Audience Wants, Needs, and Expectations

The typical website visitor:

- Prefers attractive, professional-looking sites containing credible content
- Is likely to share articles and products with others using social media
- Accesses the web using multiple device types
- Chooses sites that have easy-to-use site navigation
- Favors sites that meet web accessibility standards
- Is likely to return frequently to websites that include current content, articles, and product tips
- Responds to advice on how to make environmentally friendly choices
- Expects to pay a little more for quality products that are environmentally friendly

© 2015 Cengage Learning

Figure 3-3 A successful website meets its target audience's expectations by creating a content-rich, attractive, and usable website.

 **DESIGN TIP**   To create a successful website, you should assess your target audience's wants, needs, and expectations and then design your website to satisfy them.

Q&A

Is determining target audience wants, needs, and expectations a one-time process?
No. After creating your website, you should continually gather feedback from your target audience to update your target audience profile and fine-tune the website's content.

If you have limited resources and a tight time frame for your initial website development, begin by identifying your target audience's top two or three needs and plan your website to satisfy those needs. Then after you publish the website, continue to solicit feedback from your target audience to establish additional wants, needs, and expectations and update your website to satisfy them, as necessary.

Website Purpose Statement

After determining your website's goals, objectives, and audience, you should create a purpose statement, which is a formal written summary of reasons for publishing the website. A well-written purpose statement synthesizes into a few words the reason or reasons you are publishing your website and explains a website's overall goals and the specific objectives designed to achieve those goals. It also includes a brief summary of the target audience's demographics and expectations. Figure 3-4 illustrates the approved purpose statement for the new reusable and recycled goods website.

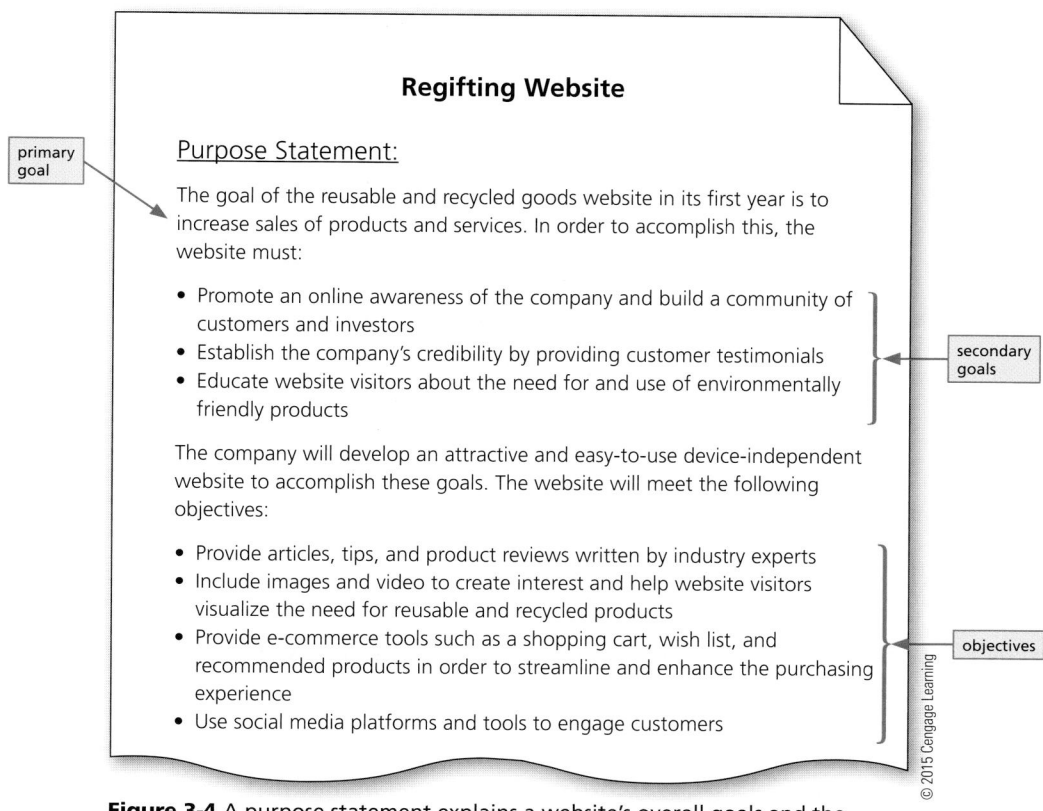

Regifting Website

primary goal

Purpose Statement:

The goal of the reusable and recycled goods website in its first year is to increase sales of products and services. In order to accomplish this, the website must:

- Promote an online awareness of the company and build a community of customers and investors
- Establish the company's credibility by providing customer testimonials
- Educate website visitors about the need for and use of environmentally friendly products

secondary goals

The company will develop an attractive and easy-to-use device-independent website to accomplish these goals. The website will meet the following objectives:

- Provide articles, tips, and product reviews written by industry experts
- Include images and video to create interest and help website visitors visualize the need for reusable and recycled products
- Provide e-commerce tools such as a shopping cart, wish list, and recommended products in order to streamline and enhance the purchasing experience
- Use social media platforms and tools to engage customers

objectives

© 2015 Cengage Learning

Figure 3-4 A purpose statement explains a website's overall goals and the specific objectives that will be used to achieve those goals.

Exploring Purpose Statements

1. Use a search engine to search for website purpose statements. Find at least two examples of purpose statements and open each in a new browser tab.
2. Make a note of your visitor expectations for the content and design of each website based solely on the information contained in its purpose statement. Do not look at other website pages before making your notes.
3. Next, review the home page and at least two subsidiary pages at each website. Does the website's content and design reflect the website's purpose statement? If yes, how? If no, what is missing? How accurate were your expectations in comparison to the site's subsidiary pages?
4. Submit your findings in the form requested by your instructor.

Formulating a well-written purpose statement requires a clear understanding of a website's goals and objectives.

DESIGN TIP

Step 2: Determine the Website's General Content

A website's general content likely will consist of multiple webpages including a combination of text, images, audio, video, animations, and multimedia elements. This section provides an overview of three types of webpages: the home page, underlying pages, and a landing or entry page. Additionally, this section introduces the different kinds of web content that might appear on these pages.

DESIGN TIP The content elements you choose for your website must support the website's purpose and satisfy your target audience's needs and expectations.

Home, Underlying, and Landing Pages

Most websites consist of two types of webpages: a home page and underlying pages. The home page is the anchor for the entire website, and the **underlying pages** provide detailed content and interest. Website visitors will access underlying pages using the navigation tools your website provides, a search box, or links from the home or landing page. You will learn more about how to structure underlying pages later in this chapter. Some websites also have a landing page, which is the page that your browser navigates to when you click a link in an ad, email, or other online promotion from a different website.

HOME PAGES As you learned in Chapters 1 and 2, a website's primary page is its home page. Generally, a home page is the first webpage visitors see at a website. A home page should indicate clearly *who* owns or publishes the website, *what* visitors can expect to find at the website, *why* they should visit this particular website, and *where* specific information or website features are located, as shown on the Hallmark home page in Figure 3-5. In designing a home page, you should include the following elements:

Q&A
Do visitors always enter a website from its home page?
No. Website visitors might follow links from other websites to view specific pages at your website or use search tools to locate specific pages at your website. For these reasons, it is critical that all pages at your website contain elements that maintain unity and visual identity.

- Who: Company name in text format, graphic logo, tag line, copyright notation, and similar elements that clearly identify *who* owns and publishes the website.
- What: Summary text and images that show visitors *what* content is available at the website, and what call-to-action is requested or required.
- Why: Text, images, or links that establish the website's value, and provide a reason *why* one should visit and interact with the website.
- Where: Easily identifiable navigational links to other pages at the website to indicate *where* specific information or features are found, and/or a method to search website content.

The answer to the Who? question should be evident throughout the website by use of corporate logos, a contact link, and copyright notices. An e-commerce website's home page could answer the What? question using a slide show or tabbed window to show a variety of the types of products or services sold at the website, or explain why a user should create an account or follow the website's social media profiles. Providing website visitors with information about accreditations or awards for an informational or organizational website or sharing customer quotes for an e-commerce website encourages visitors to choose your website over others, and answers the Why? question. The home page of a B2B website that sells web hosting services could have links to pages that detail the types of hosting services provided, fees, customer support information, privacy and security policy information, and so forth to answer the Where? question. A home page for a large website should include

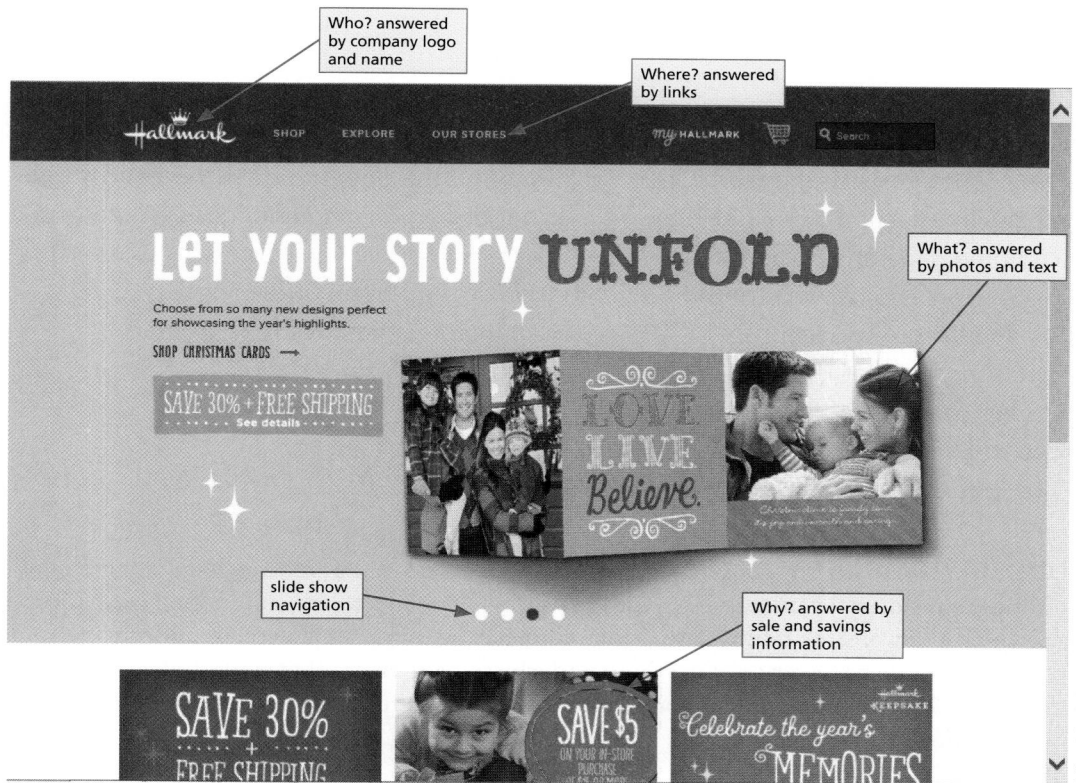

Who? answered by company logo and name

Where? answered by links

What? answered by photos and text

slide show navigation

Why? answered by sale and savings information

Hallmark Cards, Inc.

Figure 3-5 A website's home page should answer visitors' Who?, What?, Why? and Where? questions.

Q&A

What information should I put on my home page?
At its simplest, a home page tells the website visitor what content they can expect to find and how to find it. For more information about strategies for creating home pages, use a search engine to search for *home page content tips.*

Q&A

Why is branding so important?
Branding enables a company to be recognizable by its logo, color scheme, or slogan. Often, branding is so successful that the company then becomes synonymous with or symbolizes a specific product or service. For example, through successful branding, the names and logos of McDonald's are synonymous with fast food and the American Red Cross with disaster relief.

a **search feature**, which is a text box into which users enter a search term; the search tool then searches the website for that term. Search features use similar technologies as search engines, but only search within the website for matching results.

DESIGN TIP

A website's home page should contain elements that draw in the visitor and encourage further exploration or interactivity. The home page also should be different enough to stand out as the primary page, but still visually connect with other pages at the website.

Additionally, a website's home page should contain elements that establish the website's visual identity. Chapter 2 introduced the concepts of branding and using design elements to create and maintain visual identity. Organizations and companies spend a large amount of time and money defining, creating, and maintaining a positive, recognizable brand. As you learned in Chapter 2, you can exploit the power of branding on a home page using design elements — images, logo, typeface, and color scheme — alone or in combination to establish and maintain visual identity.

One way to add content to a home page without creating clutter is to use a tabbed window, slide show, or carousel to provide access to several articles, videos, or other content at once. On most pages, these elements display a rotation of articles or images and automatically advance to the next tab or screen, as well as provide user controls to navigate to or pause at a certain screen (Figure 3-5). Clicking a screen in the tabbed window, slide show, or carousel opens the complete content page in the browser.

Exploring Home Page Content

1. Use a search engine to locate the home pages for the following: Guggenheim Museum, NAPA Auto Parts, and Uvault. Open each home page in a separate browser tab.

2. Review each home page and determine how well each page's content answers the Who? What? Why? and Where? questions.

3. Summarize your home page review. Discuss the content employed at each website to address these three questions.

4. Note the website that, in your opinion, does the best job of answering these three questions and the one that does the poorest job. What design recommendations would you make to improve each home page in terms of answering these questions?

5. Submit your findings in the format requested by your instructor.

Q&A

What is a splash page?

A **splash page** uses images, animation, and sound to capture visitors' attention and draw them into the website for further exploration. Visitors can click a link on the splash page to move on to the home page or, in some instances, wait until the home page automatically appears. Many visitors strongly dislike dealing with splash pages, and they are not used frequently any more.

UNDERLYING PAGES In Chapter 2, you also learned that a website generally includes multiple subsidiary or underlying pages that provide details to the summary information shown on the website's home page. Links connect the home page with an underlying page and, where necessary, connect one underlying page to another underlying page. For example, typical underlying pages found at an e-commerce website include pages that provide the following:

- Product catalogs
- Shopping cart and checkout information
- Customer account information
- Customer service information
- Contact information
- Privacy policy and security information
- A blog

Each underlying page at a website should include the same elements — name, logo, typeface, color scheme — as its home page to provide unity and promote visual identity. Figure 3-6 depicts two underlying pages at the Hallmark website; comparing these pages

links back to home page

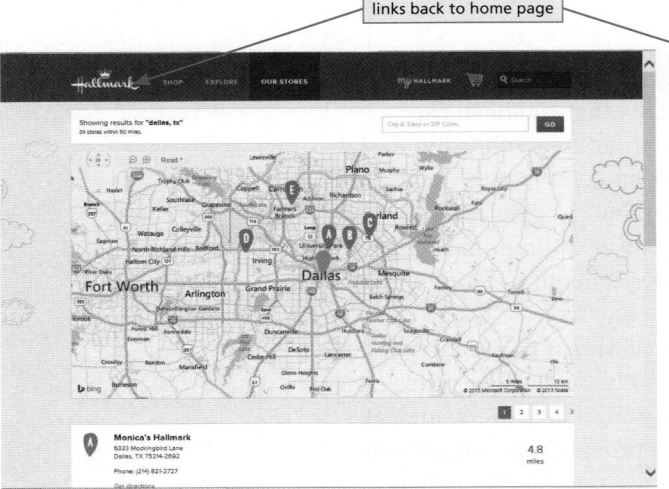
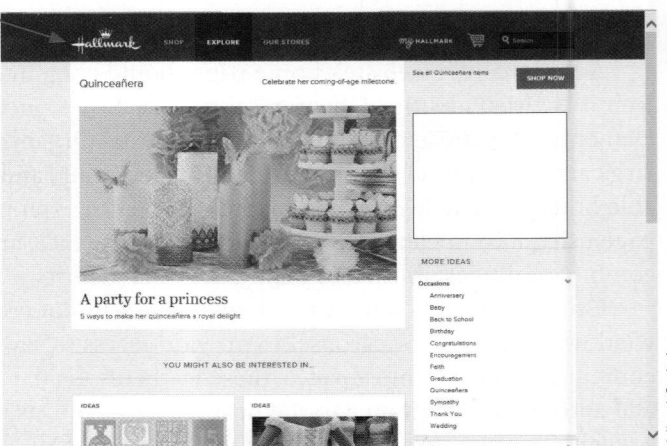

Figure 3-6 An underlying page should include most of the same visual identity elements as the home page.

with the home page shown in Figure 3-5 illustrates how Hallmark has implemented visual unity throughout its website. Additionally, like the two Hallmark underlying pages, each underlying page at a website should provide a link back to the website's home page.

Exploring Types of Underlying Pages

1. Use a search engine to locate at least five commercial websites. Include two each B2C and B2B websites and one C2C website. Open each website in its own tab.
2. Review the types of underlying pages offered at each website.
3. List the typical categories of underlying pages found at each type of commercial website. Be prepared to discuss your findings in class.

LANDING PAGES   As you learned in Chapter 1, a landing page is a page that appears when a visitor reaches a website by clicking a link, advertisement, or search result. Web marketers use social media, email campaigns, and search engine optimization (SEO) techniques to generate leads to the landing page. Websites use landing pages as marketing tools to measure the effectiveness of the advertisement by evaluating the number of times the page is visited and whether the visitor completes any transactions on the website. Landing pages generally have one of two purposes: to provide reference and specific information to customers about a product or event, or to encourage website visitors to complete a sales transaction or other specific interaction.

In the reusable and recycled goods website example, you and the team agree on a structure for the new website, which will consist of a home page and multiple underlying pages, as shown in Figure 3-7.

Q&A

What should I put on my landing page?
A landing page should include text that directly relates to the search query or ad that the website visitor uses to get to the landing page. For more information about creating effective landing pages, use a search engine to search for *landing page content*.

Regifting Website
Website Pages

The website will contain the following page types:

- Home page with slide show layout
- About Us summary page, plus Annual Report, Management Team, and History detail pages
- Customer Testimonials page
- Products pages, including categories for Lunch Boxes, Bedding, Cleaning Products, and Clothing
- Contact Us page with customer service links, phone numbers, and social media links

© 2015 Cengage Learning

Figure 3-7 The Regifting website will consist of a home page and multiple underlying pages.

Value-Added Content

Resist the temptation to fill your website with content for the sake of filling webpages. You should be selective, basing your choice of elements on how effectively they will contribute to your website's message and purpose, and how your audience will benefit

Q&A

What is an Infographic?
An **infographic** is data or information presented visually, such as in a chart or pyramid, or to show a sequence of events.

from the content. Content that furthers a website's purpose adds value to the website, and does not just fill space on a page. **Value-added content** is information that is relevant, informative, and timely; accurate and of high quality; and usable.

In general, you should create original content elements prepared specifically for the web instead of choosing existing content elements designed for print. For example, when including a written purpose statement, incorporate a short video clip of the CEO explaining the website's purpose, rather than a press release or other text.

If you must use an existing content element from another medium, you should **repurpose**, or modify, the element for the web. Repurposing content frequently involves abbreviating and rewriting text, adding hyperlinks to background or additional information, rescanning or altering photos, creating an infographic, and editing or segmenting audio and video. Most importantly, it requires creative thinking and keeping in mind the web environment and audience needs and expectations.

DESIGN TIP   Do not simply reuse content created for print on webpages. Repurpose the content so that it will add value.

Q&A

What are public domain materials?
The rights to public domain materials belong to the public at large. Examples include older material on which the copyright has expired, newer material explicitly placed into the public domain by its creator, and U.S. government work, such as publications or photographs not covered by copyright protection. Copyrights or patents do not protect public domain materials.

The following criteria help you determine if the content you plan to add is truly worthwhile, regardless of whether you are considering images, animation, multimedia, or dynamically generated content at your website. The availability of cutting-edge technology alone is never a valid reason to use it. The content element should meet all of these criteria:

- It adds value to the website.
- It furthers the website's purpose.
- It enhances visitors' experiences at the website.
- It encourages interactions.

You might use different types of value-added content on your website, including the elements briefly discussed here and covered in more detail in later chapters: text, images, audio, video, animation, multimedia, and dynamically generated content. Respect copyrights and give credit to content you repurpose from another source, where appropriate.

TEXT   Remember, visitors typically scan webpage text for information rather than read the text word for word. Avoid long paragraphs, and break up text with images, links, and multimedia. When writing original text, follow the guidelines for writing for the web introduced in Chapter 2. You can also follow similar guidelines to repurpose print publication text for the web:

- Chunk text for scannability.
- Place explanatory or detailed information on linked, underlying pages.
- Keep content to one page where possible to avoid scrolling.
- Use active voice, action verbs, and a friendly tone.
- Remove transitional words and phrases like *as stated previously*, *similarly*, and *as a result*, which might not be relevant for the chunked text.

Exploring How to Repurpose Text for the Web

YOUR
TURN

1. Use a search engine to search for tips and advice about repurposing text for the web.

2. Open a report or document you created for this or another class that includes several paragraphs of text.

3. Using the guidelines for repurposing print text for the web, repurpose at least four paragraphs from the report or document.

As an acknowledgment, cite the source of the repurposed text in a line below the text.

4. Submit the original report or document, along with the repurposed text, to your instructor. Be prepared to compare your repurposed text with the original text in class.

IMAGES   Images, which are files including graphic elements such as clip art, illustrations, infographics, diagrams, and photographs, are the most commonly used content element on webpages, after text. Photographs on a webpage can familiarize the unknown and aid in decision making. For example, imagine that you want to buy a house in a new city. Visiting websites that display photographs of available houses in your price range, such as the Keller Williams website (Figure 3-8), enables you to narrow your list before you contact a real estate agent.

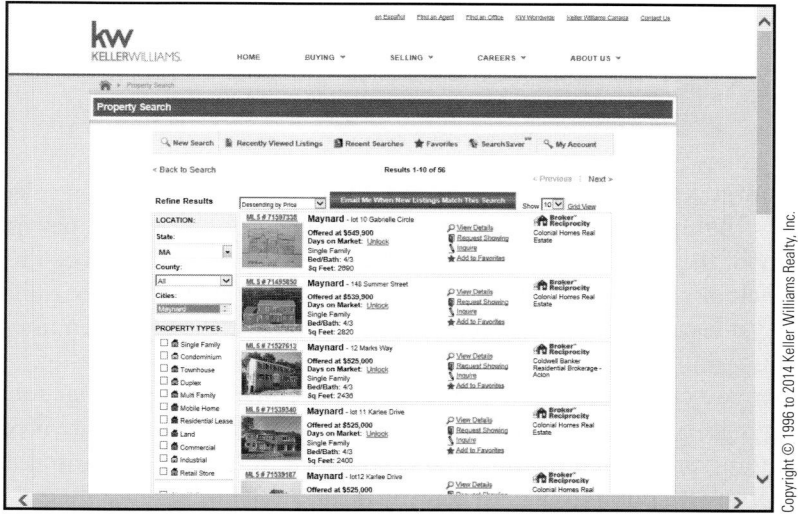

Copyright © 1996 to 2014 Keller Williams Realty, Inc.

Figure 3-8 Website images can familiarize the unknown.

You can deliver a message and/or prompt an action beyond the capabilities of text alone using images, such as clip art or photographs. Suppose you are an avid rock climber and need to lease a four-wheel-drive vehicle that can handle difficult terrain. Before you visit a dealership, you decide to shop online and visit the Jeep website. As you click through to view the photos of different Jeep models, the photo of the sleek

Jeep® Wrangler poised in the desert (Figure 3-9) captures your interest. The image prompts you to read the vehicle specifications on the website, determine that it fits your needs, and contact your local dealership to set up a test drive.

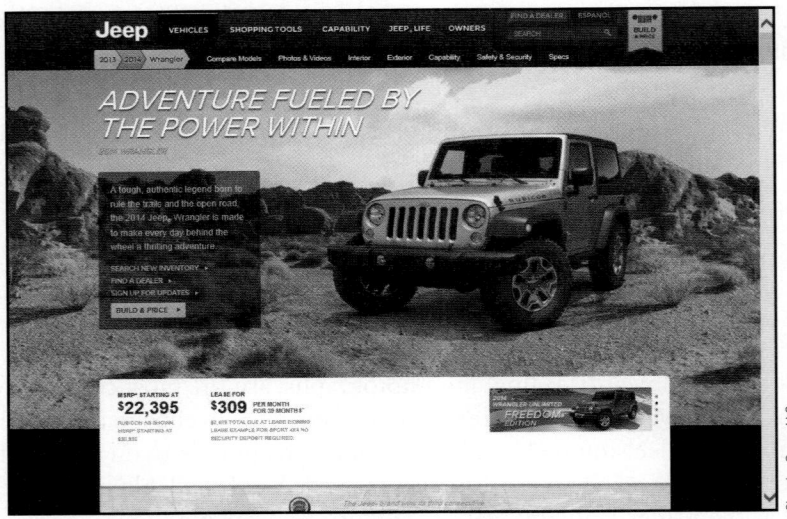

Figure 3-9 Powerful imagery can contribute to a website visitor purchasing or inquiring about your products.

 **DESIGN TIP** Webpage images can communicate and motivate powerfully. Select relevant, high-quality images that support the website's purpose.

You can draw your own illustrations and diagrams using illustration software or take your own photographs using a digital camera. Large corporations will pay for professional photography of their products to showcase them in the best light. You can find free or low-cost **stock images** — clip art and photographs — from a variety of online sources. In Chapter 5, you learn more about webpage images and the tools you can use to create and/or edit them.

Whether you create your own images or acquire them from another source, preselecting high-quality, relevant images that add value to your website is part of the website planning process. In the ongoing example for Regifting, the team asks you to research appropriate photographs to accompany articles in the reusable and recycled goods website.

DESIGN TIP Remember to ensure that content elements you use at your website are free of copyright restrictions.

Exploring Stock Photographs

1. Search the web using keywords similar to *stock photos* or *stock images* to locate at least six sources of stock photographs. Include sources of royalty-free and low-royalty photographs as well as those for which you must pay a standard licensing or royalty fee.

2. Research the selected sources' offerings for eco-friendly or recycling-related images and identify four photographs in total from the six sources suitable for the reusable and recycled goods website in the ongoing example.

3. Compare all stock photograph sources. Create a comparison table, including the following columns of information: source name, type of photographs offered, and typical cost. Add a second table that lists the four photographs selected for the reusable and recycled goods website. Include the photograph name or other identifying reference, description, source name, and cost.

4. Submit your findings in the format requested by your instructor. Be prepared to discuss the results of your research in class.

AUDIO AND VIDEO **Audio**, or sound, can vary in both form and intensity — from a child's whisper to the president's State of the Union address, or from a heavy metal band to the U.S. Navy Choir. Audio can persuade, inspire, personalize, motivate, or soothe.

Audio also enhances recall. Does a lyric that keeps playing in your head remind you of a significant life event? Does a stirring speech make you feel as if you are listening to the speaker's words live? Think of the ways that audio — with its capability of evoking emotion, prompting action, and triggering memory — can benefit your website. Imagine, for example, the persuasive effect of a glowing testimonial about your product from a satisfied customer, or recall the possibilities of a catchy jingle.

Inform visitors when a website link launches an audio file, or a video that includes sound, so that they can use a headset or turn off their speakers so as not to disturb those around them. Repetitive sounds can be irritating to frequent website visitors, so use sound sparingly.

Typically, **video**, or moving imagery, incorporates the powerful components of movement and sound to express and communicate ideas. Delivering quality video over the web efficiently can present challenges. The primary problem is the extremely large size of video files, resulting from the enormous amounts of data required to depict the audio and video. Using audio alone can be an effective, low-bandwidth alternative to video. When presenting video, web designers must decide whether to limit the size of downloadable video files or to generate streaming video. As you learned in Chapter 1, streaming media, such as audio or video, begins to play as soon as the data begins to stream, or transfer, to the browser. A user must transfer **downloadable media** in its entirety to the user's computer or device before viewing or listening to it.

If media or animations on your website require a plug-in, include a link to the plug-in manufacturer's website so website visitors can download it if necessary.

Q&A
Should I use streaming or downloadable media on my webpage? Downloadable media that you do not own can come with copyright restrictions. Downloadable media can be viewed offline once downloaded, but requires storage on the website visitor's computer or mobile device. For more information about media formats, use a search engine to search for *streaming and downloadable media.*

Q&A
What is a plug-in? Multimedia elements might require that your visitors install web browser plug-ins, software that allows multimedia elements to play in the visitors' web browsers. Many, if not most, of your website visitors will have already downloaded and installed browser media players. Most plug-ins needed to run media are free. For more information about how plug-ins work, use a search engine to search for plug-in functions.

Q&A
How does multimedia affect web accessibility? Keep in mind that some users have visual, learning, or other differences that influence their website viewing experience. For information about how the use of images and multimedia can impact web accessibility, use a search engine to search for *web accessibility multimedia.*

ANIMATION AND MULTIMEDIA   Websites often use **animated images** to attract attention and enliven webpages. A popular format is the **animated GIF** format, which adds movement to otherwise static images. Another type of animation, called **Flash animation**, is an animated movie created using Adobe® Flash® software. Adobe Flash, Apple® QuickTime, Microsoft® Silverlight®, and RealNetworks® RealPlayer® are popular, free web browser plug-ins used to play media.

Animation can add interest and appeal to your webpages; however, you must use them sparingly and only in support of your website's purpose — and only when doing so meets your target audience's expectations for content at your website. For example, a topical website promoting sports activities to a young target audience might benefit from the use of animations that encourage them to participate. However, the target audience for a B2B e-commerce website offering consulting services might find animations distracting and annoying.

Simple animations and movies are not difficult to create, as you will learn in Chapter 6. Additionally, many online vendors offer free or low-cost animations. As with any element, excessive use of animation at your website can shift your audience's focus away from the other content and mask your website's purpose. Overuse of rotating objects, scrolling text, animated advertising banners, or videos that play automatically could annoy website visitors to the extent that they might exit your website and not return.

Although definitions vary, **multimedia** typically is any combination of text, images, animation, audio, or video. Multimedia elements are popular because they can add action, excitement, and interactivity to webpages. Webpage multimedia elements can also be interactive; the website visitor participates as the multimedia plays instead of simply watching it. For example, the Weather Channel website (Figure 3-10) offers its visitors both a multimedia and an **interactive multimedia** experience. Multimedia elements such as animation, video, and music invite visitors to stay at the website by viewing photo slideshows, checking out weather forecasts, watching extreme weather videos, and more.

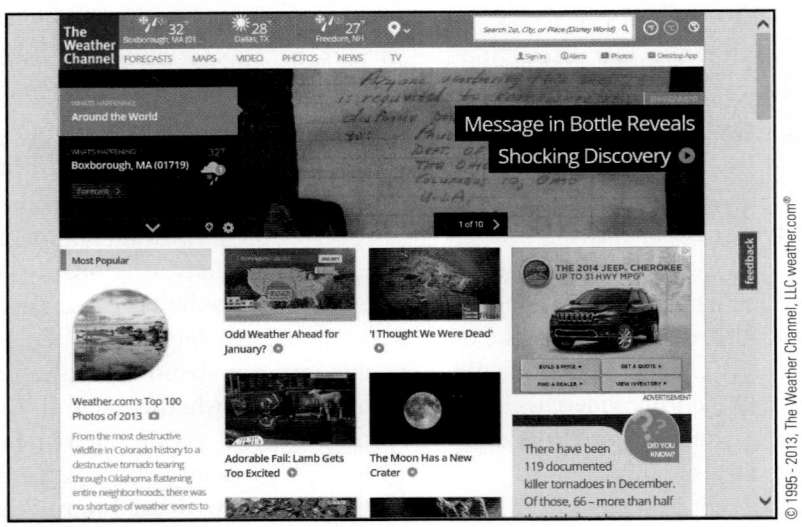

Figure 3-10 Multimedia elements can add action, excitement, and interactivity to a website.

Use animation and multimedia elements only when doing so supports your website's purpose and satisfies your target audience's expectations for content at your website. Include links to necessary plug-ins. Not all plug-ins are supported on all computers and mobile devices.

Although viewers might find your website's multimedia elements intriguing and entertaining, developing multimedia elements for your website internally can require considerable expertise, time, and money. Therefore, it might be more cost effective to purchase appropriate multimedia elements from a professional multimedia developer.

Additionally, like animated GIFs and video, you should use multimedia elements *only* in support of a website's purpose and *only* when such elements enhance visitors' experiences at the website.

TOOLKIT

Appendix C: Responsive Web Design
For information about how the use of images and multimedia can impact responsive web design, see Appendix C.

Web designers without the necessary programming resources and expertise can purchase ready-made multimedia elements from professional multimedia developers.

Exploring Webpage Animation and Multimedia

YOUR TURN

1. Use a search engine to locate the home pages for Disney, Warner Bros. Studios, and Extreme Sports Channel.
2. Open each website in a new tab. Review the home page and three of the underlying pages at each website.
3. Evaluate each website to determine how, in your opinion, the:
   a. Home page content makes clear the website's purpose.
   b. Home page content satisfactorily answers the Who?, What?, Why?, and Where? visitor questions.
   c. Animation or multimedia elements on the home and underlying pages support the website's purpose and meet target audience needs and expectations.
4. Summarize your findings by identifying each website and its purpose, and describe the animation and/or multimedia elements used. Discuss whether these elements contribute to the website's purpose and enhance visitors' experiences at the website. Be prepared to discuss your findings in class.
5. Search for websites from which you can purchase animations and multimedia for a fee. Visit one of the websites, and locate at least one element you feel would be appropriate for the Regifting website. Make a note of the cost, technical requirements, and quality of the element. Conclude whether the element meets the criteria for inclusion.

DYNAMICALLY GENERATED CONTENT   **Dynamically generated content**, unlike static information, updates periodically and can appear on a website's pages when triggered by a specific event, such as the time of day or by visitor request. Webpages that display dynamically generated content typically acquire the information from a database. A **database** is a file that stores data, such as a store's inventory or a library's card catalog, so that the contents are searchable and easily updated. Websites that use databases to generate dynamic content are **database-driven websites**. Figure 3-11 illustrates the result of a request for dynamically generated content — course and schedule information — from a Portland Community College database.

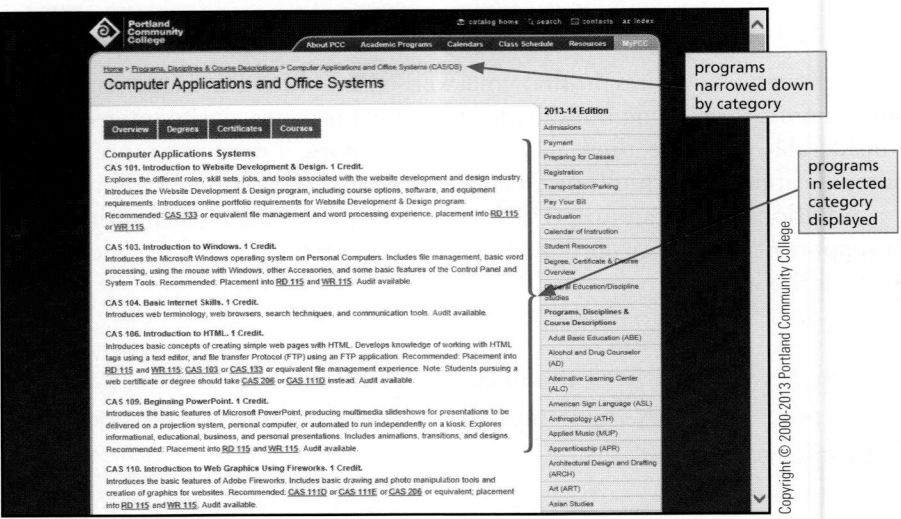

Figure 3-11 Dynamic content is updated as a result of specific events.

DESIGN TIP   Use databases to provide dynamic content to e-commerce websites to keep track of items sold and update product availability and inventory, or for an academic website to make sure online enrollment of classes falls within class-size guidelines.

What is a gadget? A *gadget* or *widget* is a fragment of code that creates dynamic content. Examples of gadgets include dynamic calendars, live weather feeds, clocks, "to-do" lists, interactive games, virtual animals, and more. Some websites allow you to copy gadget code and then paste the code into your webpage to add the gadget. Most WYSIWYG editors include widgets or gadgets. Some gadgets or widgets are specific to mobile web content.

Continuing with the Regifting example, you and the team agree that the value-added content for your website will include text articles and tips, appropriate photos and a logo image, product information, and video clips of client testimonials. Animated GIFs and multimedia are not appropriate for the website's purpose and target audience expectations, but dynamically generated content is necessary to populate the product catalog. Figure 3-12 illustrates further development of the planning document for the reusable and recycled goods website.

Regifting Website
Value-Added Content

The website's value-added content will include the following:

- Company logo
- Photos of products
- Video clips of customer testimonials and employee comments
- Current news pages with articles, press releases, and columns
- Environmental tips and tricks on most pages

© 2015 Cengage Learning

Figure 3-12 Value-added content for the Regifting website includes text, images, video clips, and dynamically generated content.

Organizing Website Files

As you develop your website, you should organize the resulting files, including HTML, image, animation, and multimedia files, to make it easier to maintain them and to publish your website. If your website is small — fewer than 5–10 total files — consider creating a single folder on your computer's local hard drive for all the files. If your website will exceed 10 files, consider creating separate, logical subfolders; for example, include subfolders for HTML code, photographs, audio, video, animation, and multimedia files. Remember that a single webpage can comprise many files, because each graphical element and article or document is its own file. For both small and large websites, create a subfolder in which you can place original files, such as word-processing files or image files that you later will convert into web-usable formats.

To protect the system of folders and subfolders that you create, you should back up your files regularly, and store the backups at a location separate from your local hard drive. For example, back up to a removable flash drive or online file storage service.

Plan an organized file system for your website files. You will work more effectively, minimize the risk of losing or misplacing content elements, and facilitate the publishing of your website if you are organized. Back up your files on a regular basis.

DESIGN TIP

Step 3: Select the Website's Structure

After you define a website's purpose and identify its target audience, you are ready to plan the structure of the website — the linked arrangement of the website's pages from the home page. The website's structure should support the website's purpose and make it easy for visitors to find what they want at the website in as few clicks as possible. The website should use navigation, links, breadcrumb trails (discussed in Chapter 4), and other methods to show website visitors their location within the website, and also should show how to return to the home page or previously visited webpages.

Planning the website's structure before you begin creating its pages has several benefits, such as the ability to do the following:

- Visualize the organization of the website's pages and linking relationships.
- Organize the pages by level of detail.
- Follow the links between pages to make certain visitors can click through the website quickly to find useful information — fewer clicks mean more satisfied website visitors.
- Detect **dead-end pages**, which are pages that currently do not fit into the linking arrangement.
- Rearrange pages and revise linking relationships, and then visualize the changes before you create the website.

An outline of a website's structure can serve as a blueprint and illustrate how visitors can follow links from page to page. Some designers use a text outline to plan a website's structure, whereas others follow the storyboard process to create a visual representation of the website's structure. A **storyboard** is a series of pages originally developed to present scenes graphically for a movie or television program. To create a simple

Q&A

Can I use Microsoft® Office® to create a flowchart?
Yes. Microsoft Word, Microsoft Excel, and Microsoft PowerPoint provide SmartArt objects, which allow you to create hierarchical or graphical representations of linked pages.

website storyboard, arrange sticky notes or index cards — each note or card representing a webpage — on a wall or corkboard to visualize a website's proposed structure. Figure 3-13 is an example of a storyboard used to plan a website's structure.

A **flowchart** is a diagram that shows steps or processes; flowcharts are another useful way to outline a website's structures. To create a flowchart, draw an arrangement of shapes and lines where each shape indicates a page and each line indicates a link from page to page. You can manually draw the structure flowchart, use application tools such as SmartArt objects, or use drawing software, such as Microsoft® Visio® Professional.

As a web designer, you should choose the method that you find most flexible to outline your website's structure. Regardless of the tool you use, your website's structure will likely follow one of three structural themes: linear/tutorial, webbed, or hierarchical.

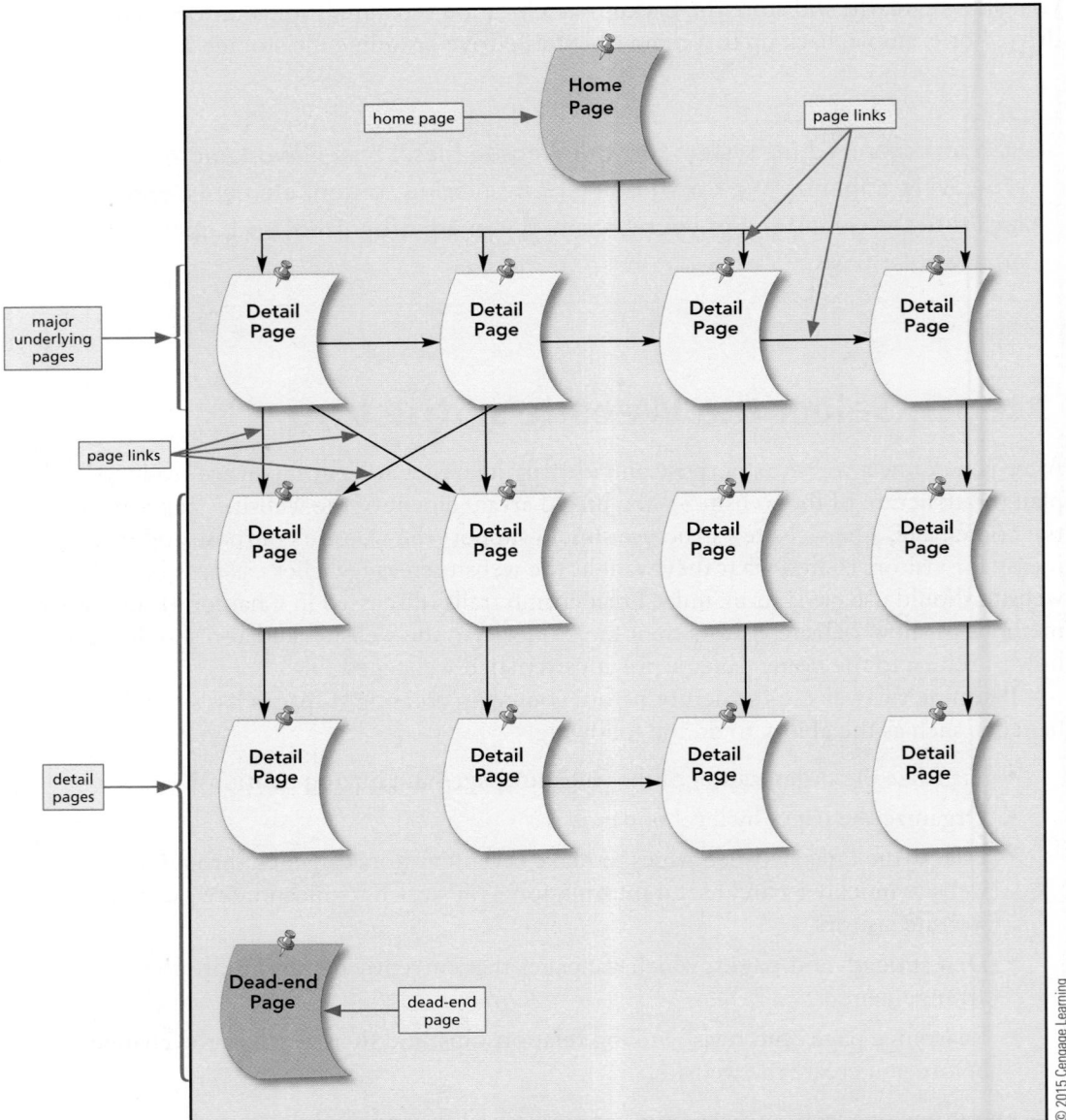

© 2015 Cengage Learning

Figure 3-13 A storyboard is a useful tool for planning a website's structure and defining the links between pages.

Linear/Tutorial Structure

A **linear/tutorial website structure** organizes and presents webpages in a specific order, as shown in Figure 3-14. A training website could use this structure to ensure that users do not miss steps or perform steps out of sequence. For example, a website that illustrates how to serve a tennis ball properly would use this structure to demonstrate the necessary range of motions in the correct order. The linear/tutorial structure controls the navigation of users by progressing them from one webpage to the next. The linear/ tutorial structure is also appropriate for information presented in a historical or chronological order; for example, a website that details the explosive growth of e-commerce might benefit from this structure.

© 2015 Cengage Learning

Figure 3-14 A linear/tutorial website structure organizes webpages in a specific order.

Webbed Structure

A **webbed website structure**, also called a **random website structure**, does not arrange its pages in a specific order. From the home page of a website organized around a webbed structure, visitors can choose any other webpage according to their interests or inclinations. Figure 3-15 illustrates a webbed website structure and shows how a visitor to this type of website could navigate to different webpages as he or she sees fit. Websites that use a webbed structure need to provide a search feature so that website visitors easily can find the information they need. Webbed structures work well for some informational websites, such as Wikipedia, or for catalogs.

Q&A | **Do all websites have multiple pages?**
No. Some web designers create one-page websites, where information is all on one scrollable page, or all of the information is viewable within a standard screen view. This is not appropriate for any content-heavy websites, and can make it difficult to apply search engine optimization (SEO) and responsive web design practices. For more information, use a search engine to search for *one-page website SEO*, and *one-page website responsive web design*.

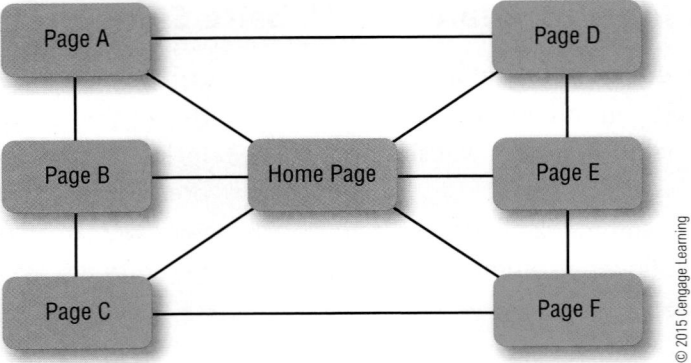

Figure 3-15 A webbed website structure does not arrange its pages in a specific order.

Hierarchical Structure

A **hierarchical website structure** organizes webpages into categories and subcategories by an increasing level of detail, as shown in Figure 3-13 (the storyboard illustration) and in Figure 3-16. Organizational and topical websites usually are well suited to a hierarchical structure. A university website, for example, might structure its webpages in three categories with multiple subcategories:

- Academics category with majors and departments subcategories
- Athletics category with teams and schedules subcategories
- Students category with current and prospective students and alumni subcategories

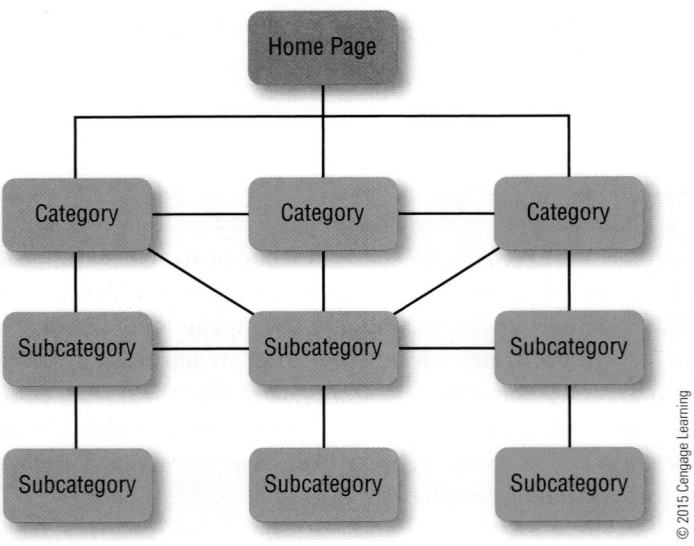

Q&A

Which website structure should I choose?
The type of structure you use is an important choice. Base your decision on the website content and how website visitors will look for information on your website. For more information about planning website structure, use a search engine to search for *website structure*.

Figure 3-16 A hierarchical structure organizes webpages into categories and subcategories by increasing level of detail.

Websites with many pages and multiple objectives, such as an e-commerce website, might use a combination of the three primary website structures rather than adhering to a single website structure to organize its pages. Returning to the Regifting website example, you and your team agree on a website structure that combines the hierarchical and linear structures. Figure 3-17 illustrates the update to the design plan to include the structure flowchart.

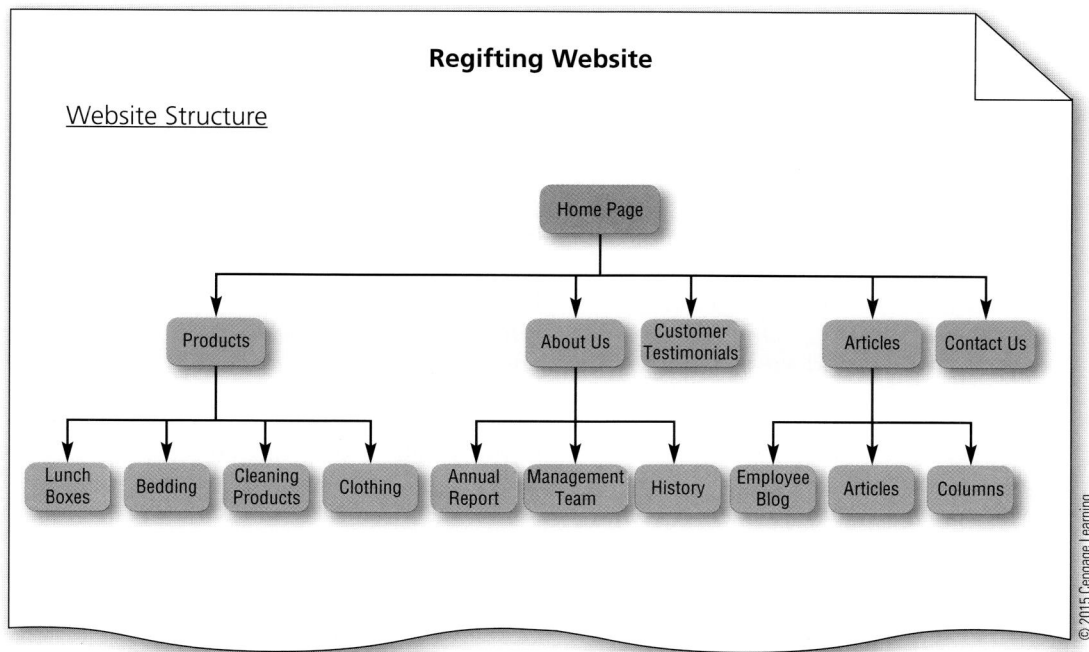

Figure 3-17 The recycled and reusable goods website's structure combines the hierarchical and linear structures.

Plan the structure of your website to support the website's purpose and make it easy for visitors to meet their needs and expectations at the website. Formalize the structure plan using a text outline, storyboard, or flowchart.

DESIGN TIP

Chapter Review

Creating a website demands a considerable investment of time and other important resources. To ensure a website's success, a detailed website plan is essential. Website planning incorporates six general steps, the first three of which you learned about in this chapter. Step 1 defines the purpose of the website, which entails determining goals and objectives. Step 1 also identifies the website's target audience, including developing a target audience profile and needs assessment. Step 2 identifies the general content of the website, including webpage selection and types of value-added content to be used. Content types include text, images, audio, video, animation, multimedia, and dynamically generated content. As you develop a website, having an organized electronic filing system for files and folders will help you work more effectively, minimize the risk of losing or misplacing elements, and smooth the process of publishing your website. Finally, Step 3 involves planning the website's structure: linear/tutorial, webbed, or hierarchical.

After reading the chapter, you should know each of these key terms.

TERMS TO KNOW

animated GIF (84)
animated images (84)
audio (83)

call-to-action (72)
database (85)
database-driven websites (86)

dead-end pages (87)	psychographic characteristics (72)
demographic characteristics (72)	purpose statement (71)
design plan (70)	random website structure (89)
downloadable media (83)	repurpose (80)
dynamically generated content (85)	search feature (77)
Flash animation (84)	splash page (78)
flowchart (88)	stock images (82)
goals (71)	storyboard (87)
hierarchical website structure (90)	target audience (71)
infographic (80)	target audience profile (72)
interactive multimedia (84)	underlying pages (76)
linear/tutorial website structure (89)	value-added content (80)
multimedia (84)	video (83)
needs assessment (74)	webbed website structure (89)
objectives (71)	website plan (70)

TEST YOUR KNOWLEDGE

Complete the Test Your Knowledge exercises to solidify what you have learned in the chapter.

Matching Terms

Match each term with the best description.

____ 1. website plan

____ 2. gadget

____ 3. dead-end pages

____ 4. database-driven website

____ 5. purpose statement

____ 6. linear/tutorial website structure

____ 7. psychographic characteristics

____ 8. plug-in

____ 9. webbed website structure

____ 10. stock image

____ 11. value-added content

____ 12. call-to-action

____ 13. hierarchical website structure

a. A website that delivers content from a collection of data based on user input, such as a library card catalog.

b. Webpages arranged in no specific order.

c. Webpages organized by categories and subcategories.

d. Social group affiliations, lifestyle choices, purchasing preferences, political affiliations, and other characteristics that explain why visitors might want to access your website.

e. A webpage that currently does not fit into the linking arrangement.

f. Information that is relative, informative, and timely; accurate and of high quality; and usable.

g. Software that allows certain content to function in a browser window.

h. Clip art and photographs available for free or to purchase.

i. Something that requires the website visitor to interact with the website in some method.

j. A fragment of code that creates dynamic content.

k. A formal written explanation of a website's overall goals and the specific objectives related to those goals.

l. A formal document that states a website's purpose, goals, objectives, general content, and structure.

m. Webpages that must be viewed in a specific order.

Short Answer Questions

Write a brief answer to each question.

1. Differentiate between goals and objectives when planning a website. Describe a purpose statement.

2. Identify the first three steps in developing the website plan for a website.

3. Discuss how to develop a target audience profile and target audience needs assessment.

4. Define the four primary questions visitors want answered by home page content and identify the types of content on a commercial website's home page that can answer visitors' questions.

5. Define psychographic characteristics and explain their role in creating a target audience profile.

6. Discuss the functions of a home page, landing page, and underlying pages.

7. What is value-added content? Discuss how the following content types can add value to a website: text, images, animation, audio and video, multimedia, and dynamically generated content.

8. Explain what a database-driven website is, and give two examples of such websites.

9. Define the term, flowchart, and explain its role in the website development process.

10. Describe three basic website structures and give examples that illustrate when each type of structure is appropriate.

Test your knowledge of chapter content and key terms.

LEARN IT ONLINE

Instructions: Reinforce what you learned in this chapter with games, exercises, training, and many other online activities and resources. Reinforcement activities and resources are available at no additional cost on www.cengagebrain.com.

Investigate current web design developments with the Trends exercises.

TRENDS

Write a brief essay about each of the following trends, using the web as your research tool. For each trend, identify at least one webpage URL used as a research source. Be prepared to discuss your findings in class.

1 | Gadgets for Mobile Devices

Use a search engine to determine what web gadgets are available for mobile devices. Are any mobile gadgets compatible with PC or laptop gadgets? If so, which ones? Research guidelines and restrictions for using gadgets for webpages that will be viewed on mobile devices.

2 | One-Page Websites

The websites with which you are familiar typically consist of several linked pages with a clear organization and an easy-to-use navigation system. However, some websites consist of only one page. Research the trend of creating one-page websites. Find an article that reviews or advises how to use one-page websites. View a few one-page websites. Are they effective or too long? How much scrolling do you have to do to view the entire page? As a web designer, what type of client would you advise to have a one-page website? How does responsive web design affect the decision to create a one-page website?

AT ISSUE

Challenge your perspective of the web and web design technology with the @Issue exercises.

Write a brief essay in response to the following issues, using the web as your research tool. For each issue, identify at least one webpage URL used as a research source. Be prepared to discuss your findings in class.

1 | Website Purpose Statements vs. Website Mission Statements

A commercial or noncommercial organization often develops an organizational mission statement to succinctly explain to its constituencies (members, customers, employees, shareholders, business partners, government agencies, and so forth) why the organization exists. The use of succinctly worded website mission statements is an outgrowth of the use of these organizational mission statements. However, some business and web critics consider formal organizational or website mission statements to be useless. After researching the arguments for and against website mission statements, create a report that accomplishes the following:

a. Compares website *purpose* statements as described in this chapter with examples of website *mission* statements. How are they alike? How are they different?

b. Describes how, as a web designer, you would advise a client on the inclusion of a website purpose and/or website mission statement at a B2B website.

2 | Web Accessibility

Research web accessibility issues with using multimedia in websites. What kinds of multimedia may cause website visitors to have difficulty viewing or interacting with your website? What types of adaptive devices and software are available for users with accessibility issues to use with mobile devices, or desktop and laptop computers? What can you do, as a web designer, to create a website that is accessible to all or most users?

Use the **World Wide Web** to obtain more information about the concepts in the chapter with the Hands On exercises.

1 | Explore and Evaluate: Database-Driven Websites

Browse the web to locate three examples of either e-commerce or academic websites that use databases to provide dynamic content. How does the website enable users to interact with the database? What user interactions may cause information in the database to update or change? Using what type of format(s) does the user interact with the database both to retrieve and input data?

2 | Search and Discover: Free or Inexpensive Animated Images

Use a search engine to identify at least five sources of free or inexpensive animated images for use on webpages. Then write a brief description identifying each source, the types of animated images offered, and, if not free, the typical cost. List any restrictions imposed on the use of free animated images. Select one animated image from each website and describe a situation in which you, as a web designer, might include it on a webpage.

Work collaboratively to reinforce the concepts in the chapter with the Team Approach exercises.

1 | Value-Added Content

Good web design involves using value-added content that attracts, informs, and entices website visitors. Team up with two other students to examine the content on the following websites. List the different types of content that appears on the home page and two underlying pages for each website. Think about what might be the target audience for each website, and the design and content choices that the website owners made to meet the audience's expectations.

a. Thirty-One Gifts

b. MapMyFitness

c. houzz

Explain how each website uses value-added content. Cite examples that support the teams' decision on how well each website uses value-added content.

2 | Website Goals, Objectives, and Purpose Statement

Join with two other classmates to create a team for this activity. Select two of the team members to form a web design team. The third team member will assume the role of the client who hires the web design team to develop his or her website.

a. The client develops an idea for a B2C website of his or her choice, for example, a bike shop or a pet grooming business.

b. The design team works with the client to develop a list of website goals and objectives, write a formal purpose statement, and develop the target audience profile and needs assessment for the website.

c. As a team, search for two websites that are similar to the one you have planned. Create a presentation for the instructor and other classmates that compares the team's website plan with the sample websites. Include in the presentation an evaluation of how the sample websites met their objectives and what changes you would make to their websites or your website plan after doing the comparison.

CASE STUDY

Apply the chapter concepts to the ongoing development process in web design with the Case Study.

The Case Study is an ongoing development process using the concepts, techniques, and Design Tips presented in each chapter.

Background Information

The three steps described in this chapter covered a lot of material — from defining the website's goals, objectives, and audience, to planning a website's content and structure. If you have carefully explored the information in each step and have worked your way through the end-of-chapter materials for this chapter, you are ready to tackle this chapter's assignment.

Chapter 3 Assignment

In this assignment, you will begin to create your own formal website plan by defining the website's goals and objectives, writing a formal purpose statement, and creating a target audience profile and needs assessment. You will also plan its general content and structure.

1. Using the report you created in the Chapter 2 Case Study as your starting point, create a formal website plan.

    a. Determine your website's goals and objectives and draft the website's purpose statement.

    b. Identify your website's target audience(s) and determine the wants, needs, and likely expectations that your website's design and content should satisfy for that audience.

    c. Identify the pages you initially plan to include at your website.

    d. Add to your website plan a list of value-added content that will help achieve your website's purpose and satisfy target audience needs. Identify possible sources for the content, keeping in mind the copyright issues discussed in Chapter 2.

    e. Determine which of the three website structures — linear/tutorial, webbed, or hierarchical (or a combination of structures) — will best meet your website's purpose. Use a text outline, or manually draw the structure, create a storyboard, or use flowcharting software to illustrate your website's structure as part of your design plan.

2. Submit your partial design plan to your instructor. Be prepared to discuss the elements of your partial design plan in class.

4 | Planning a Successful Website: Part 2

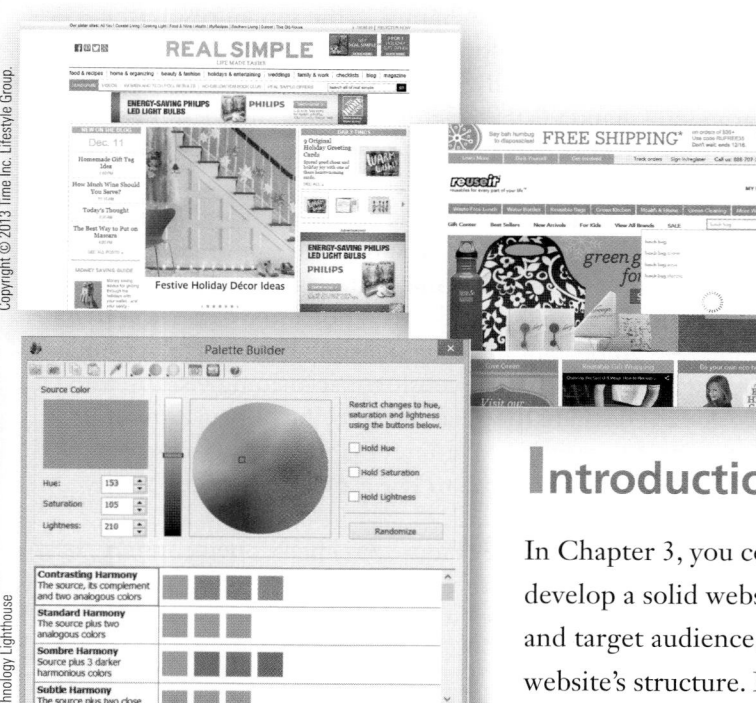

Introduction

In Chapter 3, you completed the first three of the six steps required to develop a solid website design plan: you defined the website's goals, purpose, and target audience; planned the website's general content; and specified the website's structure. In this chapter, you continue the development of your website plan by discovering how appropriately using two variables—page length and content placement—can enhance webpage usability. Then you complete Steps 4 through 6, in which you plan the navigation, select design options for your website, and plan for how you will publish and maintain the website. Finally, you use a checklist to review your completed website plan.

Objectives

After completing this chapter, you will be able to:

1. Discuss the relationship between page length, content placement, and usability

2. Complete Step 4: Specify the website's navigation system

3. Complete Step 5: Design the look and feel of the website

4. Complete Step 6: Test, publish, and maintain the website

5. Use a checklist to review your web design plan

Page Length, Content Placement, and Usability

When a website visitor views your website for the first time, he or she will see a webpage (or part of a webpage) that provides a sense of the website's contents and its ability to meet visitor needs and expectations. As you learned in Chapter 2, the screen resolution and size determine how much of a page is visible. At lower resolutions, and with smaller screen sizes, a visitor likely will need to scroll vertically and perhaps horizontally to view the entire webpage. You also learned in Chapter 2 that visitors typically dislike unnecessary scrolling and often avoid doing so. Visitors may not see any page content below and to the right of the visible screen area.

Because you cannot control visitors' screen resolution and size, you should take care to position visual identity content, such as logos and names, and important links, above and to the left of the potential scroll lines or the **scroll zone**, which is the area beyond the initial visible screen. Placing identifying page content and navigational tools above and to the left of the scroll zone is especially important for your website's home page. As you learned in Chapter 3, your home page introduces your website by informing visitors who you are, what you offer at the website, and where they can find specific information or website features. One way to maximize the initial visual content is to employ carousels or slide shows; doing so gives readers quick access to three to five articles or images in the space of one.

The web designers of the Real Simple home page (Figure 4-1) positioned content important for visual identity and links to major areas of the website above and to the left of the potential scroll lines, and used a carousel to display content.

TOOLKIT

RWD: Carousels and slide shows Carousels and slide shows help prevent webpage scrolling. See Appendix C for more information about using responsive web design techniques to create carousels and slide shows.

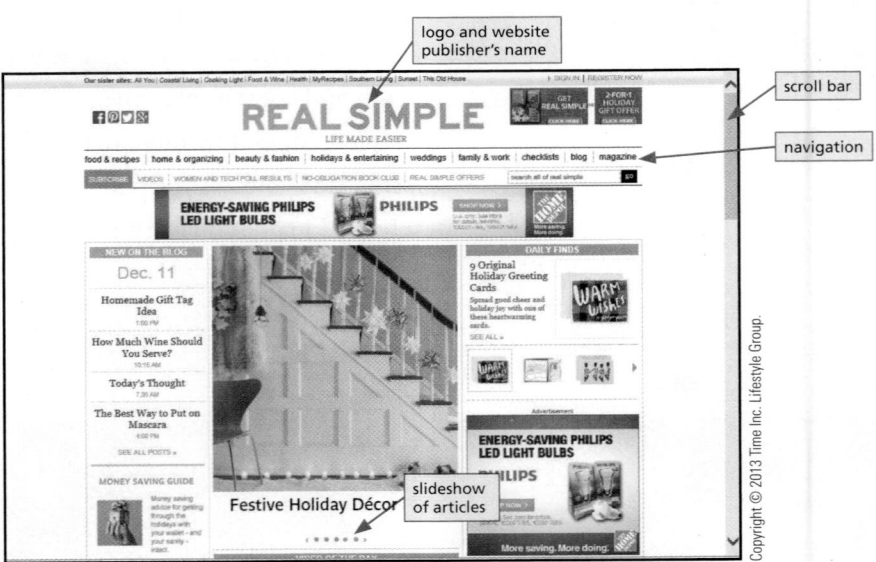

Figure 4-1 Place content important for visual identity and navigation above and to the left of the scroll zone.

DESIGN TIP You have no control over visitors' monitor resolution, screen size, or scrolling habits. To increase usability, take care to place important content, such as logos, names, and major links, above and to the left of potential scroll lines, and use RWD techniques.

To increase usability and promote unity, you follow the same guidelines on underlying pages by placing identifying and navigational elements above and to the left of potential scroll lines. By their nature, underlying pages provide greater detail in support of a specific topic or website feature and might not lend themselves to a single page of text, graphics, and other content. When it is necessary to extend webpage content beyond a single visible screen, consider limiting the page length to two screens of content. If you follow the two-screen guideline, your visitors will not need to scroll excessively to view the page's entirety, and can easily return to the top of the page and the navigation area.

If vertical scrolling is necessary, ensure a logical flow of information. Avoid horizontal scrolling on all pages. Add navigation or links at logical positions within a page that flows beyond two screens.

DESIGN TIP

Another issue to consider in content positioning is *where* visitors typically first look when viewing a webpage. **Eye-tracking studies** use various technologies to produce **heat maps** that represent data using color. Heat maps analyze the movement of a visitor's eyes as he or she views a webpage. Eye-tracking studies suggest that a website's visitors typically first look at the top and left areas of a page, and then look down and to the right. These eye-tracking studies add support to the concept of placing visual identity content and major links at or near the top and left side of a page to improve usability. Web marketing relies on data from eye-tracking studies. You learn more about website marketing in Chapter 7. Figure 4-2 illustrates the Johnson & Johnson home page with visual identity content and major links positioned at the top and on the left side of the page.

company name at the upper-left of the home page

navigation links along top of home page

Figure 4-2 Visitors typically look first at the top and left areas of a webpage.

When designing a webpage, you need to decide how to manage page width. A **fixed-width page layout** sets a specific pixel width for the page. The benefit of fixed-width pages is that the layout is consistent no matter the resolution. Fixed-width page layouts can create problems, however. On screens with lower resolution or smaller sizes, visitors may need to scroll a fixed-width horizontally. Conversely, when viewed on a larger screen, a fixed-width page may have an excess of white space, which can be distracting to the visitor. A **liquid** or **flexible page layout** sets the width of the page as a percentage of the browser window. The benefit of liquid layouts is that the page expands to fill the entire window, maximizing the viewable content; however, liquid layouts allow for less control over size or placement of images and text, which can result in awkward or unreadable placement or content. A **hybrid page layout** uses a combination of fixed-width and liquid page layouts, and takes into consideration responsive web design (RWD) techniques.

DESIGN TIP   Consider the needs of your likely website visitors and current RWD practices when deciding on a page layout format. Make sure to test your pages at different resolutions and screen sizes.

YOUR TURN

Exploring Webpage Width Options

1. Use the search tool of your choice to search using the keywords *liquid layout, fixed-width layout, responsive web design* or similar keywords. Locate three articles that discuss the benefits and downsides of different techniques.
2. Summarize your research. Discuss how you might apply what you learned about

webpage width to the design of a website, taking into consideration audience needs and how the page will look at different resolutions.
3. Submit your findings in the format requested by your instructor.

Step 4: Specify the Website's Navigation System

Q&A

What are the WAI Guidelines?
WAI is the Web Accessibility Initiative. The WAI develops guidelines to ensure all website visitors can access content on webpages. For more information about WAI guidelines for links and other webpage elements, use a search engine to search for *WAI web guidelines*.

Once you have determined the structure of your website, the next step in developing your website plan is to specify the navigation system you will use. A navigation system that is easy for visitors to understand and follow will draw them deeper into your website to view detail pages with content that can satisfy their needs and expectations. A website navigation system consists of different types of links: text links; image links; related link groups presented as menus, bars, or tabs; breadcrumb trails; and website maps. Websites often use a combination of these link types as part of a navigation system. A large website with many pages also should include a search capability, which allows visitors to search for content within the webpage. You also should keep in mind the needs of touch screen users when deciding on navigation options. No matter what combination of link types you use for your website's navigation system, the links should be both user-based and user-controlled; these concepts are described in the following section. In addition, make sure your use of links meets current WAI guidelines for accessibility.

User-Based and User-Controlled Navigation

In Chapter 3, you learned about the three common structures used to organize the pages at a website: linear/tutorial, webbed, and hierarchical. In our ongoing example, the Regifting website team has selected a combination of hierarchical and linear website structure. In Chapter 3, you also created a flowchart (see Figure 3-17) that illustrated the organization of website pages and the major links between pages. With this structure in mind, you are ready to select the link types for your pages.

A **user-based navigation system** provides a linking relationship between pages based on the website *visitors'* needs rather than the website *publisher's* needs. To develop a user-based navigation system, you can combine the target audience profile information you developed in your website plan's Step 1 and the basic website structure developed in Step 3 with an understanding of exactly how visitors will use your website. One way to get a better understanding of how visitors actually will use your website — and to ensure that your website's navigation system is user-based — is to perform usability tests as you develop the system. You will learn more about usability testing later in the chapter.

A **user-controlled navigation system** provides a variety of ways visitors can move around a website beyond the major links from the home page. User-controlled navigation allows visitors to move around a website in a manner *they* choose — and not be restricted to the website publisher's opinion of how visitors should move from page to page. For example, some visitors to a B2C website might go straight to the product catalog. Others might prefer to learn more about the company first before going to the product catalog. Some visitors might prefer to search for a specific product. Include a link back to the home page on all underlying pages and include Next Page and Previous Page links on sequential pages, such as multiple pages in a catalog. Offering various types of links in your navigation system allows website visitors the freedom to choose how they want to move from page to page at your website.

Q&A

How can I make my website touch screen-friendly? Some menus can be difficult for touch screen users to navigate. Touch screens do not have a pointing device that changes to a hand pointer when positioned over a link, so links and navigation must be obvious to all visitors. For more information about making your website accessible for touch screen users, use a search engine to search for *touch screen-friendly website navigation*.

> Create a user-based navigation system to match the way visitors move from page to page at your website. Consider all types of users and their different needs, including how they search for content and what type of devices they use.

DESIGN TIP

Link Types

To create a well-designed, user-controlled navigation system for your website, consider combining different types of links: text links; image links; groups of related links presented as menus, bars, or tabs; a breadcrumb trail; and a website map. You also should consider adding a search capability to your website.

TEXT LINKS   **Text links** are hyperlinks based on a word or words in an HTML document. Text links are a common way to navigate from section to section on the same page, from page to page at the same website, or from a page at one website to a page at another website. A text link should clearly identify its **target**, which is the webpage or content to which the link points. Avoid using ambiguous text, such as *click here*, to indicate a text link. When including text links to related content, such as an article that provides background information, create the text link using existing text that flows within the page content. This technique frequently is used in news articles, such as the one in the *PCWorld* article shown in Figure 4-3 on the following page.

As you learned in Chapter 2, the traditional formatting for a fresh, unclicked text link is blue, underlined text. After a visitor clicks a text link, the text remains underlined, but the color traditionally changes to purple to indicate a followed link. Including both underlining and color to indicate a text link helps to meet website accessibility standards.

Using traditional formatting for the text links on your pages can ensure the pages' usability, but might not fit with your webpage design. Consider using a different color for your links that matches your webpage design. Be consistent with how text links are treated throughout your website. Avoid using underlining for emphasis in body text, as underlining implies a link. Instead, use bold or italic formatting for emphasis.

Q&A

What are the WAI guidelines for links and navigation?
WAI guidelines for links specify to identify the target for a link clearly, and not to use color alone to identify links. Group related links together in navigation bars consistently across all pages at a website.

Hewlett Packard is making the case for private and hybrid clouds in Barcelona this week at its annual HP Discover user conference.

"We're seeing a significant amount of traction today in the hybrid world," said Kerry Bailey, an HP senior vice president for HP cloud services.

text link

Last month, during its own annual user conference, rival Amazon Web Services

© IDG Consumer & SMB

Figure 4-3 Within an article, use existing text to create links.

DESIGN TIP Use descriptive language in a text link to indicate the target page content. Use consistent formatting for text links throughout your website. Avoid using color alone to specify a text link. Add underlining in addition to color to meet accessibility standards.

TOOLKIT

Creating Rollover Effects
If you decide that including hidden text links serves a purpose or adds interest to your pages while still accommodating visitors' navigation needs and expectations, you can create the rollover effects with scripts or CSS. See Appendix B for more information.

Today, advances in technology and the increased sophistication of web users combine to encourage designers to add variety to text link formatting. When you browse the web or review webpage illustrations in this text, you might find text links in almost any color, sometimes underlined and sometimes not. When visiting webpages using a desktop or laptop, you also might find text links that look like body text until you hover the pointer over the text, at which time it changes color and/or is underlined indicating a link. This type of hidden link is a **rollover link** or **mouseover link**. Use caution when creating rollover links or using different color scheme colors for your text links. User-based navigation requires that you first consider the effect of hidden or differently formatted fresh and followed text links on the usability and accessibility of your website's pages. As mentioned previously, visitors using touch screen devices may not know when a hidden link is on the webpage.

DESIGN TIP Avoid hidden rollover text links unless their inclusion satisfies your target audiences' expectations for text links and there is no adverse effect on the usability and accessibility of your website's pages.

Exploring Text Link Formatting

1. Locate six websites: two e-commerce websites, two blogs about web design, and two organizational websites. Follow text links at each website.
2. Examine how each website presents text links.
   a. Does the link text clearly identify the link's target webpage or content?
   b. Does the website use traditional fresh and followed link colors and underlining to define text links? Are hidden or rollover text links used?

   c. Is there any difference in the approach to text links among the different types of websites?
   d. How easy or difficult was it for you to identify and follow the text links?
   e. Will the results of your research determine how you format text links at your website? If yes, how? If no, why not?
3. Summarize your findings and submit in the format requested by your instructor.

IMAGE LINKS   An **image link** assigns a link to a visual element, such as an illustration or a photograph. A common use of an image link is an image map. An **image map**, sometimes referred to as a clickable map, is an image that contains **hot spots**, which are areas on the image to which a link is assigned. A common use of an image map is a clickable geographic map, such as the NOAA climate map shown in Figure 4-4. Figure 4-5 illustrates an image map with hot spot links to underlying pages.

Q&A How should I use an image map? If you decide to use an image map, choose a photograph or illustration that accurately represents the target pages and meets design guidelines for visual consistency.

Q&A What are the WAI guidelines for image maps? WAI guidelines specify that you should provide a text equivalent for a graphic element, such as an image map. Use client-side image maps when possible. Provide redundant text links for server-side image map hot spots.

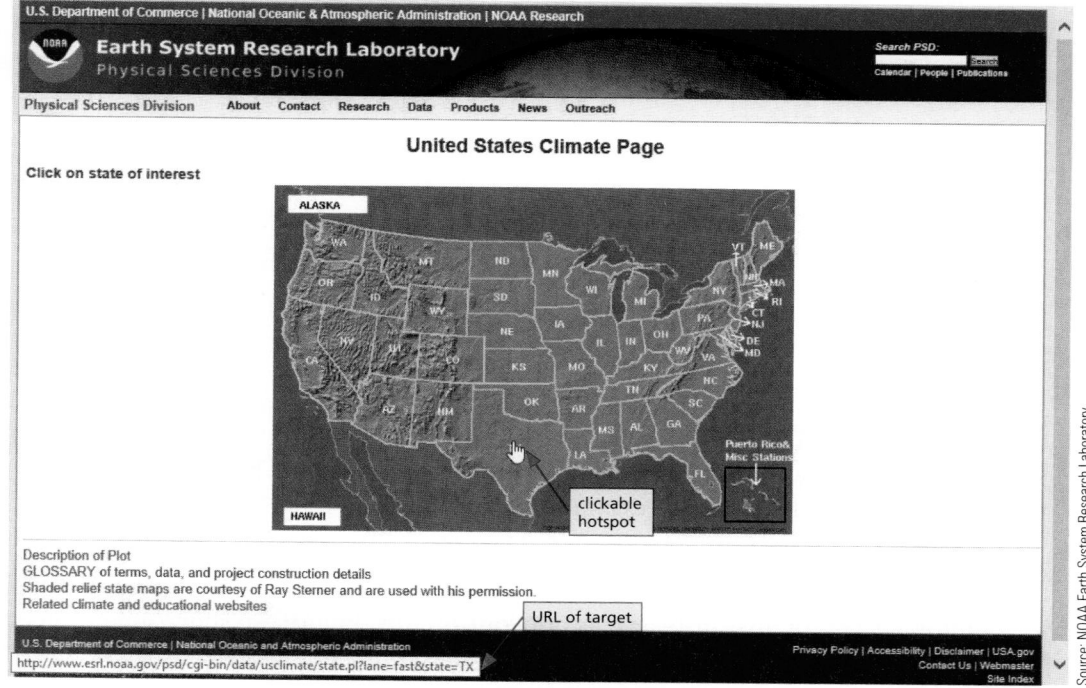

Figure 4-4 A common use of an image map is a clickable geographic map.

Source: NOAA Earth System Research Laboratory

Q&A

What type of image map should I use?
Use client-side image maps when possible. Provide redundant text links for server-side image map hot spots. For more information about client-side and server-side image maps, use a search engine to search for *client- and server-side image maps*.

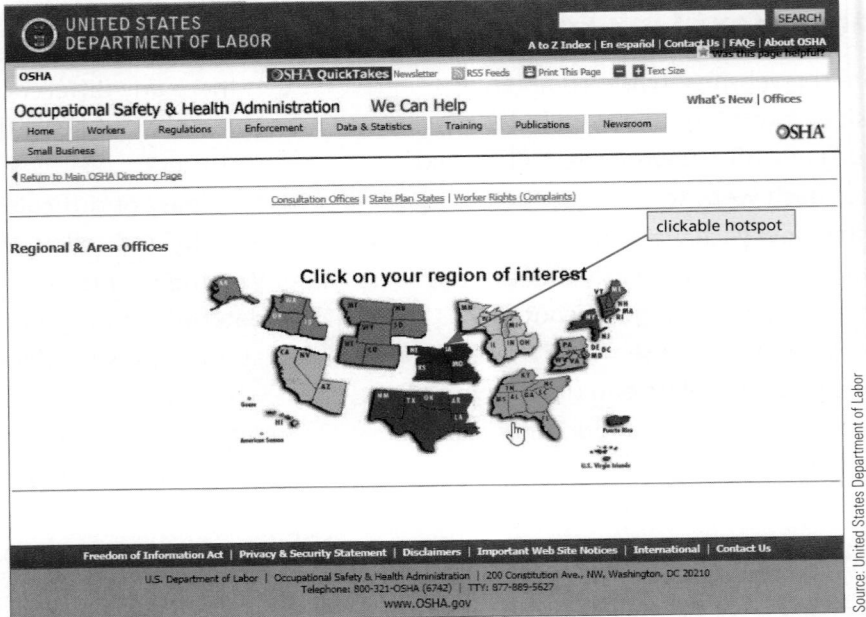

Figure 4-5 Image map hotspots also can link to a website's featured underlying pages.

Image maps can be either client-side or server-side. In a **client-side image map**, the hot spot link information resides in the HTML coding of the page, and the browser processes the code to display the image map. With a **server-side image map**, the x- and y-coordinates of the clicked hot spot report back to the server, where a script processes the hot spot link information and returns the link's target page. Server-side image maps are more complicated to create than client-side image maps, increase demands on a server, and typically have slower response times than client-side image maps.

DESIGN TIP Follow WAI guidelines for image maps. Remember to choose an image that accurately represents the target pages and follows design guidelines for visual consistency.

NAVIGATION AREAS You should group related links into a navigation area to create an eye-catching design element and help visitors identify links to a website's major underlying pages quickly. Navigation areas can group links in menus, bars, or tabs. The current trend is to use a combination of techniques. The examples in Figures 4-6, 4-7, and 4-8 may look similar, but all are excellent examples of different approaches to navigation areas.

- A **navigation menu** is a list of related links. A navigation menu might contain multiple levels of links displayed as **pop-out menus**. Figure 4-6 shows a pop-out menu from the JetBlue website.

- A **navigation bar** generally uses graphic buttons to present links. Pointing to some navigation bar buttons displays **drop-down menus**. Some websites add navigation bars with text links instead of button links at the bottom of each page. Figure 4-7 shows a navigation bar with a drop-down menu from the Zappos website.

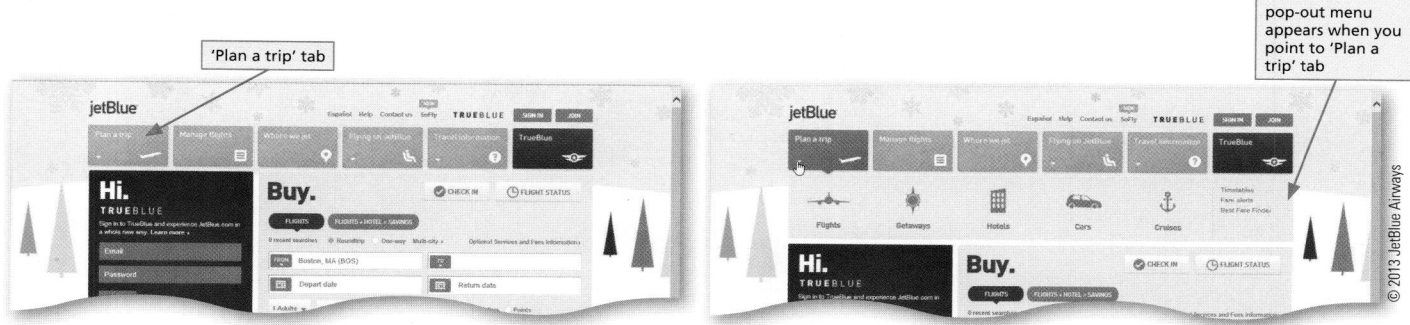

Figure 4-6 Some navigation menus contain multiple levels of links displayed as pop-out menus.

Figure 4-7 A navigation bar uses graphic buttons to present links; some navigation bar buttons also display drop-down menus of additional links.

- **Navigation tabs** present links as small tabs. Navigation tabs work best when linking to alternative views of the content. Figure 4-8 shows the Inkd website, which uses navigation tabs.

No matter which of these navigation elements you include at your website, basic design rules still apply. Use navigation elements consistently across all pages at your website. Navigation element colors should follow the website's overall color scheme to maintain visual identity. Finally, the text for a menu, button, or tab link should indicate its target page clearly.

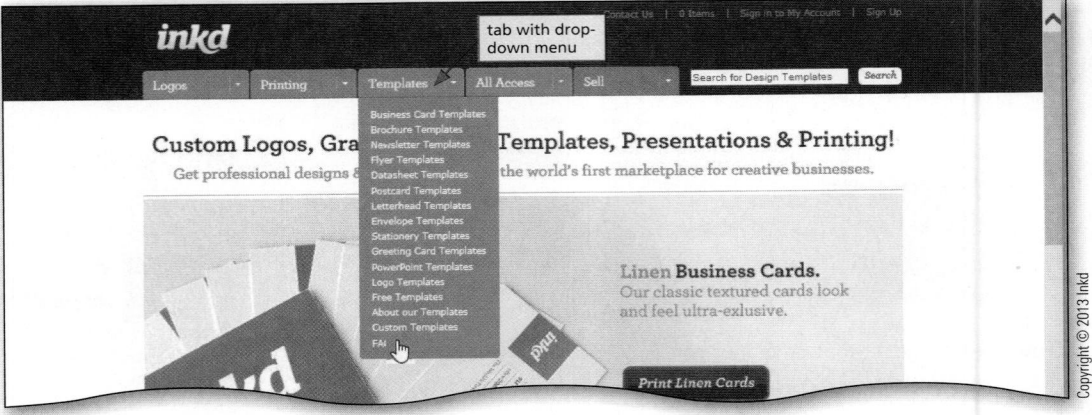

Figure 4-8 Tab with drop-down menu that appears upon hovering.

DESIGN TIP Use any combination of navigation menus, bars, and tabs to create a consistent navigation area that appears across all pages at a website. Apply the same color scheme, font, and styles for all pages. Make certain to indicate the target page clearly.

BREADCRUMB TRAIL A **breadcrumb trail** is a hierarchical outline or horizontal list that shows a visitor the path he or she has taken from the home page to the currently viewed page. A breadcrumb trail (as shown in the Centers for Disease Control and Prevention webpage shown in Figure 4-9) provides a visitor with a visual understanding of the linking relationship between pages. It also offers additional navigation tools. A visitor can click any link in the breadcrumb trail to move back to that link's target page. Breadcrumb trails do not replace navigation elements, such as menus or bars. Use breadcrumb trails to help a user find his or her way back to pages previously viewed in the website.

Figure 4-9 A breadcrumb trail shows the path between the home page and the current page.

A breadcrumb trail displays the relationship between the home page and the current page. Use a breadcrumb trail in combination with other navigation elements, such as navigation menus or bars.

WEBSITE MAP   A website with a large number of pages and a complex structure often provides a **website map**, also called a **website index**, which is a summary page of links to major pages at the website. Figure 4-10 illustrates the website map at the Apple website. Although in the past some website maps were illustrations or image maps, most website maps today consist of text links arranged alphabetically or by topic to meet the WAI standard for conveying information using text. With the use of search features, multiple navigation structures, and breadcrumbs, a website map might seem like an outdated or unnecessary feature. However, it can be helpful to visitors at a large website, and is an easy page to create and add to your website.

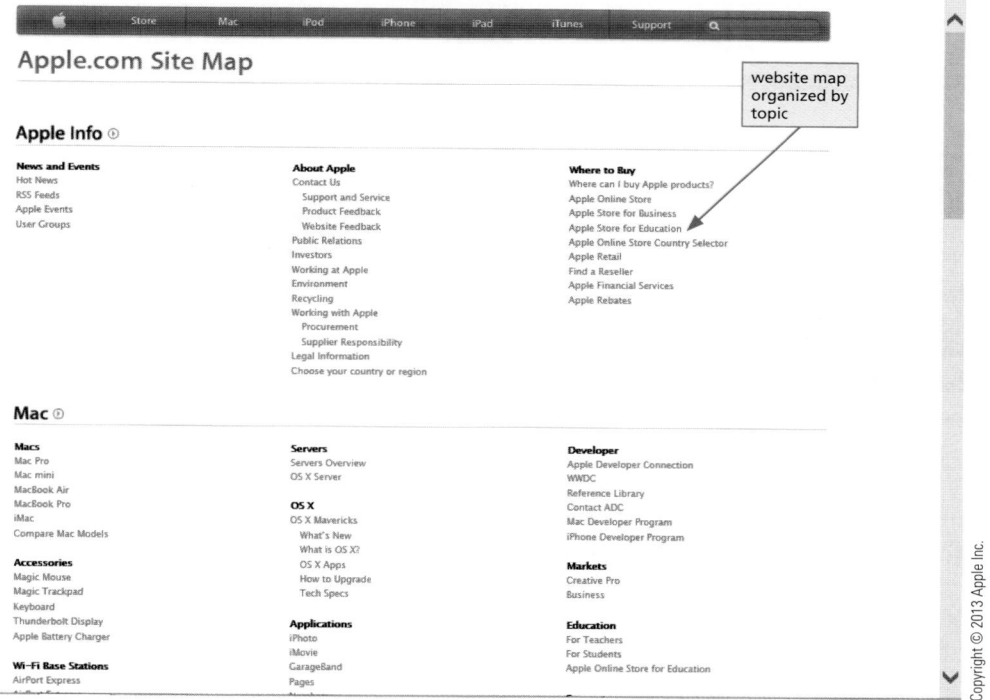

Figure 4-10 A website map provides summary links to a website's major pages.

Provide a text link-based website map for large websites with many pages. Organize a website map's text links in a logical way, such as alphabetically or by topic.

SEARCH CAPABILITY   Adding a keyword search capability and a search box to all of your website's major pages allows visitors to locate pages at your website that contain specific keywords without browsing your website page by page and maintains visual consistency across pages. Like a website map, a **website search feature** is another

Should I add search capability?
Adding search capability is important, especially for large websites. To learn more, use a search engine to search for *should I add a search feature.*

popular navigation tool for websites with a large number of pages. A large business or organization that manages its own web servers can use server-side scripts to create and maintain a searchable website index on its servers. If you do not manage your own web servers, you can contract with a hosted website search provider to provide search services. A **hosted website search provider** is a third-party company that uses spiders or other tools to build a searchable index of your website's pages and then hosts the index on their servers. You use templates and tools provided by the search provider to add a search box to your pages. Content management systems often include a search feature option. Another tool you can add to your search features is AutoComplete. **AutoComplete** is a technology that provides suggestions to website visitors by searching through the website contents to find matches as the visitor enters keywords in the search box. Figure 4-11 shows a search being conducted at the Reuseit website.

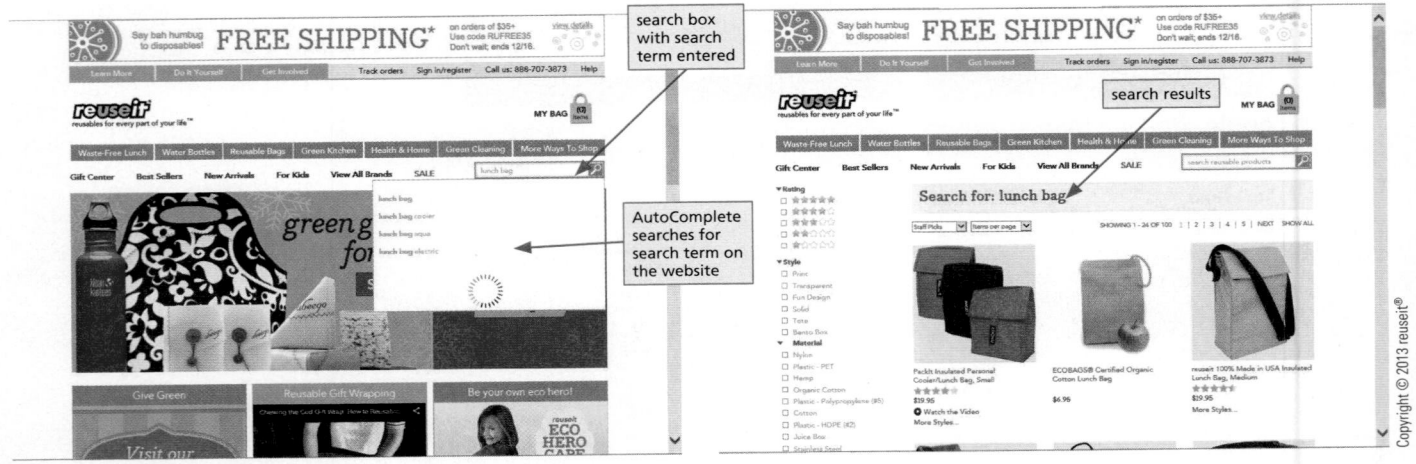

Figure 4-11 Adding search capability to your website allows visitors to locate specific information quickly.

YOUR TURN

Exploring Hosted Website Search Providers

1. Use the search tool of your choice to search for the keywords *hosted website search* or similar keywords. Identify five B2B companies that offer hosted website search services.

2. Compare the services offered by each company. Summarize the special features and cost for each company's service.

3. Choose a hosted website search service you could recommend to a client for whom you are developing a B2C e-commerce website. Give the reasons for your recommendation.

4. Submit your findings in the format requested by your instructor.

DESIGN TIP

Create a user-controlled navigation system by combining in your navigation system text links; image links; navigation menus, bars, and tabs; a breadcrumb trail; a website map; and search capability as appropriate for your target audiences.

Your Regifting website design team agrees that to meet your visitors' needs, the website's navigation system must be both user-based and user-controlled and should follow WAI guidelines. The navigation system will consist of a navigation bar at the top of each page, a navigation menu on the left side of each page, a website map organized by topic, traditionally formatted text links, links that identify their target pages, and links to the home page on underlying pages. You also will contract with a hosted website search provider to add a search feature to the website's pages. Figure 4-12 illustrates the update to the website plan.

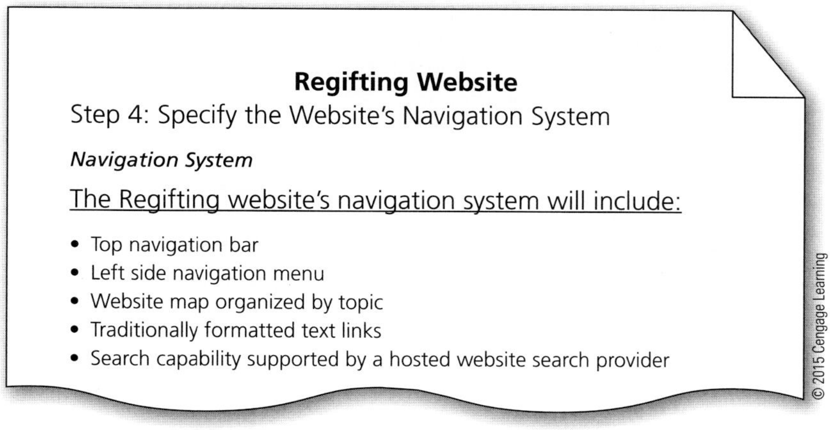

Regifting Website

Step 4: Specify the Website's Navigation System

Navigation System

The Regifting website's navigation system will include:

- Top navigation bar
- Left side navigation menu
- Website map organized by topic
- Traditionally formatted text links
- Search capability supported by a hosted website search provider

© 2015 Cengage Learning

Figure 4-12 A user-based and user-controlled navigation system enhances your website's usability.

Step 5: Design the Look and Feel of the Website

At this point, you have determined the website's purpose and audience, you have developed a plan for the website's general content, navigation, and structure, and you have gained an understanding of the roles of page length and content placement in usability. Now you are ready to tackle the next step, which is planning the look and feel of your website. Chapter 2 introduced you to the concepts of unity and visual identity and the importance of following an entity's branding specifications when planning the look and feel of a website. To promote unity and maintain visual identity across pages at your website, use visual consistency when choosing color and typeface and when positioning content across all pages at your website.

Visual Consistency

Website visitors might feel confused if a website's underlying pages fail to include common content and design features found on the home page. They might even conclude that an underlying page belongs to an entirely different website. To avoid confusing visitors, all of the pages at a website must share a visual consistency that reinforces the company's brand identity as visitors move from page to page.

You can create **visual consistency** by repeating design features across all pages at a website, including:

- Typeface
- Content position

- Color scheme
- Company or website name, logo, and major links

Repeating design features and content, as shown at the Orange Leaf website in Figure 4-13, unifies a website's pages, strengthens a website's visual identity and brand, and maintains visual consistency.

Figure 4-13 Repetition of design and content elements promotes unity, maintains visual identity, and creates visual consistency across a website's pages.

 Repeating design features across all pages at a website is one technique for creating visual consistency. Consistent elements include the color scheme, as well as content such as the logo, website or company name, and major links.

Color and Visual Contrast

In Chapter 2, you learned about the principles of color as a design tool and that a well-chosen color scheme creates unity among pages at a website. As you consider color options for a website's pages, remember the power of color to influence moods, the cultural implications of color, and your target audience's expectations for the use of color at your website.

Apply the same color scheme to the background, visual elements, and text for all webpages to build visual consistency throughout your website. Figure 4-14 illustrates a red, white, and blue color scheme across pages at the University of Kansas website. The red, white, and blue text and graphics stand out against the contrasting backgrounds, creating an effective visual contrast. The colors in the photographs add additional visual appeal. Observe that on both pages in Figure 4-14 the logo graphic, school name, and major links are positioned above and to the left of the scroll zone and at or near the top and on the left side of the page. Page length, content positioning, and use of color come together at the University of Kansas website to create attractive and usable pages.

Choose background and text colors that provide sufficient contrast to enhance readability and that permit print legibility. Studies have shown that, in general, greater contrast leads to better readability. Web designers commonly use white, gray, and cream as background colors contrasted with black or dark blue or red text colors. Alternatively, some websites use darker background colors, such as black or dark blue or dark red, and create contrast with light-colored text. These combinations can be less readable, however.

 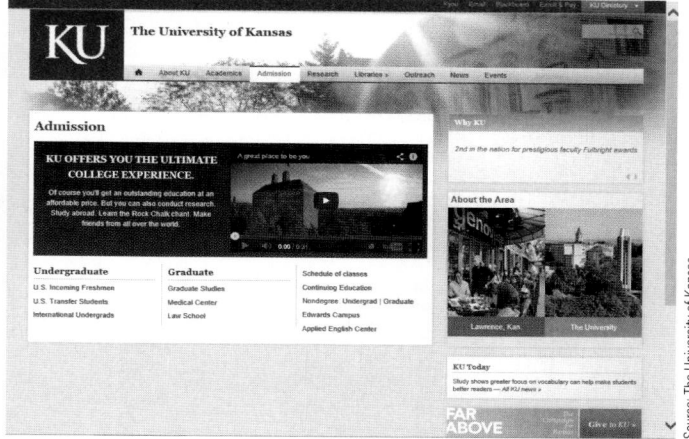

Source: The University of Kansas

Figure 4-14 Visual consistency results from standard application of color, page length, and content positioning for all pages on a website.

Exploring the Use of Color: Visual Consistency and Visual Contrast

1. Use a search engine to search for the following websites. Open each home page in a new browser tab.
   a. 1-800-PetMeds
   b. Hotels.com
   c. Anthropologie
   d. USA Today
2. Review the home page and at least three underlying pages at each website to determine how each website uses color.
3. Describe how each website uses color — including overall color scheme and individual background, graphic element, text, and image colors. Does the color scheme offer sufficient contrast between the background, foreground, and text? Does the website use its color scheme to create visual consistency across pages? Discuss how you would modify the color, if necessary, to improve readability and visual consistency.
4. Identify any messages or reasons why the website designer may have chosen the color palette. For example, if the colors reinforce a company's brand or identity, or if the colors provoke an emotional response such as feeling calm.
5. Submit your findings in the format requested by your instructor.

As you learned in Chapter 2, webpages can use color to evoke mood, stimulate interest, support a website's purpose, and meet audience expectations for the type of content found at a website. One way to select an appropriate color scheme and apply it across all webpages is to use a template. In Chapter 1, you learned that some WYSIWYG editors, such as Adobe Dreamweaver, and content management systems, such as Google Sites, offer web templates with predetermined color schemes, as shown in Figure 4-15. Online color-matching and analysis tools also are available, such as the Combo Tester on the color combos website (Figure 4-15). Using templates with a predefined color scheme can help ensure visual consistency among all pages at your website.

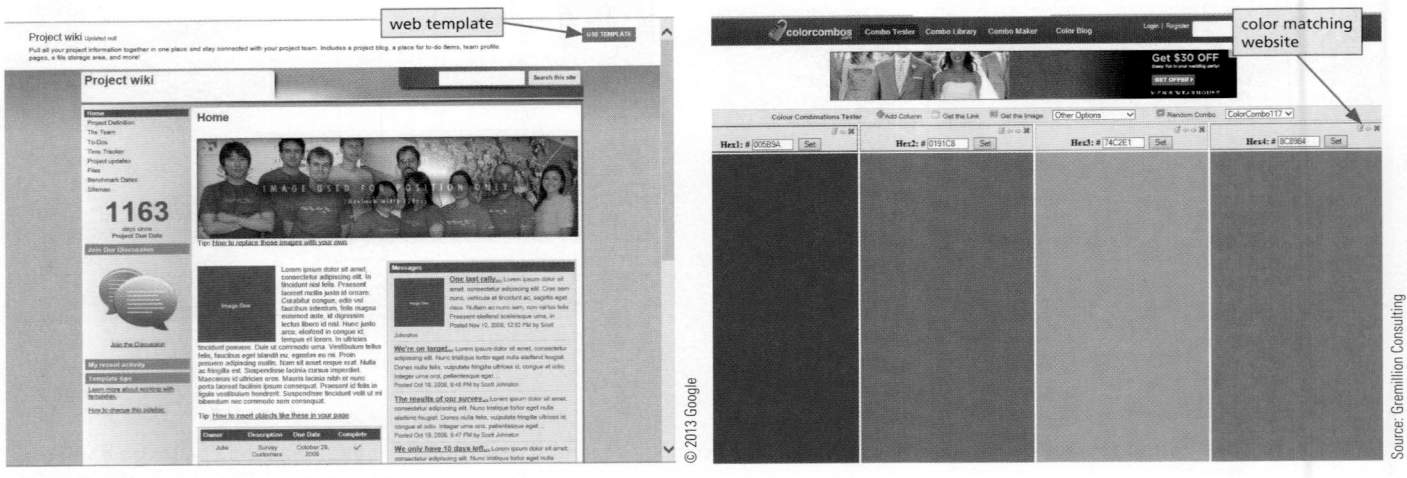

Figure 4-15 Use a web template or color matching website to apply compatible colors.

DESIGN TIP   Limit your website color scheme to three compatible colors. Choose a text color for titles, headlines, and so forth to attract the appropriate amount of attention. Test the background and text colors in your color scheme to ensure both on-screen readability and print legibility.

What are the Web Accessibility Initiative (WAI) guidelines for color usage?
The WAI specifies that color alone should not indicate information, for example, a text link. A common practice is to combine color and underlining for a link. The contrast between background and foreground colors should be sufficient for visitors with vision problems or those using a monochrome monitor. However, many website designers rely on color and bolding alone to indicate links.

Another way to choose an effective color scheme with appropriate contrast between background and text colors is to use inexpensive color-matching software, such as Color Scheme Designer®, Color Wheel Pro®, ColorShade®, or ColorCache®. **Color-matching software** and color-matching websites contain tools you can use to create sample website color schemes based on color theory, preview the color schemes in a browser, and then apply the colors in the selected scheme to your webpages.

Continuing with the Regifting example, your team meets to discuss potential color schemes that promote professionalism and the educational tone of the website's content. To assist in the discussion, your team reviews the company's print media — for example, letterhead, business cards, brochures — that illustrate the company's branding specifications for the use of color. Based on this material and your discussions with your team, you use the ColorCache color-matching software to experiment with website color schemes, as shown in Figure 4-16.

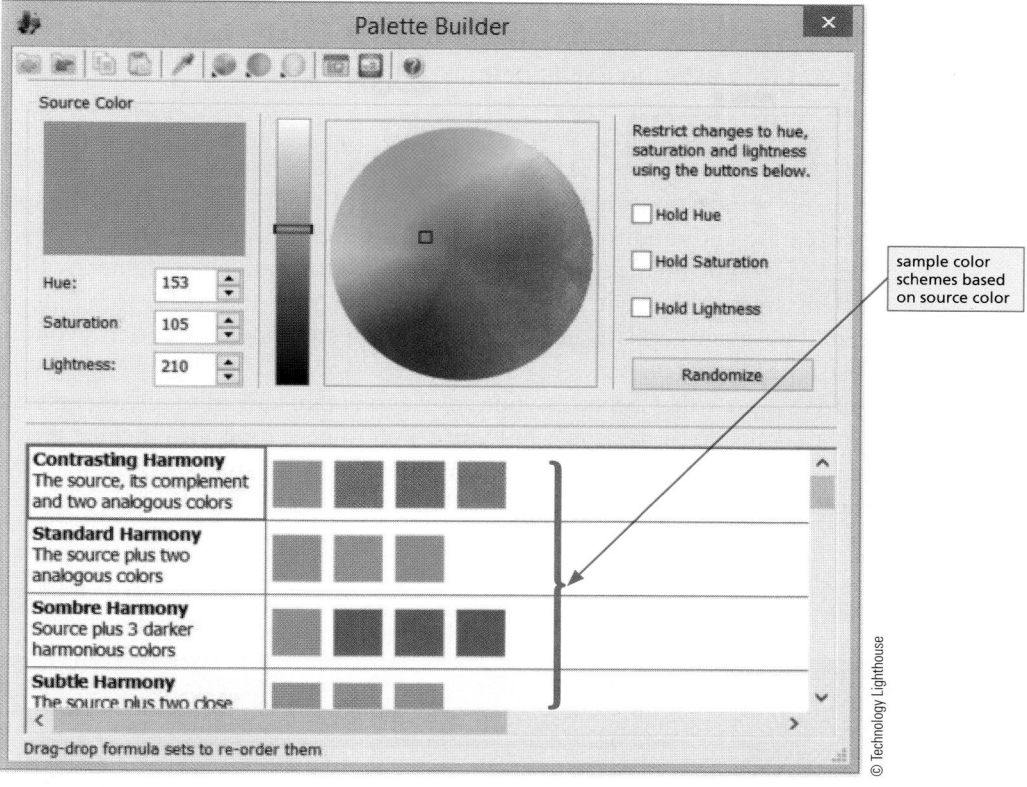

Palette Builder

Source Color

Hue: 153
Saturation: 105
Lightness: 210

Restrict changes to hue, saturation and lightness using the buttons below.

☐ Hold Hue
☐ Hold Saturation
☐ Hold Lightness

Randomize

sample color schemes based on source color

Contrasting Harmony
The source, its complement and two analogous colors

Standard Harmony
The source plus two analogous colors

Sombre Harmony
Source plus 3 darker harmonious colors

Subtle Harmony
The source plus two close

Drag-drop formula sets to re-order them

© Technology Lighthouse

Figure 4-16 Color matching software can be used to develop a website's color scheme based on color theory.

Images that you include on webpages, such as clip art, illustrations, and photos, will add more color to your pages. Choose images with colors that match or complement your website's color scheme, as well as provide contrast.

DESIGN TIP

CSS and Formatting

As you learned in Chapter 1, web designers use CSS specifications to create text documents, called **style sheets**, to control the appearance of one or more pages at a website.

A **style** is a group of formatting properties, such as bold, italic, font type, font size, or font color, applied as a group to selected text. When you use CSS, you create a style sheet containing style rules. **Style rules** are specifications that define one or more formatting properties (declarations) and their values for specific HTML tags (selectors). For example, suppose you want all the top-level heading text surrounded by the <h1> </h1> HTML heading style tag pair to be a blue color. You could create a style rule for the <h1> heading tag consisting of the heading tag itself, called the style rule's selector, and the CSS property: value combination {color: blue}, called the style rule's declaration. You can add this style rule to your pages in one of three ways:

- As an **inline style** inserted within the <h1> HTML tag on a page
- As part of an **internal style sheet** inserted within a page's HTML heading tags
- As part of an **external style sheet** saved in the folder with the website's pages and linked to them with an HTML tag

TOOLKIT

CSS standards
For more information about the W3C standards for CSS, see Appendix B.

Q&A

What is the current W3C standard for CSS?
The current W3C style sheet standards include modules for both CSS Levels 3 and 4. To learn more, use a search engine to search for *W3C style sheet standards*.

DESIGN TIP Because no current browser supports all CSS specifications, be sure to test how the webpages you format using CSS appear in different browsers.

Q&A

What does *cascading* **mean for style sheets?**
CSS prioritizes style rules to determine priority in case of conflicting rules. The first priority is for specifications the author sets in the form of inline or embedded styles, or external style sheets. The second priority includes local CSS files a user specifies. The lowest priority are styles specified by the browser. Style rules are applied in cascading order based on priority.

TOOLKIT

Order of CSS rules
To learn more about how CSS prioritizes conflicting style rules, see Appendix B.

Style sheets standardize formatting of a webpage, which saves time and simplifies the process of creating and modifying webpages. Using style sheets prevents you from having to insert HTML tag formatting attributes and values for individual elements. If you make a style change to the style sheet, such as changing the font color for all headings, the associated webpages update automatically. Using style sheets also helps you maintain visual consistency across all pages at your website. Modern WYSIWYG editors, such as Expression Web, provide CSS tools you can use to create and edit style sheets and link style sheets to your pages, as shown in Figure 4-17. These tools also include templates with style sheets already linked to them. You can also create style sheets using **CSS editor software**, such as JustStyle CSS Editor or Rapid CSS Editor®.

Figure 4-17 WYSIWYG editors provide support for inline, internal, and external style sheets.

© 2013 Microsoft

Page Layout

Earlier in this chapter, you learned how page length and content placement affect usability. With page length, content placement, and usability in mind, you should create a logical, standardized **page layout**, or arrangement of content elements, that ensures visual consistency across your website's pages. A standardized page layout fosters a sense of balance and order that website visitors find appealing and reassuring. Figure 4-18 shows the consistent layout of pages at the Samsung website:

- Logo and name in the upper-left corner of each page
- Search feature at the top of each page
- Main navigation links at the top of each page
- One- or two-column content area in the middle of the page

Not shown in Figure 4-18 are a standard copyright notation, contact phone number, and links to Legal Info and Contact Us pages at the bottom of each page. These types of links often appear below the scroll zone on a page. Observe that the visual identity content and major navigation links on the Samsung pages are above and to the left of the scroll zone.

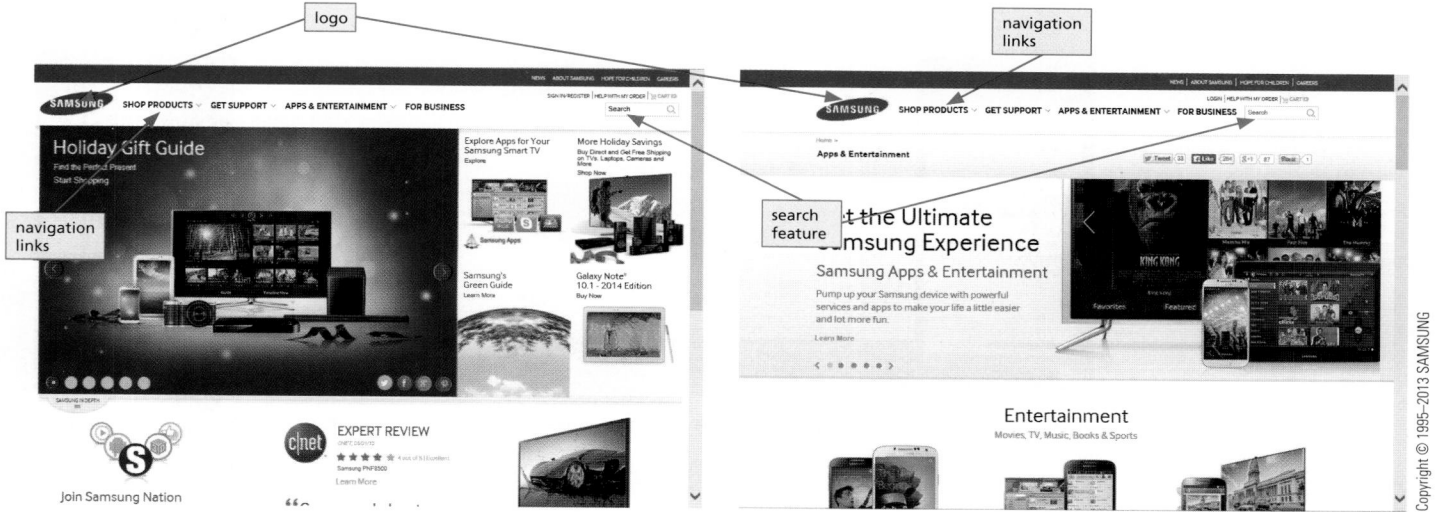

Figure 4-18 A logical, standard page layout provides visual consistency across all pages at a website.

Layout grids, Cascading Style Sheets, and tables all are used to create attractive page layouts.

LAYOUT GRIDS   Many designers use an underlying structure of rows and columns, called a **layout grid**, to position content on a page. You can precisely position and align content, set margin width, and make more adjustments using a layout grid. A layout grid is a visual guide for positioning webpage elements. It is not visible when a webpage appears in a browser.

Using a WYSIWYG editor layout grid, such as Expression Web (Figure 4-19) or Dreamweaver, it is easy to add and reposition content. You can change grid line color, spacing (pixels, inches, or centimeters), and style (dotted, solid, dashed). Additionally, you can set a command to have content automatically "snap to," or align precisely with, the closest grid line.

layout grid

grid options

Untitled 1 (Untitled_1.html) - Microsoft Expression Web 4

Page Editor Options

© 2013 Microsoft

Figure 4-19 Using a WYSIWYG editor layout grid makes it easy to position content precisely and to have elements snap to the closest gridline.

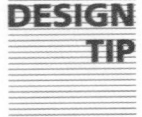

DESIGN TIP Use a layout grid to position page content that consistently appears on all pages, for example, the logo, website publisher's name, images, and major links. Then carefully add other page content that generates interest and variety while maintaining visual consistency.

Q&A

What are frames? Frames are a method for dividing the screen into multiple areas, with each area containing a separate, scrollable webpage. Designers of early websites used frames for easy maintenance. Because of accessibility issues and difficulty with setting bookmarks or direct page URLs, frames no longer are an accepted method of webpage layout.

CSS AND PAGE LAYOUT Earlier in the chapter, you learned how web designers use style sheets to control formatting across pages, creating visual consistency. Style sheets also can control page layout by dividing a page into sections, such as a header section or a navigation section. The <div> tag within a page's code specifies a section identified by the style sheet (Figure 4-20). The content tags that define a section's elements are between each <div></div> tag pair. Figure 4-21 illustrates the external style sheet for a WYSIWYG template that establishes page sections.

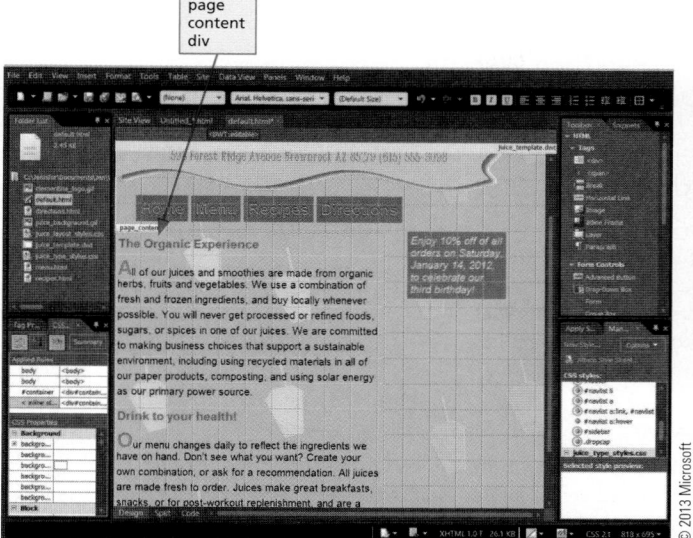

Figure 4-20 <div> tags are used to specify sections on a webpage.

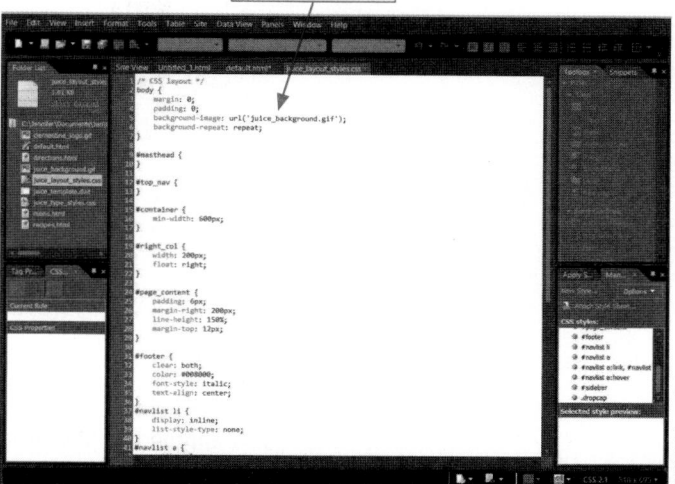

Figure 4-21 Style sheets also are used to control page layout.

TABLES   A table is an arrangement of columns and rows. Data appears in cells, which are the intersection of a table column and a row. You might be familiar with using tables in word processing software, such as Microsoft Word, or spreadsheet software, such as Microsoft Excel. Web designers might use an **HTML table** in the same way as a table in a word processing document or in a spreadsheet — as a **data table** that organizes content.

Q&A

Should I use HTML tables for layout?
HTML tables can cause issues when viewed on a smartphone or mobile device, and do not meet WAI standards. For more information about using HTML tables, use a search engine to search for *HTML tables responsive web design*.

Exploring CSS Editor Software

YOUR TURN

1. Using the search tool of your choice and the keywords *CSS editor software* or similar keywords, research different options for CSS editor programs used to create CSS style sheets.

2. Compare the features and costs of three different programs. Find and read reviews on each program if possible. Describe which you, as a web designer, might use to create style sheets for your webpages, and why.

3. Discuss whether you might prefer to use this type of software program as opposed to other methods of creating style sheets, such as text editors and WYSIWYG programs.

4. How does each program conform to responsive web design standards?

5. Submit your findings in the format requested by your instructor.

Continuing with the Regifting example, your team agrees on a color scheme based on the company's branding specifications, and a page layout for the visual identity content and major links on each page. You also agree on pursuing a liquid layout for the pages and to use CSS for both formatting and layout. Figures 4-22 and 4-23 illustrate the update to your formal website plan for Step 5.

Regifting Website

Step 5: Design the Look and Feel of the Website

Color Scheme

The Regifting website's color scheme:

- Will follow company's branding specifications for color
- Will be consistent across all pages at the website
  - Light-colored page background
  - Dark-colored foreground for graphic art
  - Dark-colored text on light background
  - Light-colored text on dark background

© 2015 Cengage Learning

Figure 4-22 The look and feel of your website can be created by an appropriate color scheme applied across all pages at the website.

Regifting Website

Step 5: Design the Look and Feel of the Website Page Layout

The Regifting website's page layout specifications include:

- Pages will use a liquid layout controlled by CSS
- Header at top of each page containing logo, tag line, company name, search tool, and Contact Us link
- Major navigational links down left side of page
- Content area in center of the page
- Contact Us page link, social media icons, privacy and security policy statement page link, and copyright notation at the bottom of each page

© 2015 Cengage Learning

Figure 4-23 The look and feel of your website can be created by a consistent and logical page layout across all pages at the website.

Step 6: Test, Publish, and Maintain the Website

A complete web design plan includes details outlining how and when you will test the website, how you will publish the website, where you will host it, and the necessary measures to maintain and update the website. These factors affect the budget and timing of your website, as well as its ultimate success. Without testing, you cannot determine if your website will work properly, or if it contains errors or broken links. If you design a website that exceeds the limit of your host web server's allotted size, you cannot publish the website. Without a plan for updating content, your website is static, and visitors have no reason to return.

TESTING　A formal website **usability test** is an evaluation that generally takes place in a structured environment, such as a testing laboratory. During the test, usability and design professionals observe exactly how visitors use a website, then use the research to create a report containing design recommendations. Formal website usability tests can be very expensive, costing perhaps several thousand dollars, and might be well beyond your budget. An informal usability test, however, involves using a team of friends, family members, coworkers, or other interested parties to test a website's navigation system or other website features and then report on their experiences. Testers should use a variety of devices, screen sizes, resolutions, and browsers to make the results more complete. Informal usability testing generally is very inexpensive, perhaps even free, but the feedback you gain can be invaluable.

You do not have to wait until your website is published to perform usability testing on the website's navigation system. You can begin by having a testing team evaluate the navigation system using a website prototype as part of the planning process. Continue frequent testing as you develop the website. Testing does not end with website development; you must continue to ensure that your navigation system works as intended through periodic testing after the website is published. In Chapter 7, you learn more about testing your website before and after publishing it.

PUBLISHING AND MAINTAINING   You will learn more about the steps involved in publishing and maintaining your website in Chapter 7. It is crucial to include these steps in your web design plan in order to create a website that meets the needs of your hosting service, and ensure that you are able to update and monitor the content to keep your website relevant and entice visitors to return frequently. Some questions you should answer include:

- Will you host the website on an internal web server or will you contract with an external vendor?
- What size limits exist for the website?
- How often will you update the content?
- Who is in charge of updating the content?
- What budget restrictions exist for publishing and maintaining the website?

Continuing with the Regifting example, your team plans strategies and budgets for testing, publishing, and maintaining the website. To ensure a focus on user-based and user-controlled navigation, your team conducts usability testing with a group of participants consisting of two employees, two representatives from the companies supplying Regifting merchandise, and two longtime customers. They will test the navigation system's usability on a regular basis during both website development and prepublishing testing. You will contract with an outside web server hosting company. The content will be updated by adding blog posts, weekly sales and coupons, and maintaining the product catalog by using a database. The updates to the website plan are shown in Figure 4-24.

Does testing end when the website is published?
No. It is important to ensure that the links on your website's pages continue to work as intended. You should plan to conduct periodic testing of the website's navigation system, making sure your website works with new devices, platforms, and browser versions.

Regifting Website
Step 6: Test, Publish, and Maintain the Website
The client will form a team to perform usability testing:

- Two employees
- Two representatives from companies supplying Regifting merchandise
- Two longtime clients

Publishing and Maintaining

- The website will be hosted by an external web hosting company
- Website content updates include):
  - Blog posts
  - Weekly sales and coupons
  - Maintaining the product catalog by using a database

© 2015 Cengage Learning

Figure 4-24 Planning how you will test, publish, and maintain the website helps you provide content that meets users' needs, as well as your budget and time resources.

Site Plan Checklist

Detailed planning is a vital step in website development and should occur before you invest time and money. Planning helps to ensure the website will meet your goals as well as the expectations of website visitors. To ensure a successful website, use the following checklist when completing your web design plan.

Step 1: Identify the Website's Purpose and Target Audience

- Identify the primary and secondary goals for your website.
- Determine the objectives necessary to meet the website's goals, including its call-to-action.
- Write a formal purpose statement for the website.
- Develop a target audience profile that identifies the demographic and psychographic characteristics of audience members.
- Perform a needs assessment to determine the target audience's wants, needs, and expectations that can be satisfied by your website.

Step 2: Determine the Website's General Content

- Determine your website's home and underlying pages, and any necessary landing pages.
- Ensure that the content on your website's home page answers visitors' *who*, *what*, *why*, and *where* questions.
- Determine the visual identity content that will brand all of the webpages in your website.
- Determine the value-added content for your pages: text, images, audio, video, animation, multimedia, and dynamically generated content.
- Plan a file folder organization for your HTML and content files.

Step 3: Select the Website's Structure

- Consider the best way to structure your website to achieve its purpose: linear/ tutorial, webbed, hierarchical, or some combination of structures.
- Create an outline of your website's structure: text outline, storyboard, or flowchart.

Step 4: Specify the Website's Navigation System

- Create a navigation system that is both user-based and user-controlled, offering a combination of text links; image links; navigation menus, bars, and tabs; a breadcrumb trail; a website map; and a search feature.
- Maintain visual consistency with the color and page placement of navigation elements.
- Follow WAI accessibility guidelines for links and image maps.

Step 5: Design the Look and Feel of the Website

- Position visual identity and vital page content above and to the left of potential scroll lines.
- Maintain visual consistency across pages with a color scheme and page layout.
- Follow WAI accessibility guidelines for the use of color.

Step 6: Test, Publish, and Maintain the Website

- Perform usability testing on the navigation system during the planning and development phases.
- Determine how and where you will publish the website, and identify any technical or budget limitations.
- Develop a content maintenance plan that includes schedule and budget.

Chapter Review

Place critical visual identity and navigation elements above and to the left of the scroll zone to reduce visitors' need to scroll. The typical website visitor looks first at the top of a webpage, then to the left, and then down and to the right. Place the content you want your visitors to see first at or near the top and on the left side of a webpage. Consider the visible screen area, and how that changes depending on the visitor's computer or device, when designing underlying webpages. Ensure that visitors never have to scroll horizontally to view webpages and that the information on underlying webpages flows smoothly and logically.

Using color and page layout to maintain visual consistency across all pages at a website promotes unity, strengthens visual identity, and reassures visitors. Apply a uniform color scheme and a consistent page layout created with tools such as grids and CSS to create visual consistency.

A user-based navigation system creates links between pages based on how visitors move from page to page at a website. A user-controlled navigation system allows visitors to move between pages in the manner of their choosing and offers both major navigation links as well as other options, such as a breadcrumb trail, website map, and search capability. Common types of navigation links include text links; image links; groups of related links presented as menus, bars, or tabs; breadcrumb trails; and website maps. After completing planning Steps 1 through 6, use the checklist to review your web design plan.

After reading the chapter, you should know each of these Key Terms.

TERMS TO KNOW

AutoComplete (108)
breadcrumb trail (106)
client-side image map (104)
color-matching software (112)
CSS editor software (114)
data table (117)
drop-down menu (104)

external style sheet (113)
eye-tracking study (99)
fixed-width page layout (99)
flexible page layout (99)
heat map (99)
hosted website search
   provider (108)

hot spot (103)
HTML table (117)
hybrid page layout (100)
image link (103)
image map (103)
inline style (113)
internal style sheet (113)
layout grid (115)
liquid page layout (99)
mouseover link (102)
navigation bar (104)
navigation menu (104)
navigation tab (105)
page layout (114)
pop-out menu (104)
rollover link (102)

scroll zone (98)
server-side image map (104)
style (113)
style rule (113)
style sheet (113)
target (101)
text link (101)
usability test (118)
user-based navigation system (101)
user-controlled navigation
    system (101)
visual consistency (109)
website index (107)
website map (107)
website search feature (107)

TEST YOUR KNOWLEDGE

Complete the Test Your Knowledge exercises to solidify what you have learned in the chapter.

Matching Terms

Match each term with the best description.

___ 1. scroll zone

___ 2. internal style sheet

___ 3. server-side image map

___ 4. breadcrumb trail

___ 5. rollover

___ 6. user-based

___ 7. target

___ 8. hot spot

___ 9. inline style

___ 10. AutoComplete

___ 11. navigation tab

___ 12. heat map

___ 13. usability test

___ 14. liquid layout

___ 15. fixed-width layout

a. A navigation system that bases linking relationships on the way website visitors actually move from page to page.

b. A way to evaluate exactly how website visitors will access website information and move from page to page at a website.

c. A text file containing formatting instructions saved within a webpage's HTML heading tags.

d. The area beyond the initial visible screen.

e. The webpage to which a link points.

f. A clickable area on an image map.

g. Specifies a webpage's width specified as a percentage of the browser window.

h. A group of related links used to display alternative views of the content.

i. A hidden link that appears when you point to it.

j. A hierarchical outline that shows the visitor the path between the home page and current page.

k. Specifies a webpage's width in pixels.

l. The colored data results of an analysis of website visitors' eye movements.

m. An image map in which the x- and y-coordinates of the clicked hot spot are processed outside of the HTML document.

n. Provides suggestions to visitors as they type in a search box.

o. Inserted within the <h1> HTML tag on a page.

Short Answer Questions

Write a brief answer to each question.

1. Describe the importance of consistency of visual elements to reinforce branding.

2. Describe eye-tracking studies and heat maps, and how web designers use them to plan webpage design.

3. What is the value of maintaining visual consistency across all pages at a website?

4. Discuss the WAI guidelines for the use of color and links.

5. Differentiate between inline styles, internal style sheets, and external style sheets, and describe the order of application.

6. Define different methods of user-based and user-controlled navigation.

7. Define five common types of links used in a navigation system.

8. Describe an image map, and explain the difference between client- and server-side image maps.

9. Explain why you would include a search feature, and how you might add one to your website.

10. List considerations when planning the testing, publishing, and maintenance of your website, and why you should include these steps in the planning process.

Test your knowledge of chapter content and key terms.

LEARN IT ONLINE

Instructions: Reinforce what you learned in this chapter with games, exercises, training, and many other online activities and resources. Reinforcement activities and resources are available at no additional cost on www.cengagebrain.com.

Investigate current Web design developments with the Trends exercises.

TRENDS

Write a brief essay about each of the following trends, using the web as your research tool. For each trend, identify at least one webpage URL used as a research source. Be prepared to discuss your findings in class.

1 | Touch Screen Navigation

Use a search engine to search for *touch screen website navigation* or similar keywords to find articles or blog posts that offer recommendations for making website navigation easy to use with touch screens. List three things that you should consider doing to a website, and at least two things that will make your website more accessible to touch screen users. If you have access to a device with a touch screen, experiment with using website navigation tools at several websites and make notes about any difficulties you encounter.

2 | Breadcrumb Trails

Using a search engine and the keywords *breadcrumb trail* or similar keywords, locate an article or blog post that expresses an opinion — positive or negative — about their use. Summarize your findings, and discuss whether you agree with the opinion stated in the article. Include any personal response you have based on your use of breadcrumb trails as a navigation tool.

AT ISSUE

Challenge your perspective of the web and web design technology with the @Issue exercises.

Write a brief essay in response to the following issues, using the web as your research tool. For each issue, identify at least one webpage URL used as a research source. Be prepared to discuss your findings in class.

1 | Cascading Style Sheets (CSS)

Cascading Style Sheets (CSS), a multifeatured specification for HTML, offers designers an expedient, powerful method to control the formatting and layout of webpages. Research the current level of support for style sheets by leading browsers and the current W3C recommendations for style sheet usage. Find an article that supports the use of CSS for creating websites that use responsive web design. Create a report summarizing your research. Explain the benefits of using CSS to design your website.

2 | Fixed-Width, Liquid, and Hybrid Page Layouts

Fixed-width and liquid page layouts each have their pros and cons. Using a search engine and the keywords *fixed-width liquid and hybrid webpage layouts*, or something similar, find two articles or blog posts discussing usage of these techniques. Create a report summarizing the articles, including any opinions expressed by the author. Conclude by stating what you might choose to use as a web designer and why.

HANDS ON

Use the World Wide Web to obtain more information about the concepts in the chapter with the Hands On exercises.

1 | Explore and Evaluate: Page Length, Content Placement, and Usability

Browse the Web to identify a website that effectively uses page length and content placement to enhance the website's usability. If possible, view the website using different screen resolutions, screen sizes, and devices. Make notes of differences in how the website pages display, and any difficulties you may encounter. Make any recommendation for ways the website could use page length and content placement to improve usability.

2 | Search and Discover: Websites and Visual Identity

Using a search engine and the keywords *website visual identity* or similar keywords, locate three different visual identity topic pages or blog posts. Write an outline for a presentation to your class on the results of your research. Include in your outline a discussion of how you would use visual identity elements at your website and whether you think it is necessary to address visual identity on a page at your website.

Work collaboratively to reinforce the concepts in the chapter with the Team Approach exercises.

1 | Website Search Features

Join with two other students to research how to add a website search feature to a website. Find examples of free and hosted solutions and reviews of each. Make notes of whether any of the websites offer AutoComplete as a part of the search feature, and any additional requirements or costs associated with using AutoComplete. Compile the team's findings and submit in the format requested by your instructor. Be prepared to present your results with the class.

2 | Usability Tests

Join with another student to create a two-person research team. One team member should research firms that offer usability tests for a fee. The other team member should research tips for conducting usability tests on your own or with a limited budget. Create a presentation for the class in which you describe the costs, benefits, and weaknesses of each. Make recommendations as to which method might work best for small websites and large, corporate websites.

Apply the chapter concepts to the ongoing development process in web design with the Case Study.

The Case Study is an ongoing development process using the concepts, techniques, and Design Tips presented in each chapter.

Background Information

Continuing with the development of your website plan that you began in Chapter 3, complete Step 4: Specify the website's navigation system, Step 5: Design the look and feel of the website, and Step 6: Test, publish, and maintain the website. Then use your design plan checklist to evaluate your complete plan.

Chapter 4 Assignment

In this assignment, you will finalize your website's plan by completing the remaining three steps discussed in this chapter: planning the navigation of your website, planning the look and feel of your website, and planning how you will test, publish, and maintain the website.

1. Review the related chapter material on page length, content placement, and usability.

2. Review the guidelines for user-based and user-controlled navigation systems, and then specify the individual elements of a user-based and user-controlled navigation system for your website.

3. Define your website's color scheme by using a WYSIWYG template or color-matching software.

4. Plan the page layout for your home page and underlying pages. Explain how you will control page layout with CSS.

5. Create a plan for testing, publishing, and maintaining your website. Include costs and schedules in the plan.

6. After completing the final three steps of your design plan, review your design plan using the design plan checklist. After your review, make any necessary additions or edits to your design plan.

7. If time permits, meet with three classmates to compare and evaluate each other's design plans and offer constructive suggestions as applicable.

5 | Typography and Images

Introduction

Once you have developed a thorough website plan that takes into consideration your audience, goals, and design needs, you are prepared to create your website. As you learned in Chapters 2 and 4, web designers primarily use text and image content elements to communicate effectively. In this chapter, you learn more about the standards for applying good typography to text in order to ensure readability. You also learn how to select appropriate images, such as photographs, diagrams, illustrations, and more, which add value to your website and support your website's message. Then, you learn how to prepare your selected images for the web.

Objectives

After completing this chapter, you will be able to:

1. Explain webpage typography issues

2. Discuss effective use of webpage images

3. Describe image file formats

4. Discuss how to prepare web-ready images

Q&A

What are the current typography trends?
Like most web design principles, typography trends evolve constantly. One current trend is to use larger, magazine-style fonts. To find out more, use a search engine to search for *web typography trends* and sort or filter the results to display the most recent.

Q&A

What are leading, tracking, and kerning?
Leading refers to line spacing, or the amount of vertical space between lines of text; more line spacing generally means greater readability. **Tracking** is a spacing technique that allows designers to squeeze or stretch text, as necessary, to fit in a specific amount of space. **Kerning** adds or removes space between two individual characters.

Q&A

What are the Web Accessibility Initiative (WAI) guidelines for font selection?
The WAI guidelines state that you should use CSS and the font-family, font-style, font-weight, and font-size properties to specify fonts instead of the HTML <font> tag and its attributes. When you specify a font, such as Verdana, you should also specify an alternative generic font, such as sans serif.

Webpage Typography Issues

In Chapter 2, you learned the importance of composing text that is accurate, easy to read, understandable, and comprehensive. You also learned that text must be concise and written or adapted for the web. You can format your text to be more readable by following the rules of typography. **Typography** is the appearance and arrangement of characters, commonly referred to as **type**, applied to text. The characteristics that define type are typeface, style, and size. Selecting the appropriate type for your webpages' text is part of the design process.

Font Sizes and Styles

A **typeface** is a group of alphabetic characters, numbers, and symbols with the same design, such as the slant and thickness. Figure 5-1 illustrates some typefaces commonly used on the web.

This is Times New Roman typeface.

This is Broadway typeface.

This is Garamond typeface.

This is Arial typeface.

THIS IS BIONDI TYPEFACE.

© 2015 Cengage Learning

Figure 5-1 A typeface is a group of characters with a common design.

Type style refers to the variations in form such as roman (regular), italic, or bold. Desktop publishing professionals and other creators of printed materials use points to measure **type size**, where 72 points = 1 inch. Web designers sometimes measure type size in pixels, where 16 pixels equals a 12-point font, approximately. In typography, a specific combination of typeface, style, and size is a **font**. For example, the general name *Biondi* refers to a typeface, and the more specific *Biondi, 14-point bold* indicates a font. Figure 5-2 on the next page illustrates three fonts.

Font Selection and Web Design

Web designers use the terms *font* and *typeface* interchangeably to identify a group of characters with the same design. When selecting fonts for a website, the main goal should be to ensure readability. Identifying the best font for your webpages requires considering how your font selection will affect visitors' reading speed and comprehension. Font selection can help establish the mood of your website — from whimsical to professional.

This is the Times New Roman 12-point (regular) font.

THIS IS THE BIONDI 14-POINT BOLD FONT.

This is the Arial 16-point italic font.

© 2015 Cengage Learning

Figure 5-2 In typography, a font is a specific combination of typeface, style, and size.

Q&A

What are TrueType, PostScript, and OpenType fonts?
TrueType is a font standard used by Windows and Macintosh operating systems. **PostScript** is a font standard developed by Adobe Systems for PostScript printers. **OpenType** is a font standard that incorporates TrueType and PostScript fonts for Windows and Macintosh operating systems.

When a webpage loads in a browser, the browser refers to the CSS specifications to determine the font the web designer specified for the text. Not all fonts are stored on all computers or devices, thus specialized fonts that you include in your website might not be available on a user's device. Using CSS to specify backup fonts or embedding fonts (described on the following page) ensures your website will be readable for all users. As a web designer, you should evaluate potential fonts based on readability, availability, and the mood you want your website visitors to experience.

READABILITY   Five generic font types exist: serif, sans serif, cursive, fantasy, and monospace fonts. Cursive, or script, fonts replicate handwriting. Web designers use fantasy fonts for decoration. Monospace fonts have equal spacing between characters, simulating characters created on a manual typewriter. Cursive, fantasy, and monospace fonts might not be appropriate for most webpage text because it can be difficult to read them online. Another reason to avoid cursive or fantasy fonts is that specific examples of these fonts are less likely to be available across different computers and devices.

The most commonly used fonts in web design are serif and sans serif. Some fonts, such as Times New Roman, have a short line extending from the top or bottom of a character called a serif; web designers refer to these as **serif** fonts. Fonts that do not have serifs, such as Arial, are **sans serif** fonts. Web designers often vary serif and sans serif fonts for heading and body text fonts to create visual contrast. Figure 5-3 illustrates characters in the Times New Roman serif font and the Arial sans serif font.

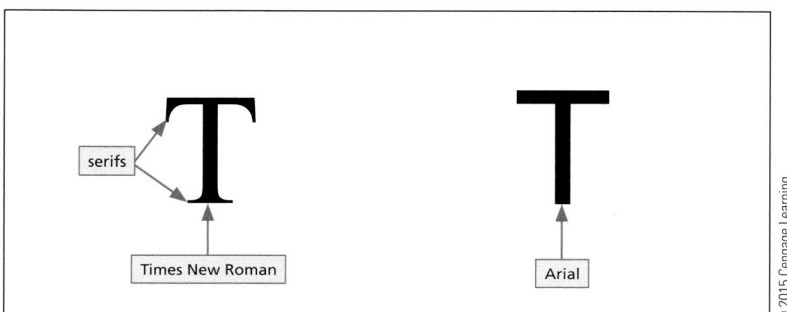

© 2015 Cengage Learning

Figure 5-3 A serif is a short line extending from the top or bottom of a character.

What is a web-safe font?
A **web-safe font** is a commonly available font that most website visitors' browsers will be able to display. Most web designers rely on CSS to specify backup fonts rather than rely on web-safe fonts. For more information, use a search engine to search for *web-safe fonts*.

Many web designers ensure the readability of website content by using commonly available fonts, such as Georgia or Arial. WYSIWYG editors, such as Microsoft® Expression Web® (Figure 5-4), allow you to use CSS to specify a **font family** or a **font stack**, which includes a default font and backup font types. If a browser cannot locate the font used on a webpage, it will attempt to replace it with the next designated **backup font** in the stack. Including a generic serif or sans serif font, which all browsers and devices can interpret, as the last backup font in the stack ensures that all browsers can display your webpage content.

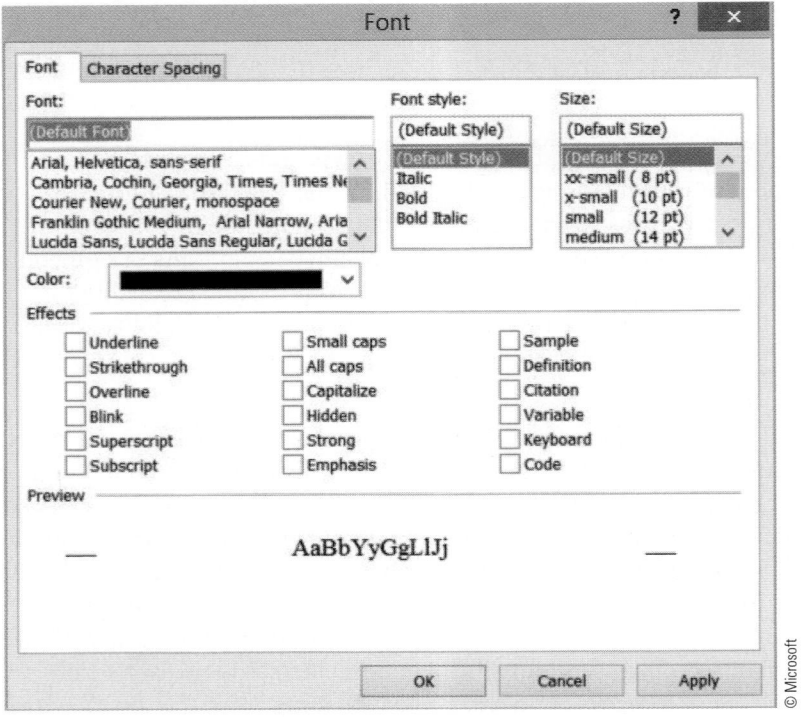

Figure 5-4 WYSIWYG editors allow you to specify a font stack.

What happens if I do not specify a font for my webpage?
Web browsers have both a default font and a default font size setting. If you do not specify a font or font size using an HTML tag and attributes or CSS properties and values, browsers will use the default font to display text.

Another method web designers use is to include **embedded fonts** in the website. Embedded fonts are included in the code for the webpage and must be downloaded to the user's device before the webpage text can appear. Embedded fonts often increase the time it takes for a page to load. The delays can cause the website visitor to become annoyed and possibly abandon the website for another option. When using embedded fonts, web designers often will use a tool such as Google® Font Loader® (Figure 5-5) to specify backup fonts while the embedded fonts download.

How do serifs affect readability?
Many web designers use serif fonts for webpage body text, although they are equally likely to apply serif and sans serif fonts to headlines. For more information about research on the sans serif and serif readability debate, use a search engine to search for *sans serif and serif readability*.

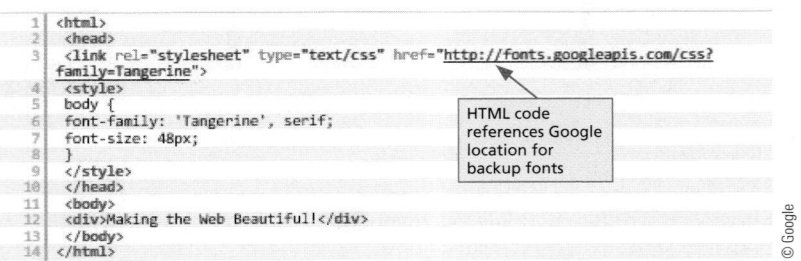

Figure 5-5 When using embedded fonts, specify backup fonts while the embedded fonts download.

Despite a number of research studies, no clear direction exists regarding serifs and online readability. Although some early studies point to sans serif fonts as more readable for online text, more recent studies suggest that style, size, spacing between characters, contrast, white space, line length, readers' familiarity with the font, and other characteristics might play a larger role in readability than the presence or absence of serifs.

Font size also plays an important role in your selection of a font. A webpage's font size is either absolute or relative. **Absolute font sizes** do not change when visitors change their browser font size settings. While absolute font sizes allow designers to maintain control over the size of page text, they do not comply with responsive web design techniques. **Relative font sizes** adjust to the user's screen and resolution. Web designers traditionally measured relative font sizes in pixels (relative to the viewing screen) as a percentage in relation to the font size of surrounding text, or as a percentage of an em unit, where one **em unit** equals the font size. The third version of CSS specifications, known as CSS3, introduced **rems** (root em). Like an em unit, a rem allows for flexible font sizing, but the percentage specification for rems appears in the HTML document's root, or top level heading, rather than for each font style or type.

To emphasize a word or phrase, such as a paragraph heading or an important part of a paragraph, use bold and italic font styles. Use bold and italic font styles sparingly, to make the key points in your webpage stand out. Recall from Chapter 2 that you should never use underlining for emphasis because underlining typically indicates a link. Additionally, avoid using all uppercase characters for words or phrases, as this can reduce scannability and viewers often interpret it as shouting.

Q&A
Do all browsers support rems?
Rems are a newer specification, and older browser versions might not support them. For more information about rems, use a search engine to search for *rem browser compatibility*.

TOOLKIT
Applying rems using CSS3
See Appendix B to learn more about using CSS3 and rems to specify relative font size.

Use relative font sizing to follow responsive web design practices and enable your website to be accessible to users with varying screen sizes and resolutions.

DESIGN TIP

MOOD   Just as with a web color scheme, font selection can help establish an emotional connection with your visitors by suggesting a specific mood or state of mind. A website's mood should always promote and not detract from the website's message. For example, a topical website on snowboarding or a website that offers online games for preteens requires a font that contributes to a mood of fun, excitement, and challenge. However, the font used at a B2B website selling technical products or services should convey professionalism, not whimsy. Figure 5-6 illustrates how font selection for two websites — Schwab, an investment company and KidRex, a search engine for children — helps convey the website's mood.

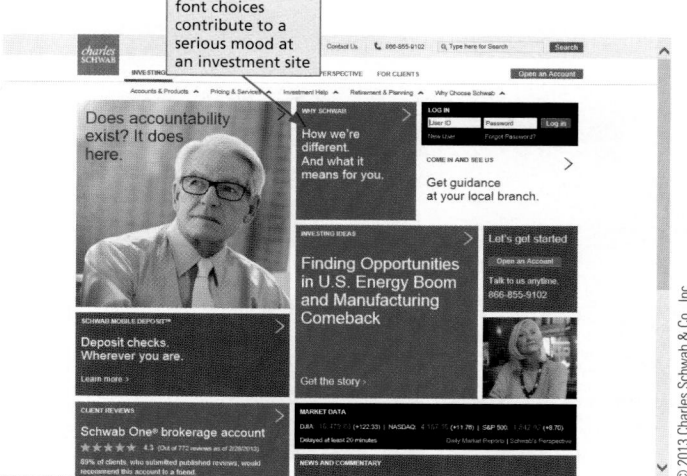
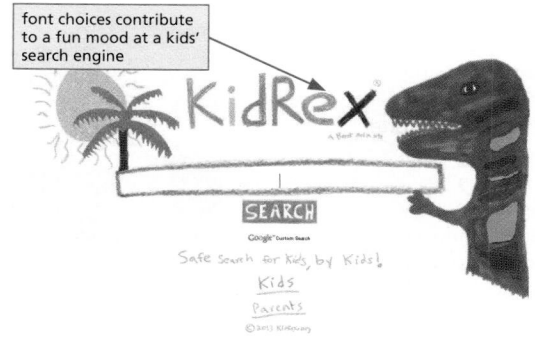

font choices contribute to a serious mood at an investment site

font choices contribute to a fun mood at a kids' search engine

© 2013 Charles Schwab & Co., Inc.

©2013 KidRex.org

Figure 5-6 Fonts can help set the mood for a visitor's website experience.

Exploring Fonts

1. Use a browser to open three websites in separate tabs. Choose any website in the following categories: a gaming website, a health care website, and an investment website.

2. Review the home page and two underlying pages at each website. How do fonts and font sizes set the mood for website visitors?

3. If possible, view the websites using a different device or at different resolutions. How does changing the screen size or resolution affect the readability of the fonts?

4. Explain how the website's choice of fonts, font styles, and font sizes does or does not set a mood that matches the website's content and message. Submit your findings in the format requested by your instructor.

Q&A

Do font choices affect web accessibility?
To make your website accessible, use readable fonts, relative font sizing, sufficient contrast between background and text color, and avoid using the appearance of text to convey its meaning. For more information, use a search engine to search for *fonts and web accessibility*.

Q&A

Can I use clip art images on my webpages?
Even if the clip art you want to use is provided for free in a word processing, desktop publishing, or WYSIWYG website editor program or app, it often has restrictions on any material produced for commercial use or public-access, such as a webpage. If you have access to a program or app that includes clip art, use the program's Help feature or a search engine to see if there are restrictions to using the clip art.

Image Text

Some image-editing software and apps contain features that allow you to create images from text or add text to an image. For example, you can use headlines or larger text paragraphs to add to an image or create a new image, and then use editing tools to give the text shape, color, fade effects, or opacity to make the image more interesting. Web designers often save text as an image to create logos for brands, such as Coca-Cola, that use proprietary fonts not available on visitors' browsers.

Adding text to an image, or creating an image from text, is much like working with webpage body text or text in a word-processing document. First, you select an editing tool that allows you to type the text. Then, you select the font, font size, font style, and font color options you want for your text. Next, click an area of the image where you want the text to appear, and type your text. The text appears in a box, called a **bounding box**. You can alter the shape of the bounding box to add interest. The Ocean Alliance webpage shown in Figure 5-7 shows an example of an image created from text. Do not use images

Figure 5-7 Text can be used to create an image.

alone to convey information on a webpage. Make certain to include the information you are trying to convey with image text also as body text and as alternative text that screen readers and other assistive technologies can read and interpret.

Webpage Images

In Chapter 3, you learned how webpage images, such as illustrations, diagrams, and photographs, can personalize and familiarize the unknown, deliver a message, and prompt visitors' actions. When you select images, be sure you select high-quality, relevant images that achieve the following:

- Add value to your website.
- Match or complement your website's color scheme.
- Accurately represent the content to which they link, if used for image mapping.
- Support the website's message.
- Contribute to the overall mood you want to set.

Be creative in the use of images on your webpages. For example, tilt a photograph slightly in image-editing software and apps to add visual interest to a page. Besides enlivening a page, a tilted photograph creates white space between it and the text. Removing a photograph's background will produce an eye-catching silhouette that can serve as a focal point.

Remember to follow best practices for images and web usability and accessibility: include redundant text links for image map links, add an alternative text description for each image, and avoid background images that obscure text. Also make sure only to use images to which you own the copyrights, or secure the copyrights and give proper credit to the image owner or creator if using an image from another source.

Keep web accessibility in mind as you select images for your webpages. Include redundant text links for image maps and add an alternative text description for each image.

DESIGN TIP

Exploring the Effective Use of Webpage Images

YOUR TURN

1. Use a browser to open the following three websites in separate tabs: whale.org, baylorhealth.com, and aicpa.org.
2. Review the home page and two underlying pages at each website.
3. Examine how the website uses images. Do the images add value? Do they match or complement the color scheme? Do the images contribute to the overall mood of the website and promote the website's message?
4. Do any of the websites use text images? If so, how did they address accessibility concerns?
5. Summarize your review and submit in the format requested by your instructor.

You can acquire images for your website by creating your own image files or, as you learned in Chapter 3 when you researched available stock photographs, by purchasing or acquiring images online. If you are creating your own images, you will use some combination of these tools: a digital camera, a smartphone with a camera, screen capture software or app, and illustration software or app.

Digital Cameras

How can I take high quality photos using my smartphone?
Smartphone cameras are convenient, and can be used to take photos that are ideal for sharing digitally (such as on a webpage) or printing smaller sized copies, such as 5x7 inches. You can use photo-editing apps, or attachments, such as lenses, to improve the quality of smartphone photos. To learn more, use a search engine to search for *high resolution smartphone photos*.

A **digital camera** records an image electronically. Many smartphones have built-in digital cameras that can take quality photos. Professional photographers or those without a camera on their smartphone can purchase a standalone digital camera. The quality and price of digital cameras varies. Professional photographers typically purchase digital cameras that include the ability to switch lenses, adjust settings, and produce high resolution images. A digital camera allows the photographer to view the images while they are still in the camera, thereby allowing the photographer to reshoot the picture if needed. Because there are no expenses associated with purchasing or developing film, the photographer can take as many shots as necessary to get the perfect one. Digital cameras store images internally or on memory cards or other storage devices. You can transfer the photos to your computer, or directly to photo-sharing websites or social media sites.

The transfer process from camera to computer varies depending on the camera and the storage method. You can download internally stored images using a connecting cable from the camera to the computer. You can also transfer images stored on memory cards using a wireless or connected reading device. Many standalone digital cameras, and virtually all smartphones, include Bluetooth or wireless transfer capabilities that enable you to transfer images to a computer or the Internet. If using a **photo-sharing website**, such as Shutterfly (Figure 5-8), you can order printed copies, create photo albums, and share links to the photos with friends and family.

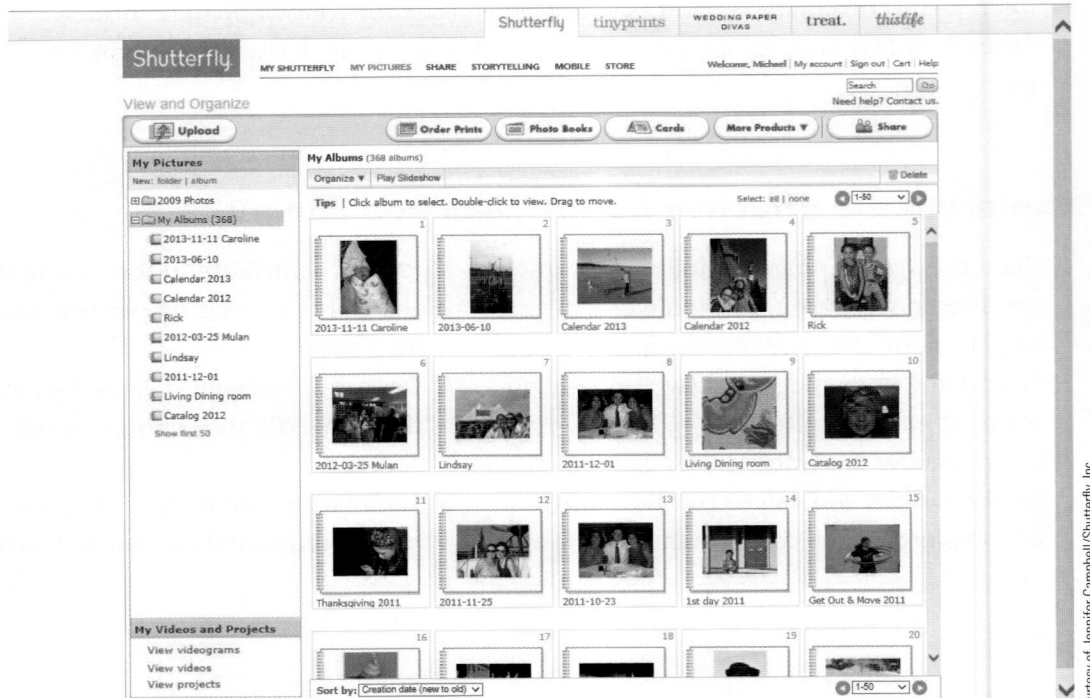

Figure 5-8 Photo-sharing websites enable you to store, share, and organize digital photos.

If you are purchasing a new standalone digital camera or a smartphone with a camera, you should familiarize yourself with your camera's features and modes. Read the manual to learn about the camera's capabilities and features and how to use them to take quality photos. Most digital cameras offer default options for the majority of their settings that are adequate for general use. Use the auto options until you have mastered the potential capabilities and greater control of the customized settings. Remember to transfer your digital images from your camera to your computer or the Internet and back them up. You can manipulate and fine-tune photos using image-editing software on your computer, or using photo-editing apps directly on your smartphone.

Exploring Photo-Sharing Websites and Apps

YOUR TURN

1. Use a browser to open three photo-sharing websites of your choice, such as Shutterfly or Flickr, in separate tabs. Alternatively, you can explore photo-sharing apps, such as Instagram, if your smartphone has that capability.

2. Note the features of each website or app, including sharing, printing, and storage. Does the website or app charge a fee for its services or use? What privacy settings does the website or app use to protect your images?

3. Determine whether the website or app appeals to amateur photographers, professional photographers, or both. How might you use the photo-sharing website or app to store, link to, or add photos to your website?

4. Summarize your findings, as well as any experience you have with sharing digital photos. Submit in the format requested by your instructor.

Screen Capture and Illustration Software and Apps

You can use **screen capture software**, such as SnagIt®, !Quick Screen Capture®, and FullShot®, to create an image of computer screen contents. Many smartphones include screen capture capabilities (Figure 5-9), or enable you to download or purchase a screen capture app. Web designers use screen captures, also called **screen shots**, in print media (like the computer screen illustrations in this text) and online to show the contents of a computer screen at a point in time. Technical blogs, webpage software tutorials, and technical support webpages often use screen shots. Most screen capture software and apps also contain features for editing the images.

Web designers and graphic artists use **illustration software and apps**, such as Adobe Illustrator®, Xara Xtreme®, and SketchBook® Mobile (Figure 5-10), to create images, such as diagrams and drawings, by drawing shapes, lines, and curves. You learn more about images created using illustration software and apps in the next section.

Q&A

What are megapixels and how do they affect digital image quality?
One **megapixel** is equal to a million pixels. Professional photographers use digital cameras with higher megapixel capabilities to produce larger quality images, such as poster-sized. If you have a digital camera or smartphone with a camera, check the camera settings to see the megapixels per image.

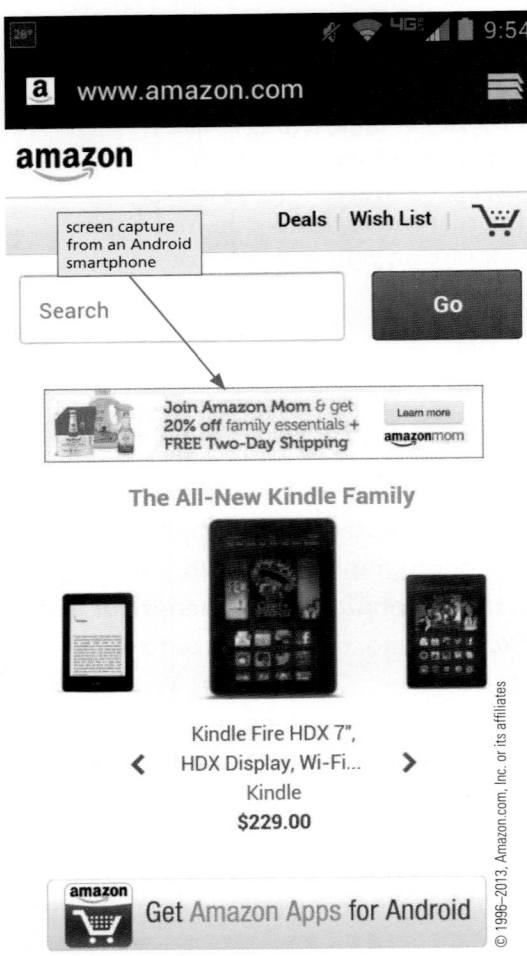

screen capture from an Android smartphone

Figure 5-9 Screen capture software and apps create an image of the contents of a screen.

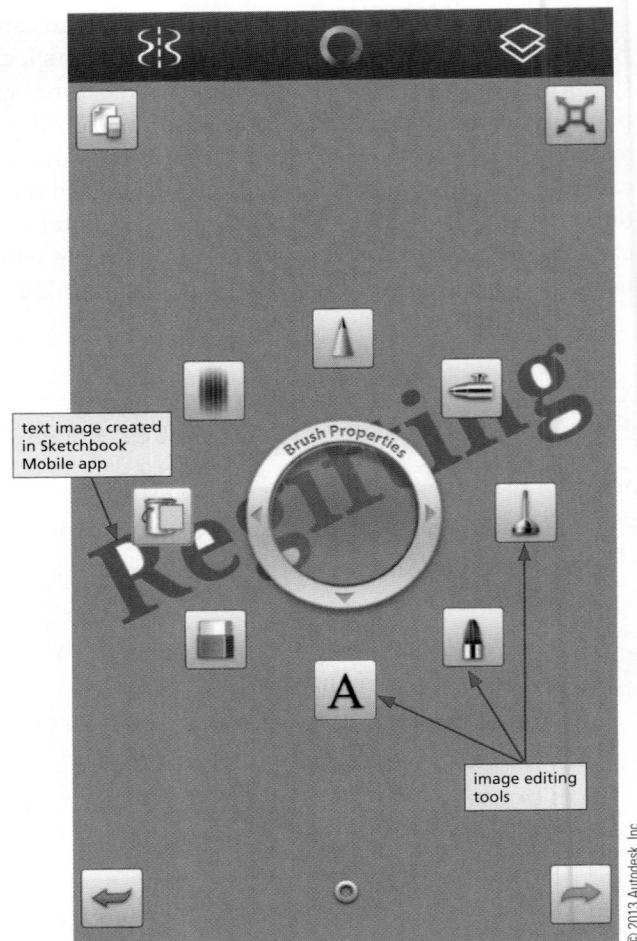

text image created in Sketchbook Mobile app

image editing tools

Figure 5-10 Designers use illustration software and apps to draw and format an image.

How can I transfer a printed photo to digital?

A **scanner** is a computer input device that reads printed text, images, or objects and then translates the results into a digital file. Three common scanner types are flatbed, sheet-fed, and drum.

If you are unable to create your images because of restrictions on time, available resources, or expertise, you can use various sources for graphics files created and/or provided by individuals or companies that specialize in graphic design. WYSIWYG editors, image-editing software and apps, or illustration software and apps often provide sample images or drawing templates. You can search online by category, such as sports or medicine, and by photo type (clip art and photography, for example) to purchase individual digitized images or a library of images. You can download images offered for a fee at some websites or download free public domain images, such as those found at many U.S. government websites. Websites such as morgueFile.com (Figure 5-11) include archives of artist-provided images available for free and with limited copyright restrictions.

Before you download images or include an image on your website, locate any terms or conditions for using the image. The copyright owner might require you to provide a link to the page that offers the image. You should add a credit line for images from other sources, even those in the public domain.

Figure 5-11 Searchable archives of images from multiple artists exist on the web.

> Before downloading photos or illustrations from the web, ensure that you are not violating copyright restrictions, and pay any royalty or licensing fees for the images' use.
>
> **DESIGN TIP**

Image File Formats

The variety of devices used by website visitors and the range of sizes of these devices create challenges for web designers. Including an image file that has specific dimensions and file resolution means that some visitors to the webpage will see a full image, while other visitors will see a partial image or none at all. Although most image file formats are readable on mobile devices, the size and download time can cause issues with page loading. Currently, no single solution exists for this problem. Web designers have developed some interim methods to address the issue. One approach includes specifying options within the HTML <picture>…</picture> tags that instruct the website to display different images (or no image) based on the size of the screen. Web designers are exploring possibilities for developing a mobile-friendly file type that enables an image to adapt in size to the display device.

Image files are either raster or vector. **Raster images**, or **bitmaps**, consist of a series of individual pixels. At the optimal resolution (based on image quality and size), the pixels are not visible. You can create and edit bitmaps using **image-editing software and apps**, such as Microsoft Paint®, Adobe® Photoshop®, and ProCamera®. A bitmap contains a specific number of pixels measured as pixels per inch (ppi) and is **resolution dependent**, meaning that resizing the image affects the image quality. Figure 5-12 illustrates a bitmap image zoomed to show the individual pixels in the image.

TOOLKIT

Responsive web design and image file formats
For more information about responsive image file formats, see Appendix C.

Q&A

Why are raster images called bitmaps?
Raster images are called bitmaps because they are created one bit at a time using a process called **rasterizing**. One bit equals one screen pixel.

Courtesy of Jennifer Campbell

Figure 5-12 Individual pixels are visible in a zoomed bitmap image.

A file name includes a **file extension** — a period (.) and a file format identifier. Web designers commonly refer to bitmap files by their file extensions, such as GIF or JPEG. Figure 5-13 lists common bitmap file types. You can save an image created originally in one bitmap format in another bitmap format in your image-editing software or app.

Bitmap Formats and File Extensions

Format	File Extension
Windows Bitmap	.bmp
Graphics Interchange Format	.gif
JPEG File Interchange Format	.jpg or .jpeg
Portable Network Graphics	.png
Macintosh	.pict
PC Paintbrush Exchange	.pcx
Tagged Image File Format	.tiff
Adobe Photoshop	.psd

© 2015 Cengage Learning

Figure 5-13 Bitmap images are commonly referenced by their file extensions.

Vector images, or **vector graphics**, consist of a group of separate drawing objects, such as shapes, curves, and lines, combined to create a single image. Vector images are **resolution independent**. You can resize a vector image with no loss of image quality. With illustration software and apps you can draw vector images such as the one shown in Figure 5-10 earlier in this chapter. Some illustration software and apps use specific vector image file extensions, such as *.ai* for Adobe® Illustrator®.

To use a vector image on the web, you must rasterize it by saving it in a bitmap file format. Some illustration and image-editing software and apps contain features for working with both vector and bitmap images. The images you choose for your website likely will be in the Graphics Interchange Format, Joint Photographic Experts Group, or Portable Network Graphics bitmap formats. Most web browsers support these formats.

Graphics Interchange Format (GIF)

CompuServe created the **Graphics Interchange Format (GIF)** bitmap image file format in the late 1980s. The GIF image file format was the original image format used on the web. GIFs contain a compression algorithm that reduces file size. GIF images are 8-bit color images, meaning they have a maximum of 256 colors. This color limitation makes the GIF format inappropriate for complex images, such as photographs. GIFs are most suitable for basic, solid-color images, such as cartoons, diagrams (Figure 5-14), and navigation buttons. Different types of GIF images include interlaced, transparent, and animated.

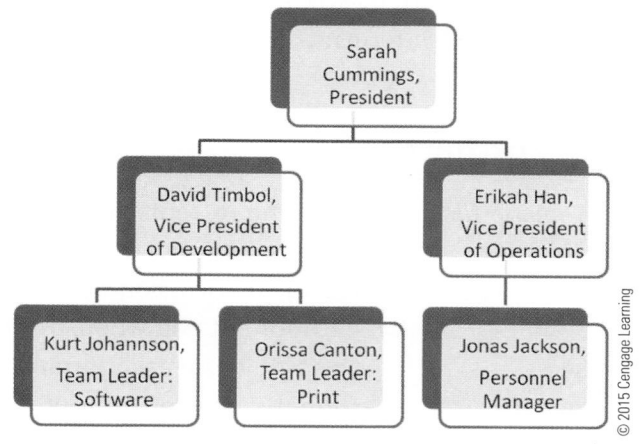

Figure 5-14 GIFs are most suitable for basic, solid-color images, such as cartoons, diagrams, or navigation buttons.

An **interlaced GIF** image appears on the screen in a sequence of passes. Each pass displays the whole image at a higher resolution than the previous pass. Gradually, the image changes from blurry to distinct. An interlaced GIF gives a preview of the image to come without extensively affecting file size. You should use interlacing only for large images that might require more time and bandwidth to download completely, unlike smaller images that typically can be displayed in one pass. Turning on or off a single color in a **transparent GIF** image, such as the image background color, allows the webpage background color to show through. You can use image-editing software and apps to create both interlaced and transparent GIFs. Animated GIFs consist of a series of frames that repeat to simulate movement. You will learn about animated GIFs in Chapter 6.

JPEG File Interchange Format (JFIF)

The **Joint Photographic Experts Group (JPEG)**, an international committee sponsored by the International Organization for Standardization (ISO), published the **JPEG File Interchange Format (JFIF)** image compression format standard. Most people

Q&A **What type of image is created with screen capture software and digital cameras?** Images created with screen capture software and apps and digital cameras are bitmaps.

Q&A **Which image file format should I use?** Choose image file formats that are appropriate for the image you are showing, and that you can adjust, delete, or adapt to make your website responsive. For more information about image file formats, use a search engine to search for *image file format responsive web design*.

Q&A **What is antialiasing?** **Antialiasing** of fonts and bitmap images is a technique for smoothing jagged edges by adding shaded pixels that make the image appear to have smooth lines and curves.

Q&A **What is a progressive JPEG?** A **progressive JPEG** is similar to an interlaced GIF and appears on the screen in a sequence of passes. The progressively improved image quality allows the viewer a preview of the image while it downloads. Progressive JPEGs and interlaced GIFs are not in common use today because more people have access to high speed Internet, which improves download speed more than the use of these two file formats would.

refer to JFIF images as JPEGs. Web designers use the JPEG image format for digital photographs, photo-like paintings, watercolors, and complex illustrations requiring more than 256 colors. JPEG image files, containing millions of colors, are compressed. The compression creates smaller files, which results in some loss of quality, usually undetectable. Because of smaller file sizes, JPEG images are a good choice for photographs and other high-quality digital images used on webpages.

DESIGN TIP

Use the GIF image format for basic, solid-color images that do not require more than 256 colors, such as cartoons, diagrams, and navigation buttons. Use the JPEG image format for photographs or art-like images.

Portable Network Graphics (PNG) Format

The **Portable Network Graphics (PNG)** image format is a free open source image format developed to replace the GIF format. The PNG format has two primary advantages over the GIF format: the PNG format supports more than 16 million colors, giving it a greater range of colors than the GIF format; the PNG format also has superior transparency capabilities compared to other formats.

YOUR TURN

Exploring Web Image File Formats

1. Use a search engine to search for *image file formats responsive web design*. Find two articles that discuss image file formats for responsive websites.
2. Describe the most commonly used image file formats and techniques for

   adapting or replacing images based on screen size.
3. Include a discussion of the pros and cons of each format and when, as a web designer, you would use each format. Submit in the format requested by your instructor.

Q&A

Why was the PNG format developed? As the popularity of GIF images on the web grew, CompuServe and Unisys, the company that developed the technology used to compress GIFs, announced that anyone using GIF images had to pay a license fee for doing so. Although you no longer need a license fee to use GIFs, PNGs remain a popular alternative.

Web-Ready Images

Creating **web-ready images** involves using image-editing software and apps to refine and enhance the images as necessary, selecting the right format for the type of image, and then optimizing the images or providing multiple options for different screen sizes to find the balance between the smallest possible image size and the highest possible quality.

If you include images without optimizing them for size, visitors using mobile devices might experience excessive webpage download times and become frustrated. Additionally, using image files that that are larger than necessary wastes server storage space. Failure to optimize images will give your website an unprofessional appearance and detract from your website's message. You can use image-editing software and apps to optimize your images by achieving a balance between compressing your image files into a smaller size and maintaining the best possible image quality.

Refining Images

Image-editing software and apps can help you refine your images to improve their quality. For example, if an image contains more subject matter than you want to include, you can crop the image using use image-editing software and apps. When you **crop** an image, you select the part of the image you want to keep and remove the unwanted portion. Another benefit of cropping an image is reduced file size. Figure 5-15 illustrates cropping an image in SnagIt.

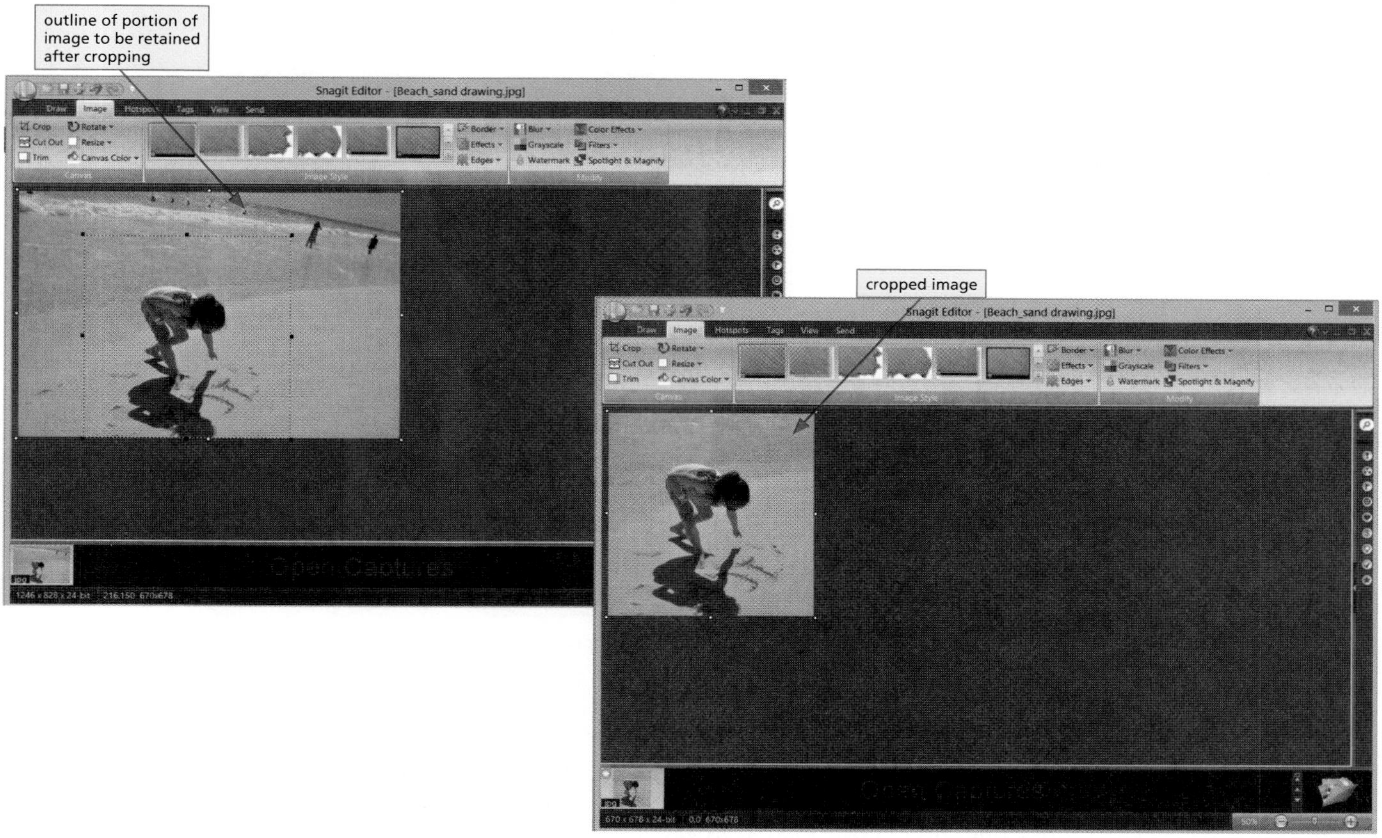

Courtesy of Jennifer Campbell

Courtesy of Jennifer Campbell

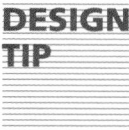

Figure 5-15 Cropping an image creates a focal point and reduces the file size.

Cropping an image eliminates distracting background elements and establishes a focal point. Discarding unwanted portions of an image also results in a smaller file size. Crop an image using a photo-editing app or software before including it in your website to ensure the smallest file size.

DESIGN TIP

Image-editing software and apps have image-enhancement features ranging from predetermined, automatic settings to very precise, sophisticated, customizable adjustments. For example, you can manipulate the levels of shadows and highlights in an image. Additionally, you can use image-editing software and apps to correct an image that is too dark, blurry, or has unwanted spots or markings. Figure 5-16 illustrates enhancing a photograph using the Photo Editor app.

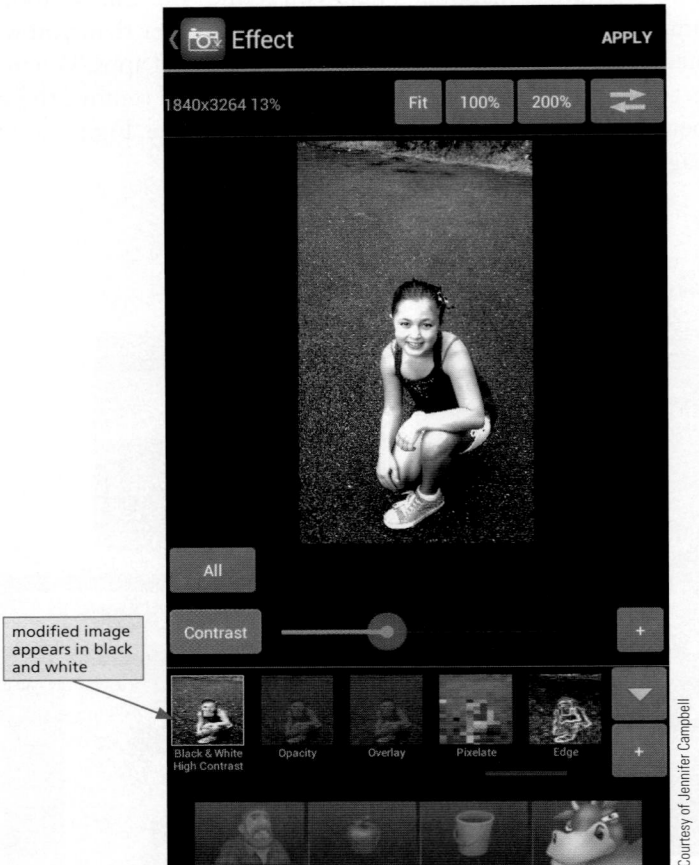

Figure 5-16 Image-editing software and apps offer image-enhancement features.

Optimizing Images for Size and Quality

The three most popular image file formats for webpages — GIF, JPEG, and PNG — all contain a compression feature that reduces the size of an image file during saving. The GIF and PNG formats offer **lossless compression**, which retains all the image data during compression. Image data retention maintains the quality of the image. As you have learned, the GIF format is not suitable for photographs or images containing more than 256 colors. The PNG format supports millions of colors, but creates files that might be too large for efficient webpage downloading. Some designers suggest using the PNG format for editing photographs or other images containing millions of colors, but then saving the images in the JPEG format to reduce the file size.

The JPEG format provides **lossy compression**, meaning that some image data is lost permanently during compression. Using a low level of compression results in a loss of data that is undetectable by the human eye; there is no apparent deterioration in the image quality. You can control the level of JPEG compression with digital camera settings or by using the optimizing feature in image-editing software and apps.

JPEG compression values and the resultant image quality have an inverse relationship: a greater compression value yields a smaller file size, but also leads to poorer image quality. If you are selecting a JPEG image compression value for your webpage images and your primary concern is image quality, a lower compression value will result in a higher image quality, but at the cost of a larger file size. If you need smaller, faster-loading image files, use a higher compression value. Higher compression values lead to a greater loss of image data, called image degradation or **compression artifacting**. Compression artifacting can result in areas of an image that appear blurred or distorted.

Note that each time you reopen, edit, and resave a JPEG image, the loss of data due to compression artifacting increases and becomes more visible in the image. To protect image quality in an image that requires multiple edits, some designers suggest saving the image in a lossless compression format, such as PNG, until editing is complete. You then can save the image in the JPEG format to reduce its file size. Although it is important to keep a backup copy of all your original unedited images, it is critical to do so for a JPEG image. Because of the progressive compression artifacting that takes place each time you save a JPEG, you should make a copy of the original unedited JPEG file to maintain it.

You should make a copy of your unedited original image and consider doing interim edits in a lossless compression format, such as PNG. Save your image in a lossy format, such as JPEG, only after you have finished editing.

DESIGN TIP

Image-editing software and apps provide the capability to refine and optimize any image — whether from a digital camera, created with illustration software and apps, or purchased from a website that sells predesigned images. Many popular image-editing software and apps contain features for manually or automatically optimizing images for use on webpages. You can use these optimization features to help find the best balance between image file size and image quality. Image-editing software and apps offer a variety of quality settings of the same JPEG image. Typically, the quality settings range from very high quality to low quality. Figure 5-17 summarizes the file size, estimated download speed, and quality value for different quality settings.

JPEG Compression and Image Quality Comparison

Image #	Quality Setting	File Size	Download Speed @28.8Kbps	Compression Value
1.	Very High	116.5K	42 seconds	80 quality
2.	High	71.68K	26 seconds	60 quality
3.	Medium	37.89K	14 seconds	30 quality
4.	Low	23.18K	9 seconds	10 quality

© 2015 Cengage Learning

Figure 5-17 Compare file size, estimated download speed, and image quality.

Exploring Image-Editing Software and Apps

1. Use a search engine to search for *image-editing shareware.* If you are using a mobile device, search for *image-editing apps.* Identify at least two image-editing shareware (free to try and then purchase) or freeware (free to use) software programs or free mobile apps.

2. Compare the features offered in each software program or app. Find professional and user reviews of each software program or app. If possible (and permissible if using a computer or device that belongs to your school), download and try a shareware or freeware image-editing software program or app. Explore ways to refine an image and optimize an image for size and for quality.

3. Summarize your findings and submit in the format requested by your instructor.

Chapter Review

Text for webpages is most effective when you follow the rules of good typography — the appearance and arrangement of the characters that make up text. The features that define type include typeface, type style, and type size. Combined, these three features are known as a font. As a web designer, you should evaluate potential fonts based on the readability, accessibility, and availability of the font along with the mood you want website visitors to experience. Include font stacks to ensure all computers, mobile devices, and browsers can read your website content, even if they do not include your preferred font. If you are creating your own images, you can use a digital camera (standalone or part of a smartphone), screen capture software and apps, and illustration software and apps. You also can purchase or locate free predesigned images online.

When you choose images, be sure to select quality and relevant images that add value to your website, match or complement your website's color scheme, accurately represent the content to which they link (if used as an image link), support the website's message, and contribute to the overall mood you want to set for visitors. Consider responsive web design practices, and include options for adjusting or replacing images depending on screen size. Choose GIF, JPEG, or PNG compression file formats in which to save your images and, if using image-editing software and apps, take advantage of the built-in file optimization features. Creating a web-ready image involves refining the image, selecting the right format for the type of image, and then optimizing the image for both image size and image quality.

After reading the chapter, you should know each of these Key Terms.

absolute font size (131)
antialiasing (139)
backup font (130)
bitmap (137)
bounding box (132)
compression artifacting (143)
crop (141)
digital camera (134)
em unit (131)
embedded font (130)
file extension (138)
font (128)
font family (130)
font stack (130)
Graphics Interchange Format (GIF) (139)
illustration software and apps (135)
image-editing software and apps (137)
interlaced GIF (139)
Joint Photographic Experts Group (JPEG) (139)
JPEG File Interchange Format (JFIF) (139)
kerning (128)
leading (128)
lossless compression (142)
lossy compression (142)
megapixel (135)
OpenType (129)

photo-sharing website (134)
Portable Network Graphics (PNG) (140)
PostScript (129)
progressive JPEG (139)
raster image (137)
rasterizing (137)
relative font size (131)
rem (131)
resolution dependent (137)
resolution independent (138)
sans serif (129)
scanner (136)
screen capture software and apps (135)
screen shots (135)
serif (129)
tracking (128)
transparent GIF (139)
TrueType (129)
type (128)
type size (128)
type style (128)
typeface (128)
typography (128)
vector graphics (138)
vector image (138)
web-ready image (140)
web-safe font (130)

Complete the Test Your Knowledge exercises to solidify what you have learned in the chapter.

Matching Terms

Match each term with the best description.

____ 1. resolution independent

____ 2. lossless compression

____ 3. embedded font

____ 4. antialiasing

____ 5. relative font sizes

____ 6. PNG

____ 7. JPEG

____ 8. bitmap

____ 9. rem

____ 10. bounding box

a. CSS specification that includes a default font and backup font types.

b. A font standard that incorporates TrueType and PostScript fonts.

c. A file compression method that results in permanent removal of image data.

d. Images created pixel by pixel; also known as raster images.

e. The container in which text added to an image appears.

f. You can resize a(n) _____ image with no negative effect on image quality.

g. A short line extending from the top or bottom of a character.

continued

___ 11. compression artifacting

___ 12. serif

___ 13. crop

___ 14. OpenType

___ 15. font stack

h. A font that must first download in order to allow the webpage text to display.

i. A technique for smoothing jagged edges by adding shaded pixels that make the image appear to have smooth lines and curves.

j. To remove portions of an image to emphasize certain parts of the image.

k. The font size specified as a percentage in relation to the font size of surrounding text.

l. The image file format most suited for photographs.

m. An image file format originally designed to replace the GIF file format.

n. Retains all image data and maintains the quality of the image.

o. Font specification that appears in the HTML document's root, or top level heading, rather than for each font style or type.

Short Answer Questions

Write a brief answer to each question.

1. Describe the characteristics that define type and describe how web designers use typography.

2. Compare the terms *type style* and *font* as used in web design.

3. Describe the five generic typeface or font families and when to use each.

4. Discuss the role of font stacks when specifying website fonts.

5. Discuss responsive web design guidelines for determining website font sizes.

6. List five factors to be considered when selecting relevant, high-quality images for webpages.

7. Describe tools you can use to create your own webpage images.

8. Identify methods for transferring image files from a digital camera to a computer or the Internet.

9. Compare and contrast lossless and lossy compression methods for image files and identify which image file types provide lossless compression and which provide lossy compression.

10. Describe how to optimize your images to create web-ready images; discuss four ways to help ensure your images are web-ready.

Test your knowledge of chapter content and key terms.

Instructions: Reinforce what you learned in this chapter with games, exercises, training, and many other online activities and resources. Reinforcement activities and resources are available at no additional cost on www.cengagebrain.com.

TRENDS

Investigate current web design developments with the Trends exercises.

Write a brief essay about each of the following trends, using the web as your research tool. For each trend, identify at least one webpage URL used as a research source. Be prepared to discuss your findings in class.

1 | Smartphone Digital Cameras

Research digital camera options for smartphones. Compare the characteristics of the highest-quality smartphone digital cameras to those of professional digital cameras. Explore options for enhancing smartphone digital images using apps or attachment devices. If possible, determine the image size of a photo taken with your smartphone's digital camera and the printing or resolution restrictions or recommendations that apply to such photos.

2 | Typography, Images, and Visual Identity

As you learned in Chapters 2 and 3, using design to establish a visual identity or brand for a corporation or organization can contribute to widespread recognition of the corporation's or organization's products and/or services. Locate a real-world website of your choice that has a very well-known visual identity (for example, a recognizable logo, such as the Nike swoosh, or font, such as Disney). Discuss how typography and image selection contribute to the website publisher's visual identity and brand.

AT ISSUE

Challenge your perspective of the web and web design technology with the @Issue exercises.

Write a brief essay in response to the following issues, using the web as your research tool. For each issue, identify at least one webpage URL used as a research source. Be prepared to discuss your findings in class.

1 | A Question of Integrity

Image-editing software and apps are evolving constantly, increasing web designers' capabilities to apply highly sophisticated techniques. Cloning, editing, blending, and image-correction tools can reconfigure an image so even experts have difficulty perceiving whether the image is an original or an altered version. The negative aspect to these evolving capabilities is the potential to misrepresent reality. For example, it is possible to place an individual in a photo to suggest he or she was present when the photo was taken. This capability to alter images raises the question of integrity. Identify one or two legal and moral issues surrounding misrepresentation using altered images. In addition, discuss the responsibility of web designers to protect against misrepresentation using altered images.

2 | Choosing Responsive Font Sizes

What do you need to consider when choosing font sizes for a website in order to follow responsive web design practices? List and define the methods described in this chapter, and outline pros and cons for each. Use a search engine to learn more about font size trends and choosing responsive font sizes. List current practices and recommendations. If possible, view a website on devices or computers with different screen sizes and/or resolutions, and evaluate the responsiveness of the font sizes.

HANDS ON

Use the World Wide Web to obtain more information about the concepts in the chapter with the Hands On exercises.

1 | Explore and Evaluate: Image Compression

Create a table or other comparison tool in which you list five image file types used on the web. Use the information in this chapter, and/or a search engine to include the following information about each image type.

a. Does the image file type use lossless or lossy compression?

b. Is the image file type owned or under the control of any company or organization? If so, are there any restrictions upon its use?

c. Find recommendations for the type of image, resolution, or other use for the image file type.

2 | Search and Discover: Images in the Public Domain

Use a search engine to identify sources of images in the public domain. Create a list of public domain image sources, including the website name, URL, type of images, and required credit information, if any. List factors you should consider when using public domain images. Explain how an image becomes part of the public domain.

TEAM APPROACH

Work collaboratively to reinforce the concepts in the chapter with the Team Approach exercises.

1 | Using Font Stacks

Use a search engine to find a list of fonts and font stacks considered to be web safe. Join with another student to research how to use CSS to create font stacks. Include discussion about techniques, tools, and commonly used font stacks. Explore the use of generic fonts. Explain why or why not you might use embedded fonts in your website. Discuss why including similar backup and generic fonts can meet the website's design goals, and why it is important to include them in your website.

2 | Create Vector Images

Join with another student to create or describe a vector image you would add to an existing website of your choice, such as a personal website you have created, or your school's website. If available, use an image-editing software program or app to create a vector image that you could use on the website. If you do not have access to image-editing tools, sketch an image by hand. Discuss the website for which you would use the image, and explain how your image's colors, lines, and size meet the needs and support the goals of your website.

CASE STUDY

Apply the chapter concepts to the ongoing development process in web design with the Case Study.

The Case Study is an ongoing development process using the concepts, techniques, and Design Tips presented in each chapter.

Background Information

In this Case Study assignment, you begin to create, gather, and prepare some of the content you have determined in your website plan that will help achieve your website's goals and objectives. First, you need to review guidelines and principles presented in this chapter and previous chapters. Specific sections for review are detailed in the assignment.

Chapter 5 Assignment

1. Review the guidelines in Chapter 2 for writing for the web. Then, use word-processing software and apps to create the text for your webpages. Remember to check the text's spelling and grammar. If possible, wait at least one day after creating your text before proofing your pages, and have at least one other qualified person proofread your pages.

2. Select the fonts you will use for your webpage text. Determine the backup fonts you will use in your font stack.

3. Gather or create value-added images for your website. Ensure that your images are free of copyright or usage restrictions.

4. Prepare your web-ready images by using image-editing software and apps to refine the images and then optimize them for size and quality.

5. Save your text and images in the appropriate folders in the directory structure you have created for your website.

6. Save a backup copy of your files to an external storage device.

6 | Multimedia and Interactivity Elements

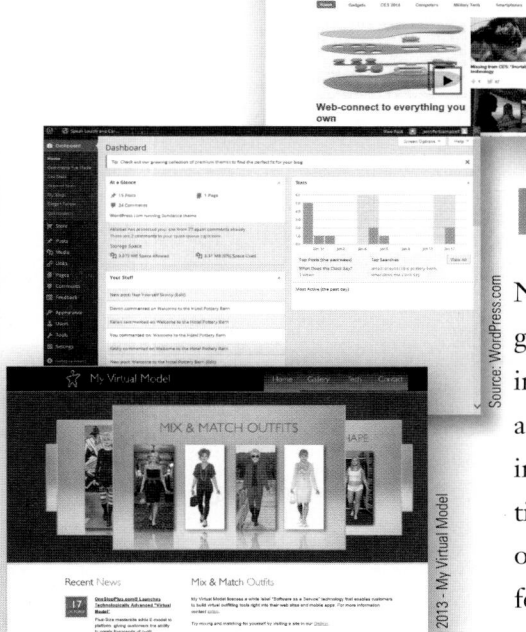

© 2014 FOX News Network, LLC

Source: WordPress.com

© 2013 - My Virtual Model

Introduction

Now that you know how to develop a website plan, understand the rules of good typography, and are familiar with the methods to prepare and optimize images for your website, the next step is to learn how to use multimedia and interactive elements to enhance your webpages. Multimedia elements, including audio and video, add interest and excitement to a website. Interactive elements allow you to connect with your target audience. Strategic use of multimedia and interactive elements can provide a means for collecting feedback from and entertaining your website visitors.

You can download or link to ready-made multimedia and interactive elements available for purchase or for free on e-commerce and sharing websites. With the proper tools and expertise, you can create your own multimedia and interactive elements. As with any website element, you should consider the value it adds to your website and ensure it helps you meet your website goals before adding it.

Objectives

After completing this chapter, you will be able to:

1. Explain webpage multimedia issues

2. Describe types of webpage animation

3. Discuss adding and editing webpage audio and video elements

4. Identify ways to effectively use interactive elements

Multimedia Issues

In Chapter 3, you learned that multimedia elements typically are some combination of text, images, animation, audio, and video used to produce stimulating, engaging webpage content, as shown in the Fox News website in Figure 6-1. Video clips might be used to play an interview that supports a news story or demonstrate how to use a product correctly. Audio can present a personal greeting or teach the proper pronunciation of a foreign language. WYSIWYG editors, such as Microsoft® Expression Web® and Adobe® Dreamweaver®, include tools for incorporating multimedia with ease. Most mobile and web browsers support the plug-ins needed to view and play a variety of multimedia elements.

Figure 6-1 The Fox News website effectively incorporates multimedia elements.

Although multimedia can add value and interest to your website, it is not essential. Many well-designed websites achieve their objectives without it. Drawbacks associated with using multimedia include longer download time for visitors using mobile devices, the need for browser plug-ins, and the use of substantial storage space on your website's host server. In addition, multimedia elements might not be accessible for visitors with disabilities, such as those who have hearing or visual impairments, or on certain mobile devices. Lastly, creating professional quality multimedia often exceeds the expertise and budget of many designers.

Instead of including multimedia in your website, you might consider embedding, or adding a link to multimedia elements in their source program or website. For example, linking to a video on YouTube enables you to show the video while maintaining a link to its original source. Linking to the original source not only keeps a connection to the video's credit information (author and so on), but also enables the video to play without any additional programming or support from you. Figure 6-2 shows a Google employee's blog with links to embedded YouTube videos. Other websites such as Flickr (photography) and Rhapsody (music) enable you to incorporate media content by adding a link to the media they host onto your webpage or blog.

Q&A

Are most multimedia elements compatible with all browsers and devices?
No. Some devices and browsers include proprietary multimedia players that might not play all types of multimedia files. For more information, use a search engine to search for *multimedia browser compatibility*.

Q&A

What is a podcast?
A podcast is digital audio or video available to listen to remotely. Originally called webcasts, they more commonly are known as podcasts due to the popularity of the Apple® iPod® player. Examples of podcasts include radio shows, interviews, and classroom lectures. NPR offers a library of podcasts available to download or stream to a remote device or computer.

Q&A

What are the Web Accessibility Initiative (WAI) guidelines for multimedia?
Within your webpages, you should provide a text equivalent for every nontext element, including all multimedia elements. For more information, use a search engine to search for *multimedia WAI guidelines*.

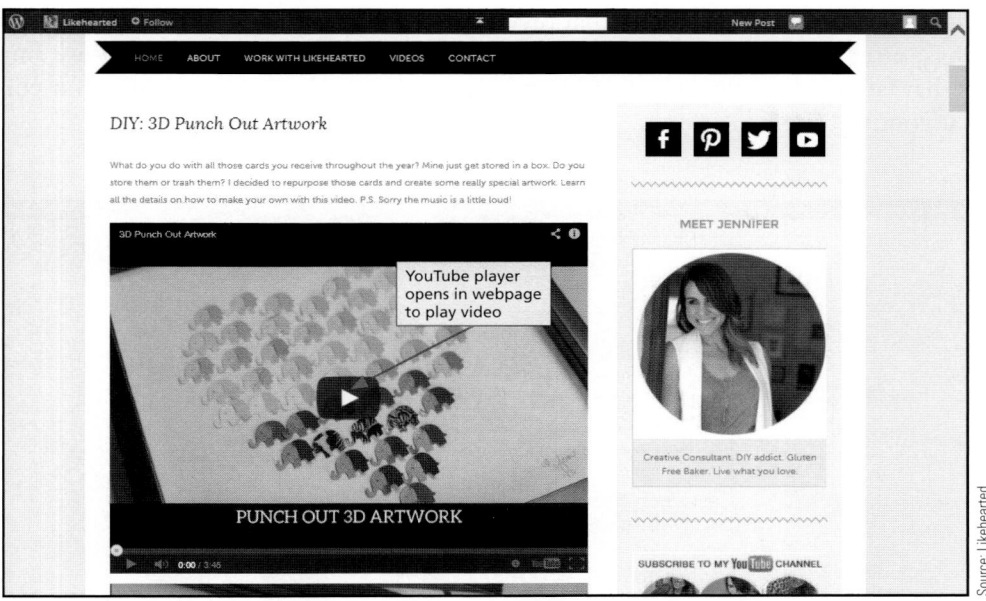

Source: Likehearted

Figure 6-2 Embedding a YouTube video opens the video player and plays the video within the webpage.

> Use multimedia only when its use supports your website goals. Ensure that it adds value and satisfies target audience expectations for content at your website.

DESIGN TIP

You will learn about optimizing multimedia elements for efficient web delivery later in this chapter. However, consider these general guidelines for using multimedia at your website:

- Give website visitors a choice of high- or low-bandwidth content, such as audio instead of video, as well as streaming or downloadable multimedia content.
- List any necessary plug-ins and provide links to download if necessary.
- If possible, provide options for full-screen viewing of videos or animations.
- Provide text equivalents for all multimedia elements to meet accessibility standards.
- Do not waste bandwidth on an uninteresting video clip with little action if an audio clip alone will convey the real content of value.
- When developing original multimedia, break audio or video files into short segments to create smaller files.

Animation

Webpage animation can catch a visitor's attention, demonstrate a simple process, or illustrate change over time, such as the metamorphosis of a butterfly. You can purchase ready-to-use animated elements from countless websites, such as Animation Factory, shown in Figure 6-3. Once purchased, you then can download the file and embed it in your webpage. Costs for animated elements vary, as do restrictions on usage. For example, some animation developers place restrictions on use in commercial websites. Before purchasing an element, read the terms of use to ensure that your intended usage meets with the developer's guidelines. Ensure that the developer does not require you to renew your purchase after a certain amount of time has passed. Select only those ready-to-use animations that fall within your budget and satisfy your target audience's expectation for content at your website.

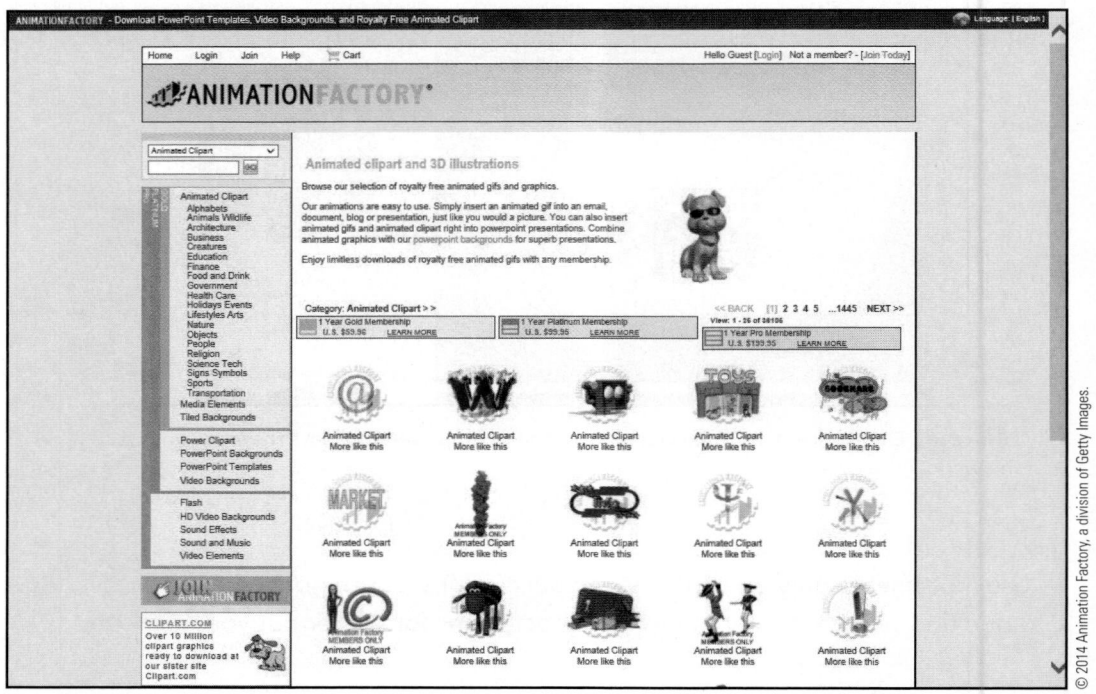

Figure 6-3 Select ready-to-use animations that promote your website's message and satisfy your target audience's expectation for content.

Webpage animation can take many forms, for example, animated GIFs, movies, avatars, and gadgets.

Animated GIFs

Q&A

What are the copyright guidelines for creating animated GIFs?
Websites such as Tumblr provide platforms for posting user-created animated GIFs. Often these animations use images from TV shows or movies for which the creator does not own the copyright. Use a search engine to locate Tumblr's copyright guidelines and policies. To learn more, use a search engine to search for *animated GIF copyright restrictions*.

Chapter 3 introduced you to animated GIFs. Animated GIFs are popular and prevalent web elements. An animated GIF is a single file that stores separate images within multiple **animation frames**. Displaying these animation frames in sequence over a specified time interval, usually stated in **frames-per-second (fps)**, gives the illusion of movement or animation. An individual animated GIF file also contains the instructions and timings to display the image in the browser.

Animated GIFs, like standard GIFs, include up to 256 colors and support transparency. Most browsers support animated GIFs without requiring a browser plug-in. Selective use of animated GIFs can add visual appeal to your webpages. If you choose to use animated GIFs, consider limiting them to one per webpage.

You can download inexpensive software specifically designed to create animated GIFs, such as Easy GIF Animator® and GIF Construction Set Professional™. You also can use high-end image-editing software, such as Adobe® Photoshop®, to create animated GIFs. Some GIF animation software contains **wizards**, which are step-by-step instructions for creating commonly used animated GIFs, such as banners and buttons. Figure 6-4 illustrates the frame-by-frame preview of an animated GIF button created with a wizard in the Easy GIF Animator software.

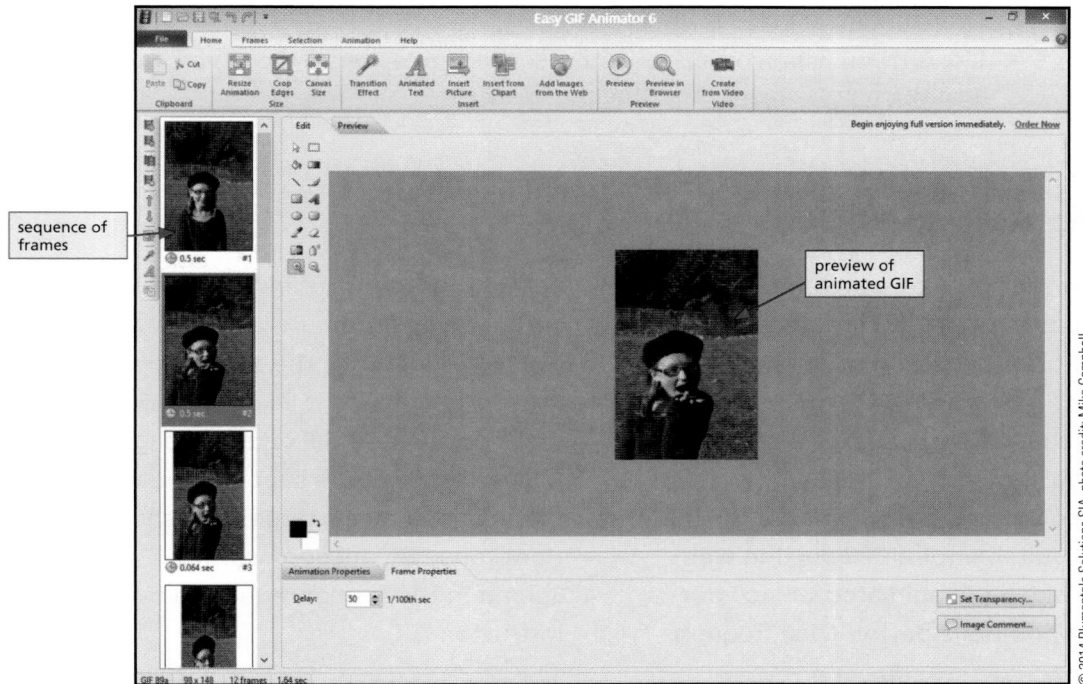

Figure 6-4 You can download inexpensive software specifically designed to create animated GIFs as shareware from vendor websites.

In general, when creating animated GIFs, you perform the following steps:

1. Identify the sequence of the GIF images you want to animate. Use predesigned GIF images, photos for which you own the copyrights, or create original images using illustration or image-editing software. Some animated GIF software allows **tweening**, in which you only create a beginning and an ending animation frame. With tweening, the software creates all the animation frames in between.

2. Specify the time interval between frames, typically in seconds or fractions of a second.

3. Specify whether the animation should **loop**, or repeat. *Keep in mind that endlessly looping animations annoy most visitors.*

4. Set background transparency, and add a layer of text, or a caption, if desired.

5. Test the animation and make color, transparency, timing, and looping adjustments as necessary.

Q&A

What should I consider when modifying GIF colors?
When possible, decrease the bit depth or number of colors of images. Instead of 8-bit/256 colors, experiment to see if 6-bit/64 colors or 4-bit/16 colors yields satisfactory images. To learn more, use a search engine to search for *GIF color bits*.

Using multiple animated GIFs or an endlessly looping animated GIF can distract and annoy visitors. Follow good design practice. Include no more than one animated GIF per webpage, and limit the number of loops.

DESIGN TIP

To optimize your animated GIFs for size and quality, apply the following guidelines:

• Plan ahead to determine the essential animation effects that you want to achieve to limit the number of animation frames.

• Limit image colors for each frame to the same or similar palette of colors selected from the available 256 colors.

- Crop unwanted pixels from the image.
- Use GIF animation or image-editing software to optimize the file for size and quality when saving or exporting it.

YOUR TURN

Exploring Animated GIFs

1. Use a search engine to search for *animated GIFs* or similar keywords. Locate websites that offer predesigned animated GIFs. Identify the URLs of three resource websites that offer royalty-free or low-cost animated GIFs.
2. Identify one royalty-free animated GIF that would be suitable for a C2C auction website. Download the animated GIF to your computer or mobile device. (First, request permission from your instructor if using a school-owned computer or device.)
3. Name the source of the animated GIF you chose and describe it. Explain how including the animated GIF on a webpage at a C2C auction website supports the website's message and meets target audience expectations for a C2C auction website.
4. Submit in the format requested by your instructor.

Q&A

What is meant by the term, sticky content?
Sticky content is any content that entices website visitors to return frequently. Examples include blogs or daily quotes or quizzes.

TOOLKIT

HTML 5
To learn more about HTML 5 and RIAs, see Appendix A.

Q&A

What should I consider when deciding how to add animations and multimedia to my website?
For a variety of reasons, including past conflicts between Apple and Adobe, web designers more often rely on HTML 5 for movies and animations. For more information, use a search engine to search for *Apple iOS and Adobe Flash*, and *Microsoft Silverlight and HTML 5*.

Rich Interactive Applications

Rich interactive applications (RIAs) are web-based computer applications that contain interactive multimedia elements. RIAs use a browser window for the application's user interface and store the application's internal instructions on an application server. Web designers use RIAs to provide valuable content that incorporates video, images, and audio to instruct or entertain the website visitor.

Historically, web designers have relied on Adobe® Flash® and Microsoft® Silverlight® to support web animations and movies. Flash tools enable you to create an entire website or to generate quick-loading, scalable vector animations, which adjust to different browser sizes without degrading quality. Visitors must have the free Flash media player plug-in installed to view Flash movies. Silverlight is a browser plug-in technology designed to play the multimedia content found in rich interactive applications. Silverlight is a cross-browser and cross-platform RIA plug-in, which means that you can use it with many popular browsers.

Because both Flash and Silverlight are proprietary tools, they are not compatible with all devices and browsers. Web designers increasingly are relying on HTML 5 standards to create browser- and device-independent animations and movies. One issue with using HTML 5 is that different browsers or devices can interpret the standards differently. In addition, fewer WYSIWYG platforms exist to support creation of HTML 5 animations and movies.

HTML 5 has many advantages. It is an open format, so it does not need proprietary viewing or creation tools. Screen readers and adaptive devices can interpret the content more easily. HTML 5 also uses the <audio> and <video> tags to enable multimedia content to run within a webpage.

RIA animations use a fast-paced presentation of changing static images to simulate motion. The software records the changing images in frames along a timeline. Web designers create animations using either frame-by-frame animation or animation with tweening.

With **frame-by-frame animation**, the designer must change the image manually, such as by erasing a portion or increasing the size of the image. With **animation with tweening**, the beginning and ending frames identify the original and final location and/or appearance of an image. Then, the software automatically creates the necessary frames within the changing image in between the beginning and ending frames. Animation with tweening is a more expedient, less-intensive method than frame-by-frame animation.

When deciding whether to incorporate movies at your website, consider these guidelines:

- Determine whether you have the necessary expertise and resources. The creation of web movies is often part of the multimedia producer role discussed in Chapter 1.
- Use movies only if they contribute to your website's purpose in a way that other website elements cannot.
- Indicate on your website the necessary plug-in, if needed. Provide a link to the plug-in download website.

DESIGN TIP

Use animations and movies on your website only if they add value to the visitor's experience or enhance page content. Provide information about and links to the necessary plug-in to ensure that visitors can access the content.

Exploring HTML 5 Animation Capabilities

YOUR TURN

1. Use a search engine to locate websites that discuss HTML 5 capabilities for including animations and movies on a website. Find articles or blog posts that discuss the advantages and disadvantages of HTML 5 over Flash and Silverlight.
2. Make a list or table to compare the three technologies. Include information about available tools for creating animations and movies, browser and device support and incompatibilities, speed and quality of animations and movies, and other criteria for comparison that you come across in your research.
3. Conclude which technology is best, and why. Submit your findings in the format requested by your instructor.

Avatars

In Chapter 1, you learned that millions of gamers interact with each other by playing massively multiplayer online games (MMOGs) or by participating in 3D virtual worlds. These gamers create **avatars**, also known as **alternative personas** or **virtual identities** for MMOGs or 3D virtual worlds. You also might find avatars used in email marketing campaigns, on business or personal blogs, or at e-commerce websites. Companies such as My Virtual Model (Figure 6-5) provide e-commerce websites with the tools necessary to create avatars called **virtual models.** Customers can use a virtual model to "try on" clothing before purchasing it. Depending on your intended usage, you may find that adding an avatar does not fit within your budget.

Other e-commerce websites use avatars to welcome website visitors, provide a "virtual salesperson" to promote products and services, personalize customer support responses,

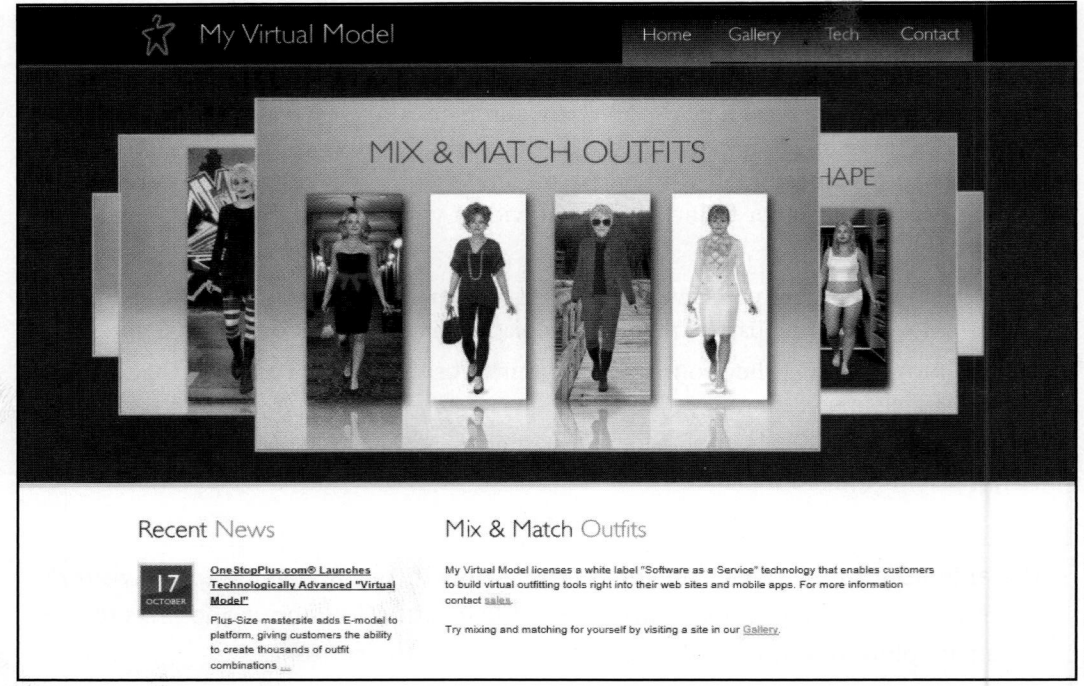

Figure 6-5 Website avatars are alternate virtual identities.

direct visitors to specific website pages, provide instructions for webpage tutorials, and more. Websites, such as SitePal™ (Figure 6-6) or Media Semantics, provide low-cost tools you can use to create an avatar quickly, and then copy and paste the HTML code for the avatar to your website's pages.

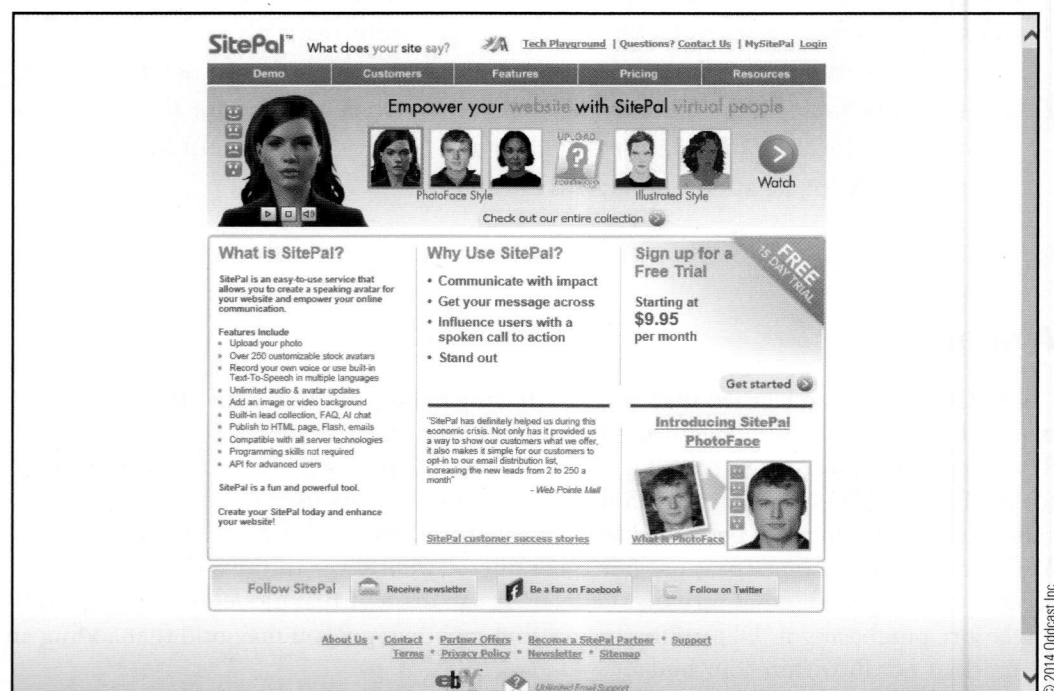

Figure 6-6 Websites such as SitePal provide low-cost tools to create and maintain avatars.

Avatars have other uses, such as in social media and e-learning platforms. You can create an avatar for use in multiple websites, social media sites, and apps, using services available from a number of companies.

Gadgets

Chapter 3 introduced you to **gadgets**, also called **widgets**. Website gadgets are small code objects that provide dynamic web content, including clocks, weather reports, breaking news headlines, and more. On a personal webpage or a blog, you might add a gadget to display the current weather or to launch a slide show to add interest or enhance your visitors' website experiences. To add a gadget, you can copy and paste HTML code to your page from a source such as Google Gadgets, shown in Figure 6-7.

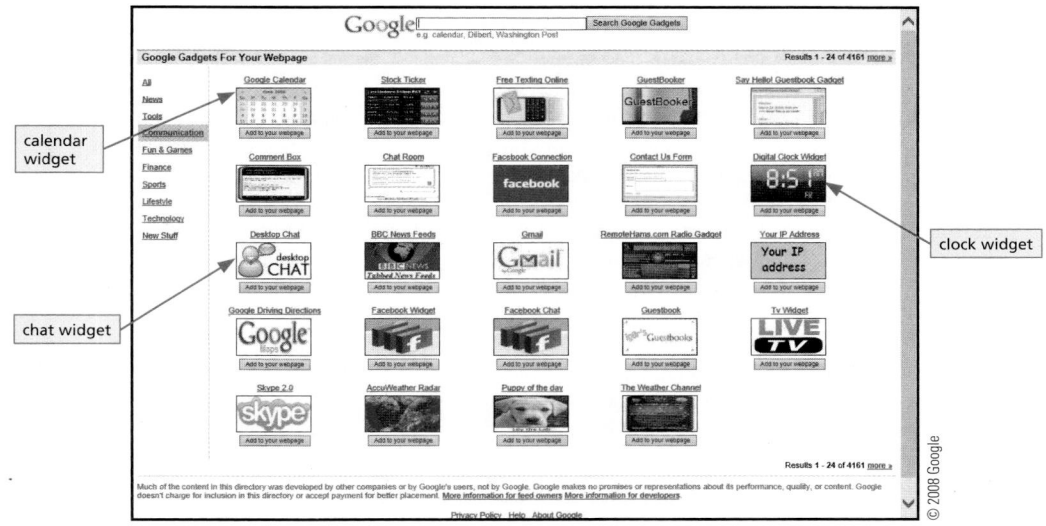

Figure 6-7 You can search for specific gadgets and then copy the HTML code for a specific gadget and paste it on your webpage.

E-commerce avatars and webpage gadgets can add interest to a website. Use both only to further the website's message and purpose and enrich the target audience's experience at the website.

DESIGN TIP

Exploring Gadgets

YOUR TURN

1. Use a search engine to locate sources for webpage gadgets. Identify different gadgets suitable for personal, organizational/topical, and e-commerce websites.
2. Note the platforms, browsers, and devices for which the gadgets you identify are compatible. Note any costs, copyright or usage restrictions, or credits needed to add the gadget to your website.
3. List the gadget resources you reviewed, the types of gadgets suitable for the three types of websites, the guidelines for including a gadget on a webpage, and how to add a gadget to a webpage.
4. Submit your findings in the format requested by your instructor.

Audio and Video Elements

Q&A

Why is it called pseudo streaming?
The term, pseudo, means fake, or simulated. Because the media plays as it downloads, it appears to be streaming. Once downloaded, it resides on the computer or device and can be played in its entirety without interacting with the host server.

You can include audio and video on your website either as downloadable or streaming media. As you learned in an earlier chapter, you must store downloadable media in its entirety on your computer before you can access it. In contrast, streaming media begins to play as soon as the data starts to stream, or transfer from the server to the browser. **Progressive downloading**, or **pseudo streaming**, allows the media to play while it downloads. Because the entire media file is not downloaded at once, there may be delays in playback while the entire file downloads. Each media type has specific advantages and disadvantages, as illustrated in Figure 6-8.

Downloadable versus Streaming Media

Media Type	Advantages	Disadvantages
Downloadable	Downloaded files can be accessed again and again; utilizes the HTTP protocol to transfer the data and, therefore, does not require a specific media server.	Files typically are extremely large, resulting in a long download time and taking up considerable storage space on the user's computer or device.
Streaming	Users can choose the file portion they want to play using the player's control buttons; consumes RAM only while being played.	Very high bandwidth requirements; frequently requires a specific media server to transfer the data.
Pseudo streaming	Users can access the content as it downloads, without waiting for the entire file to begin playback; users can access the files offline once the download is complete.	Once downloaded, files typically are extremely large, resulting in a long download time and taking up considerable storage space on the user's computer or device. Playback during download may be interrupted if the speed at which the media plays exceeds the download speed.

Figure 6-8 Advantages and disadvantages of downloadable and streaming media.

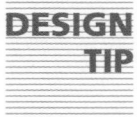
DESIGN TIP Avoid copyright infringement when incorporating media at your website by researching public domain media, or securing permission from the artist or copyright holder. Always give proper credit and citation, even for free or public domain materials.

Audio Elements

Adding audio files to your webpages enables you to add sound effects, entertain visitors with background music, deliver a personal message, or promote a product or service with testimonial statements. You can provide a webpage link to download an audio file, or embed the audio file in the page's HTML coding. Sources of web-deliverable audio include websites that offer royalty-free and copyright-protected audio files as well as message-creation services you can purchase from vendors. E-commerce avatars and movies also often use audio.

Many website visitors dislike background audio or sound effects. Ensure that website visitors can turn off sound, and give them a warning before sound plays. Avoid repeating or looping audio. Only include audio when it supports your website's message and the mood you want to achieve.

DESIGN TIP

If your computer or device has a sound card or capability, a microphone, and speakers, you can create your own audio easily and inexpensively. You will also need to use audio-recording and editing software or apps, such as RealNetworks' RealProducer® or the freeware product Audacity®. Ensure that your recordings are high in quality. Poor-quality audio makes your website look unprofessional.

Exploring Audio Products and Services

YOUR TURN

1. Use a search engine to research vendors that provide audio creation and editing software and apps.
2. Compare and contrast the products or services offered by at least three vendors. Find reviews of the products or services. Examine costs, file quality, and features of each product or service. List any known incompatibilities with devices or platforms.
3. Submit your findings in the format requested by your instructor.

Streaming audio begins playing as the server delivers the audio file to the computer or device. Visitors must have a plug-in or app installed, such as Xbox Music (Figure 6-9) or Apple QuickTime Player®, to listen to audio. To stream audio, your webpage files must be stored on a server that also has streaming software to deliver the audio stream when requested by the browser. Figure 6-10 lists common audio file formats.

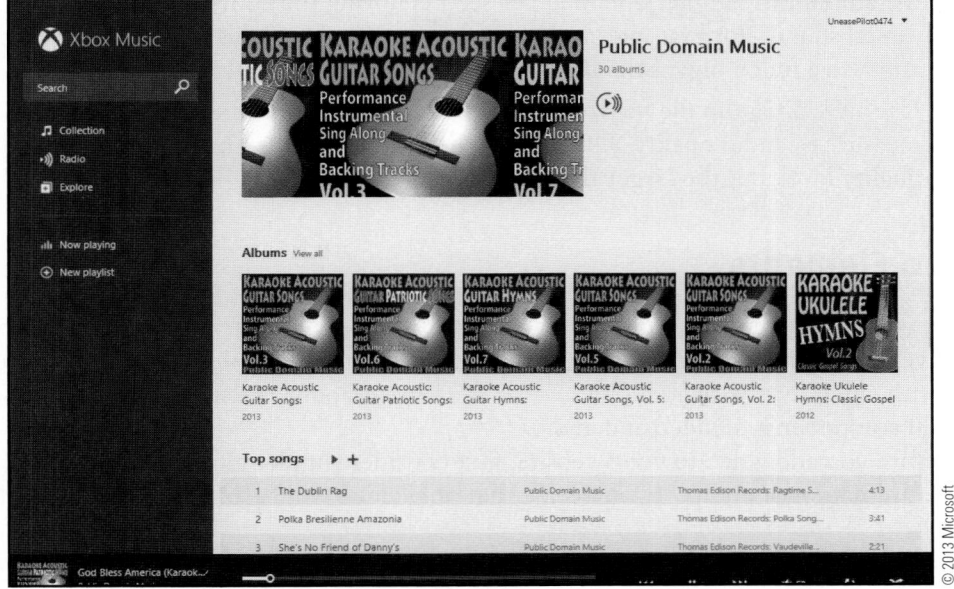

© 2013 Microsoft

Figure 6-9 Xbox Music is one tool used for streaming audio.

Web Audio Formats

File Format	Description
.AIFF	Apple's standard audio file format
.Au	Audio file format used by Sun, Unix, and Java
.mp3	Most common file format
.ogg	Free, open source audio format type similar to mp3
.ra, .rm	Online streaming audio format developed by RealAudio
.wav	Audio file format commonly used by Windows PCs
.wma	Microsoft-created Windows Media Audio Format

© 2015 Cengage Learning

Figure 6-10 Common web audio file formats.

Q&A

How can I add streaming audio and video to my website?
A variety of sources exist online to help you add your own streaming media, or link or embed existing streaming media that plays within its source program and gives proper credit to the source. For more information, use a search engine to search for *streaming audio and video sources.*

Q&A

How can I ensure my audio content is digital?
Using sound-editing software, such as Audacity or WaveLab®, you can digitize, or **encode**, analog (non-digital) audio files. You edit digital audio files by manipulating certain audio aspects, including message size and audio channel selection.

Q&A

Why should I worry about the audio channel?
Selecting a mono audio channel reduces the file size approximately by half over a stereo audio channel. A mono audio channel also is the best choice for an audio message. Whether to choose mono or stereo for a music file depends in part on the desired sound quality and the type of file compression.

EDITING AUDIO FILES   Although you might never need to edit audio files, understanding certain aspects of audio file editing can help you make better choices when selecting audio files for your website. Web audio must be in digital format. Keep in mind these guidelines for creating and editing audio files for the web:

- Keep recorded audio messages or music clips short, such as 15 seconds, and only include necessary content in the audio message. Shorter audio messages equal smaller files.

- Consider the audio channel type when editing an audio file. **Mono (one-channel)** and **stereo (two-channel)** are the two more well-known audio channels. A mono audio channel has a smaller file size, but might not provide the best listening experience for your website visitors. Sound-editing software enables you to change the audio channel of an audio file.

- Use an 8 kHz sampling rate for voice-only audio and 22 kHz sampling rate for music audio. **Sampling rates** are measured in kilohertz (kHz). A sampling rate is the amount of samples obtained per second during the conversion from analog to digital sound. For example, a sampling rate of 48 kHz yields higher quality audio and also a much bigger file than a sampling rate of 11.127 kHz or 8 kHz.

- Use an 8-bit audio file for voice and 16-bit audio file for music. **Bit depth** is a measure of audio quality. The greater the number of bits, the higher the audio quality level, but the larger the file.

Video Elements

Downloadable or **streaming video** can have a powerful impact, but it is a challenge to deliver streaming video content over the Internet efficiently. File size is a much greater issue with video than with audio because of the large amount of data necessary to describe the dual components of video and audio.

Before you add video to your website, first consider simpler alternatives to video, such as animation or audio. If you decide that only video will best further your website's purpose, you can download royalty-free video files from the web, or create your own video files with a good quality **digital video camera** or smartphone with video recording capabilities, and video-editing software or apps, such as Adobe® Premiere® Pro, Pinnacle Studio™ Ultimate, or Windows Movie Maker® (Figure 6-11). Figure 6-12 lists common video file formats.

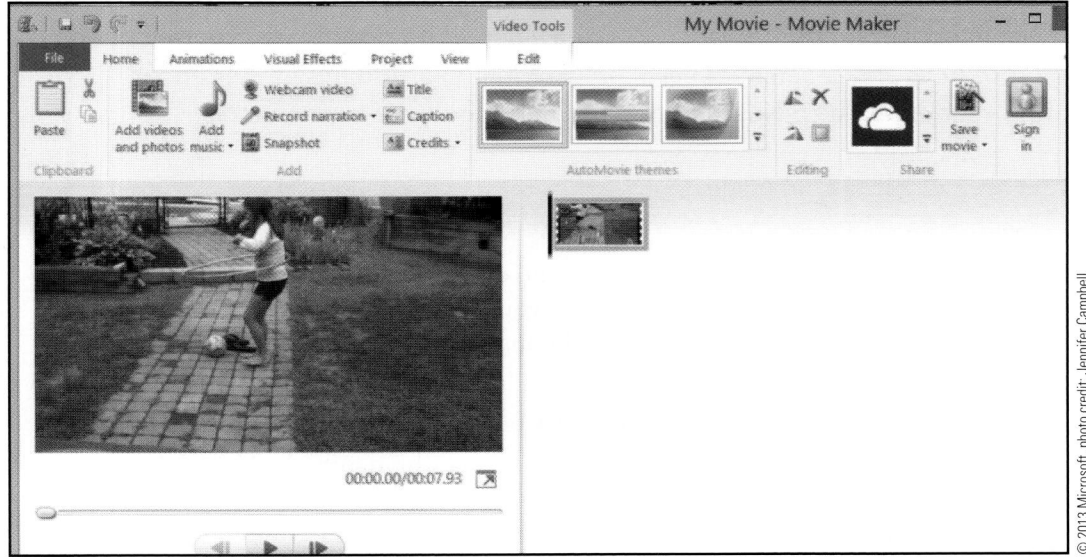

© 2013 Microsoft, photo credit: Jennifer Campbell

Figure 6-11 Windows Movie Maker is video-editing software that enables you to create and edit videos.

Web Video Formats

File Format	Description
.avi	Name comes from audio/video interleaved; common format used by digital video cameras
.mov	Originally designed for Apple systems, now usable with the free QuickTime player on most devices and platforms
.mpeg	Platform-independent file format created by the motion Pictures Expert Group
.rm	One of the first streaming media formats, used with the Real Player
.wmv	Windows Media Video format, available for streaming or download

© 2015 Cengage Learning

Figure 6-12 Common web video file formats.

Exploring Video-Editing Software and Apps

1. Use a search engine to search for video-editing software and apps. Research at least three video-editing software programs or apps. Compare the features and cost for each. Make certain that each software or app has features for creating videos optimized for the web.

2. Review the procedures and capabilities each has for sharing your edited web videos using social media, or uploading directly to your blog or website.

3. Examine the results of your research. Include a recommendation, based on your research, for purchasing or downloading a video-editing software program or app. Submit your findings in the format requested by your instructor.

Q&A

What is a screencast?
A screencast is a video of a computer screen's changing content over time. You can use software such as Camtasia Studio to create screencasts for web-based training videos and demonstrations.

EDITING VIDEO FILES   You can manipulate certain aspects of video — frame size, frame rate, bit depth, compression scheme, and overall video quality — to optimize web videos. Although you might never edit video yourself, understanding these aspects can help you make informed choices about including video on your website. For web-based videos, consider the following:

- The **frame rate** for web video ranges from 10 to 15 frames per second (fps).

- As with audio, the greater the number of bits or bit depth, the bigger the file size. If you decrease a video segment from 16-bit to 8-bit, the file size will decrease significantly, as will the quality. Experiment with different settings to find a balance that produces quality videos optimized for playback on various computers, download speeds, and devices.

- You can define the general quality level of your video by adjusting the compression. Similar to editing photographic images, video compression can be lossy or lossless. A lossy compression reduces the file size of your video by removing data, but may not produce the best quality of video. If you define the quality between low and medium, you will achieve a good balance between sufficient compression and video quality that is suitable for the web.

Interactive Elements

In Chapter 2, you learned that a well-designed website should include elements that enable the website publisher and website visitors to engage in interactive, two-way communication. You also learned about a variety of elements you can use to promote interactivity, such as contact pages, social media integration, and web-based forms.

Web-based forms allow visitors to submit information to a website publisher using email or directly to a database or spreadsheet. Scripting languages, applets, and servlets play a role in creating interactive elements, such as rollover buttons or games, for webpages. Enabling your visitors to post comments to an article, or share it using social media, provides you with feedback about users' reactions and interest in a topic. Many e-commerce websites encourage communication and promote interactivity by using live chat.

Web-Based Form Guidelines

In Chapter 2, you learned that web-based forms are structured web documents in which a website visitor can enter information or select options. Common form elements include text boxes, check boxes, option buttons, drop-down list boxes, and a Send or Submit button. Web designers include forms to obtain comments and feedback or to enable customers to order products or services.

Breaking your form into multiple form pages can help by chunking the information into smaller, screen-sized forms. One benefit is that if a visitor makes an error on one part of the form, he or she only has to go back to that page to find and fix the error. An example of multiple, sequential form pages is an e-commerce website shopping cart. A series of shopping cart form pages allows an online shopper to review purchases, enter shipping information (name, address, and phone number), enter billing information (third-party payment service or credit card number), and, finally, verify entered information and submit the form.

To create attractive, usable web-based forms, you should:

- Require that visitors complete fields containing essential information before submitting the form. Prompt visitors to provide the missing information.
- Make text boxes large enough to hold the approximate number of characters for a typical response. Restrict responses to characters or numbers or both as appropriate.
- Use an **input mask**, where appropriate, to limit the number and type of characters, and provide parentheses, hyphens, or other characters to guide the user to properly format a phone number or Social Security number when entering data into the form.
- Use check boxes to allow users to submit more than one response to a query.
- Provide space for additional comments or requests for further information.
- Use color to highlight and segment information.
- Include a reset button so that the user can clear the form quickly and reenter the information if necessary.
- Add a button that allows the visitor to confirm the information he or she has entered in the form.
- Send an email confirmation notice informing the user that the server received the form data.

When creating a form, you also must plan how you will collect, store, analyze, and use the data. For example, an e-commerce form should connect to the inventory and sales database to ensure that the product is available, and then update the inventory. A form that collects website visitor information to create or add to a mailing list should feed the information into a spreadsheet or database that enables you to sort and filter the data, as well as create custom mailings. Google Forms (Figure 6-13 on the next page) is one example of a web-based tool that assists you in creating a web-based form, and provides data storage in the Google Drive spreadsheet program.

TOOLKIT

HTML 5
Appear IQ, Google Web Toolkit, and Worklight are three web development tools that use HTML 5 to assist you in creating web-based forms. HTML 5 form features include autocomplete, placeholders, and specifying the input type (such as email). To learn more, see Appendix A.

Q&A

What fields should be required in my forms?
Required information might include name, address, telephone number, and email address. Optional information might include position title, income, or marital status.

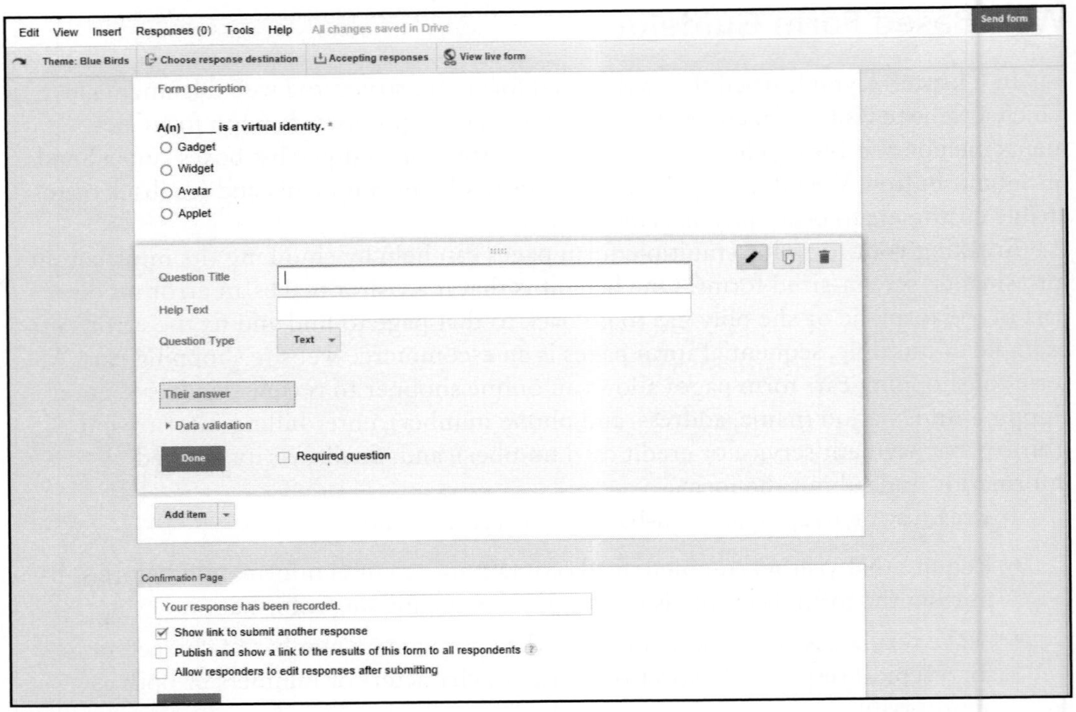

Figure 6-13 Web-based tools can assist you in creating web-based forms.

JavaScript, Applets, and Servlets

JavaScript, applets, and servlets all are programming tools that web designers use to create interactive content elements. JavaScript, ASP, PHP, and MySql, which you learned about in Chapter 1, are examples of scripting languages. Web designers use JavaScript to create customized interactive webpages. Web designers frequently use JavaScript to verify form information and to create rollover buttons, advertising banners, and pop-up windows. Programmers insert JavaScript scripts directly into a page's HTML code.

Applets are small programs that execute in a browser. The server sends the applet files to the browser as a separate file together with the related webpage. Web designers use applets in developing games, flight simulations, specialized audio effects, and calculators. Applets do not require a browser plug-in for viewing. A **servlet** is similar to an applet. A servlet, however, executes from the server instead of within the visitor's browser. To create most applets and servlets, you must have professional programming experience.

Blogs

In Chapters 1 and 2, you learned about blogs, which are online journals. Millions of Internet users now are bloggers, promoting their small business or publishing thoughts and anecdotes about their lives. Thousands of businesses use blogs to promote their products and services, and provide valuable information to their customers.

Sites such as Blogger, Typepad, and WordPress provide tools you can use to create a blog hosted on your own server or on the tool provider's server. Creating a blog using one of these tools can be as simple as entering an email address and password, selecting a layout template for your blog, and specifying where to host the blog. All of these tools offer methods for tracking your website statistics and taking advantage of social media sharing and more, as shown in the WordPress blog in Figure 6-14.

Q&A

How can I protect myself from malware when using JavaScript? A number of websites offer free JavaScript scripts for rollover buttons and banners. You should use caution before downloading any type of free dynamic content from an unknown source to prevent downloading malware to your computer. To learn more, use a search engine to search for *JavaScript malware concerns.*

Q&A

What is a sandbox? A sandbox is a browser feature that restricts a script from running on the computer or device to protect the device from malware risks. To learn more, use a search engine to search for *sandbox security.*

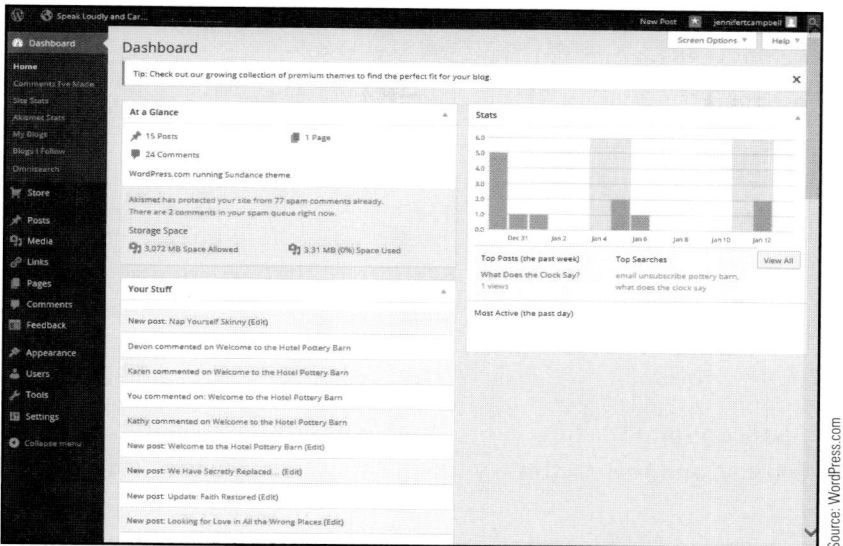

Source: WordPress.com

Figure 6-14 A blog is a powerful tool to enhance communication and promote website interactivity.

◁ Q&A

Where can I find blogs on a specific topic?
Blog hosting services, such as WordPress, enable you to search for blogs by area of interest, keyword, and other criteria. You can follow and read blogs and blog posts directly from within the host website, add the blog to your RSS feed, or sign up to receive email alerts when the author submits a new blog post.

Comments

Adding a comments feature to your website enhances interactivity by enabling visitors to comment on articles and by creating a sense of community. News websites allow visitors to comment on a specific article and to respond to others' comments. Entertainment news websites that regularly feature recaps or information about a specific television show use the comments feature as a venue in which viewers can discuss characters, story lines, and other aspects of the show. Blogs use comments features extensively to promote interactivity. A blog such as CakeWrecks (Figure 6-15) can receive hundreds of comments per day. Comments help the website's creators gauge interest in each day's posting. To add a comments feature to a website or specific website content, you can add a premade script available from many online sources to your website code.

It is important to monitor comments posted to your website for spam or malicious content. Many websites have a disclaimer stating that the website owner will remove anything offensive. Some websites permit visitors to rate the comments made by other visitors. Spam often appears in comments as well. Having someone monitor comments before or as they post gives you control over any postings that might be offensive or that

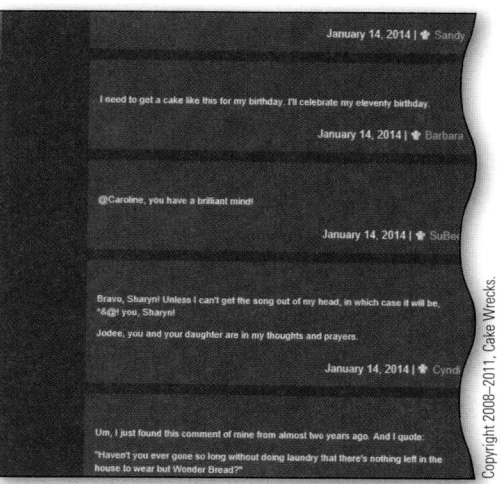

Copyright 2008–2011, Cake Wrecks.

Figure 6-15 Comments features allow site creators to gauge visitors' reactions to postings on a blog or to an article.

may contain links to malware or phishing websites. Consider requiring users to create an account before posting comments. Doing so helps you keep track of or block users who may violate the code of conduct by introducing spam or using inappropriate language.

YOUR TURN

Exploring Comment Features

1. In separate tabs in a browser, open the following websites:
   a. Entertainment Weekly
   b. TV Line
   c. ABC
2. On each website, find a recap for a specific episode of a television show, and review the comments features.
3. Describe one show recap for each website you visited. In what way do comment

postings promote interactivity between the website publishers and the visitors who read and post comments to the blog? How would a website creator find these postings helpful? How do the comment features of the three websites differ and how are they similar? What restrictions or disclaimers regarding comments does each website have?

4. Submit your findings in the format requested by your instructor.

Live Chat

Q&A

What software or apps can I use to include live chat on my website?
LiveChat, Website Alive, and Live Person are a few of the many chat tools available. To learn more, use a search engine to locate the website of any of these tools, or search for *live chat software and apps*.

Another popular tool for interactivity at organizational or e-commerce websites is live chat. **Live chat** allows visitors to ask questions and receive answers in real time using text, voice, or video. Web designers include live chat features to enable website visitors to query product information, ask for customer service, or troubleshoot problems with a computer or device. Websites either offer **broadcast** live chat, in which visitors initiate the chat, or **proactive** live chat, where a chat window opens automatically. Live chat uses a browser window in which a visitor exchanges messages with a **chat agent**, a customer service representative who handles the visitor's query. Chat agents can be in-house or they might be outsourced chat agents located in a call center. Figure 6-16 illustrates the live chat window at the Lands' End e-commerce website.

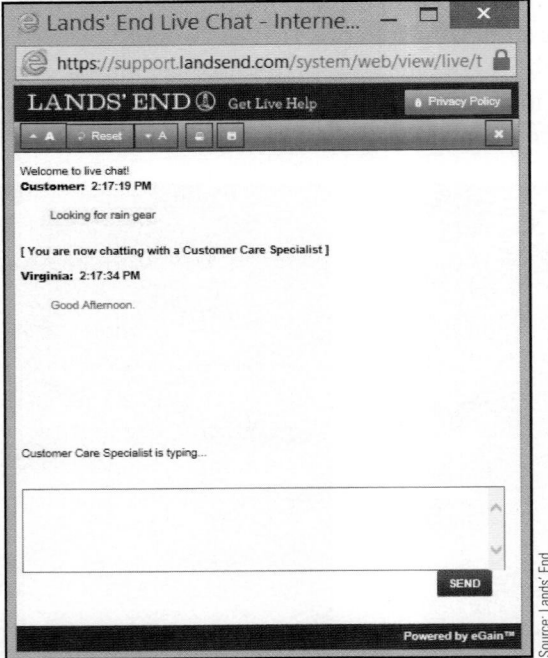

Figure 6-16 Live chat allows website visitors to interact with chat agents in real time.

Blogs and live chat are two useful content elements that add interactivity to a website. If you do not operate your own servers, you can purchase hosted blog or hosted live chat software or services. You also can purchase outsourced chat agent services.

DESIGN TIP

Exploring Live Chat

YOUR TURN

1. Use a search engine to search for *live chat tools* or similar keywords. Research live chat options for a B2C e-commerce website. Identify at least four live chat services: two software or scripted services and two hosted services. Note the features and costs involved with each service.
2. Describe the live chat solutions you have researched. Include a recommendation for a live chat solution for a B2C website that hosts its own servers and a B2C website that requires a hosted live chat solution. Be prepared to discuss your research and recommendations in class.
3. Submit your findings in the format requested by your instructor.

Chapter Review

Multimedia generally is defined as some combination of text, images, animation, audio, and video. Interactive elements promote communication between a website publisher and website visitors. A combination of multimedia and interactive elements can generate exciting, entertaining, and more useful webpages. Multimedia and interactive elements are not essential for the success of a website. Only include them on a website to add value, further the website's message and purpose, and meet the target audience's expectation for content.

Effective uses of animation can include catching a visitor's attention, demonstrating a simple process, or illustrating change over time, such as the metamorphosis of a butterfly. Animated GIFs are the most popular, widely used form of animation on the web. You can use software and apps specially designed for creating web graphics to create animated GIFs. RIAs are interactive multimedia animations and movies that entertain and inform visitors. Web designers increasingly use HTML 5 to include RIAs and other interactive content.

Web audio and video can be either downloadable or streaming, or use pseudo streaming to combine the two technologies. Each has distinct advantages and disadvantages. Designers should consider alternatives to video that would circumvent issues related to delivering video on the web. Popular interactive elements include web-based forms, avatars, gadgets, applets, servlets, blogs, comments, and live chat.

After reading the chapter, you should know each of these key terms.

alternative persona (157)
animation frames (154)
animation with tweening (157)
applet (166)
avatar (157)
bit depth (162)
broadcast (168)
chat agent (168)
digital video camera (163)
encode (162)
frame rate (164)
frame-by-frame animation (157)
frames-per-second (fps) (154)
gadget (159)
input mask (165)
live chat (168)

loop (155)
mono (one-channel) (162)
proactive (168)
progressive downloading (160)
pseudo streaming (160)
rich interactive applications (RIAs) (156)
sampling rate (162)
servlet (166)
stereo (two-channel) (162)
streaming audio (161)
streaming video (162)
tweening (155)
virtual identities (157)
virtual models (157)
widget (159)
wizard (154)

Complete the Test Your Knowledge exercises to solidify what you have learned in the chapter.

Matching Terms

Match each term with the best description.

___ 1. proactive
___ 2. animated GIF
___ 3. input mask
___ 4. tweening
___ 5. broadcast
___ 6. rich interactive application (RIA)
___ 7. avatar
___ 8. pseudo streaming
___ 9. comments
___ 10. sampling rate
___ 11. wizard

a. Manually creating a beginning and ending animation frame; the software creates the missing animation frames.
b. Live chat where a chat window opens automatically.
c. A web-based computer application containing multimedia elements.
d. Live chat in which visitors initiate the chat.
e. Technology that allows media to play while it downloads.
f. A virtual identity.
g. A feature that enables website creators to gauge visitors' reactions to content.
h. The amount of samples obtained per second during the conversion from analog sound to digital sound.
i. A single file in which separate images in multiple animation frames are stored.
j. Step-by-step instructions for creating commonly used animated GIFs.
k. Limits the number and type of characters, and formats data entered into a form.

Short Answer Questions

Write a brief answer to each question.

1. List the general guidelines for adding multimedia to a website.

2. Define tweening and how it is used to create objects. In your definition, include the type of object that can be created and software and apps that enable tweening.

3. Discuss advantages and disadvantages of using HTML 5 to add RIAs to a website.

4. Describe the roles avatars can play at e-commerce websites.

5. Discuss guidelines for adding and monitoring comments for a website.

6. Discuss the guidelines for creating and editing audio for the web.

7. Describe how an e-commerce website would use live chat. Include the difference between proactive and broadband.

8. Describe how to optimize video for the web in terms of frame size, frame rate, bit depth, compression scheme, and overall video quality.

9. Explain the design guidelines for creating attractive and usable web-based forms.

10. Discuss how JavaScript, applets, and servlets are used to add interactivity to a website.

Test your knowledge of chapter content and key terms.

LEARN IT ONLINE

Instructions: Reinforce what you learned in this chapter with games, exercises, training, and many other online activities and resources. Reinforcement activities and resources are available at no additional cost on www.cengagebrain.com.

Investigate current web design developments with the Trends exercises.

TRENDS

Write a brief essay about each of the following trends, using the web as your research tool. For each trend, identify at least one webpage URL used as a research source. Be prepared to discuss your findings in class.

1 | Website Design Trends Blogs

Find two blogs that discuss website design trends. On each website, find blog entries on a specific interactive feature, such as comments or gadgets. On each blog, read a few entries on the subject to get information about current trends. Evaluate the blogs' interactive and website features, such as comments and multimedia. List three things that you learned from each blog's content. What does each blog do well? What changes might you make to the layout or features? Evaluate each blog as a source of information.

2 | Gadgets and Widgets

Research the types of gadgets and widgets website designers can add to their website. Find two sources for reputable, safe gadgets or widgets. List the concerns website designers and website visitors have with making website content accessible to users of all devices and platforms, and address any restrictions or guidelines for including gadgets and widgets. Discuss the advantages of including this type of content on a website.

Challenge your perspective of the web and web design technology with the @Issue exercises.

Write a brief essay in response to the following issues, using the web as your research tool. For each issue, identify at least one webpage URL used as a research source. Be prepared to discuss your findings in class.

1 | Avatars for Multiple Platforms

Avatars are not a new web technology, and have been used in gaming and other web areas for many years. A new development is services that enable users to create avatars that they can use in multiple platforms, including social media. Research this current trend, including available software and apps for creating multiplatform avatars, as well as platforms that integrate these avatars. What security and privacy concerns did you uncover in your research, or can you imagine happening? Are there copyright issues with using avatars for multiple platforms? What do you think of this trend?

2 | Streaming versus Downloadable Multimedia

Describe the differences between streaming, downloadable, and pseudo streaming multimedia. List the advantages and disadvantages of each. Use a search engine to find websites, forums, or blogs where web professionals discuss which method is best. Describe any experience you have with watching or listening to multimedia on the web, and what type of delivery was used.

Use the World Wide Web to obtain more information about the concepts in the chapter with the Hands On exercises.

1 | Explore and Evaluate: Embedding Video or Audio Content from Other Sources

Browse the web and locate three websites that effectively include links to video, audio, or images from YouTube or other original sources.

a. Describe the multimedia element and explain how the element is used by a visitor.

b. Describe the advantages and disadvantages of including this type of content on your website.

c. Which of the three websites does the best job of incorporating multimedia?

d. What might you change about how any of the websites link to external multimedia sources?

2 | Search and Discover: HTML 5 and Rich Interactive Applications

Research how web designers are using HTML 5 developments to include rich interactive applications for websites. List specific tags and techniques that HTML 5 offers, how they are used, and any advantages or disadvantages over using Flash or Silverlight. Discuss the effect of HTML 5 in RIAs and other multimedia and interactive elements in web design.

Work collaboratively to reinforce the concepts in the chapter with the Team Approach exercises.

1 | Evaluate Forms

Join with another student to evaluate the use of multiple forms at two e-commerce websites.

a. Fill out the forms using fake information, but do not submit the forms. Skip information, such as your name or email address, which should be required to see what kind of response is generated. Make a note of any input masks you come across.

b. Describe how the forms are broken into multiple parts and what information is required.

c. Describe the steps needed to complete the form and review your experience.

2 | Apply Your Knowledge

Join with two other students to form a team to identify a list of interactive elements that you should add to the Regifting sample website discussed in previous chapters.

a. As a team, write a report for your instructor that lists five interactive elements in the order of priority (from most to least effective).

b. For each element, briefly describe the technical skills you would need to employ to add the element.

c. For each element, describe what its purpose would be as part of your website, and how adding it meets your website goals.

Apply the chapter concepts to the ongoing development process in web design with the Case Study.

The Case Study is an ongoing development process using the concepts, techniques, and Design Tips presented in each chapter.

Background Information

In the Case Study assignments in the previous five chapters, you have created your website plan, generated the text content for your webpages, and created or gathered and optimized the images for your website.

Chapter 6 Assignment

In this chapter's Case Study, you will create your website. In the final part of the process, you will apply the concepts presented in this chapter and gather or create any multimedia and/or interactive elements that will help achieve your website's purpose. Remember that multimedia and/or interactive elements are not required elements for a successful website. Using the website plan you created in Chapters 3 and 4, and the guidelines in Chapters 2, 5, and 6, complete the following steps to create your website.

1. Decide whether you will generate your pages with HTML code and a text editor such as Notepad or with WYSIWYG software, such as Expression Web or Dreamweaver. You may use a WYSIWYG template, if desired.

2. Begin to create your webpages. As you add your text and position your optimized images, do the following:

   a. Use responsive web design techniques to ensure your website will be effective on multiple devices and screen sizes.

   b. Apply the rules of good typography.

   c. Include alternative text descriptions for images and follow other WAI accessibility guidelines.

   d. Develop your home page and underlying pages according to your chosen website structure.

   e. To achieve unity, establish and apply a consistent page layout and color scheme for all pages at your website. Limit the color scheme to no more than three complementary colors.

3. Download from the web, purchase, link to, or create any multimedia you want to include on your webpages. Insert the elements into your pages following the guidelines for multimedia. Give proper credit where necessary.

4. Develop any web-based forms you want to include on your webpages following this chapter's guidelines for creating usable forms.

5. Download from the web, purchase, or create interactive elements. Incorporate the interactive element(s) into your website.

6. Save your completed website files. Submit your work in the format requested by your instructor.

7 | Promoting and Maintaining a Website

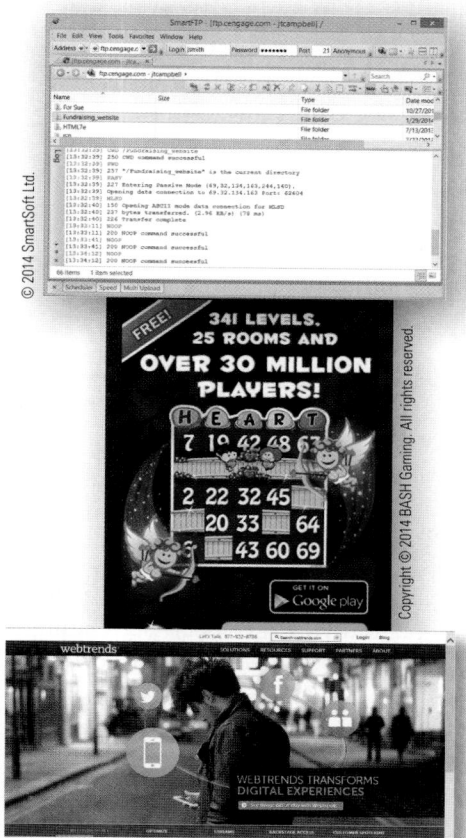

Introduction

Chapter 1 introduced you to Internet and web fundamentals and how businesses and individuals use the web for communication, commerce, and more. In Chapters 2 through 6, you learned about essential design guidelines for creating a website's structure and adding page content such as text, links, images, and multimedia. You also read about how to use color and layout effectively to promote unity and visual identity at your website. You learned about responsive web design and the importance of designing webpages that work with a variety of devices and screens. Along the way, you created a website plan. At the end of Chapter 6, you used your website plan to create pages for your website.

Next, you must test your website to make certain that all elements work as intended, that your website accomplishes the website plan's stated goals and objectives, and that the content satisfies your target audience's needs and expectations. After you thoroughly test your website, you are ready to publish it to a web server to make it available to your audience. As you have learned, a website's content should be dynamic and interactive. Once you publish your website, you then start the ongoing processes of maintaining and promoting it.

Objectives

After completing this chapter, you will be able to:

1. Explain how to test a website before it is published

2. Describe how to publish a website to a web server

3. Identify ways to promote a published website

4. Discuss the importance of maintaining and evaluating a published website

Website Testing

In Chapter 4, you learned why it is important to perform usability testing during website development to ensure that your website's navigation system is both user based and user controlled. Before publishing your website to a web server, you must test the website thoroughly to identify and fix any undetected problems with navigation. Testing also identifies any structural problems or content issues. Failure to test your website thoroughly might lead to loss of credibility with your website's visitors, which would be embarrassing and could lead to your website's failure.

Many organizations and businesses publish **staging websites** to a temporary web server, called a **staging server**. A staging website is a new or revised version of a website, on which you will conduct testing before publishing or republishing new web content. A staging server enables testing in an environment similar to that of a live web server. Thoroughly testing a website prior to publishing incorporates both self-testing and testing by interested parties not involved with the website's design and development.

Self-Testing

The first phase of prepublication website testing is **self-testing**. During this phase, you test your website's structure and page layout, color scheme, and other elements. Prepublication testing helps you ensure the website's pages look and function as designed and confirm that you have satisfied all aspects of the design plan. If you have been performing usability testing during your website's development and creation, you should find few problems during the self-testing process. If you are using a WYSIWYG editor or an online content management system, use the program-specific tools to test links, browser versions, spelling, and accessibility.

As part of the self-testing process, you should do the following:

1. Ensure that all images and multimedia elements work as intended. Verify that the page code does not contain misspellings of the image or multimedia file names and does not link to an invalid folder location or external webpage.

2. Test the navigation and search tools and examine the website's structure to determine whether visitors can find all pages easily.

3. Test all internal and external links to make certain they work properly and none are broken. A **broken link** is one that does not work. Verify that the link text identifies its target clearly and that the correct page opens when clicked. If relevant, make sure that the new page opens in the same browser window, a new tab, or a new window as specified.

4. Include a text equivalent for all nontext elements to satisfy WAI guidelines for images and multimedia.

5. Use any optimization tools provided by your WYSIWYG editor or content management system. Possible tools include: HTML validation, HTML cleanup, accessibility testing, and website speed testing.

6. Correct any problems uncovered by testing, and retest to verify your corrections solved the issues.

7. Use different browsers, devices, and screen sizes to perform Steps 1 to 5. You can expect a reasonable range of variances as long as the page appears legible and looks well laid out in each instance.

Target Audience Testing

The second testing phase involves recruiting a small group of people to act as testers. Include colleagues not involved in the website development, people who represent your target audience, and other interested parties. The testers should review your website and test its navigation, links, and other features. For an e-commerce website, target audience testers might be employees, vendors, and other business partners.

Using an outside group of testers to evaluate your website can help provide insight about how potential visitors will respond to your website and use its pages. Additionally, the testers might find problems that you, as the designer, could not identify because you were too close to the process. If possible, you and others in a designated observation team should watch some (preferably all) of the testers to record their experiences as they explore your website. Testers should use a variety of devices and screen sizes. Observe the testers to determine the following:

- Which pages appear to appeal to them?
- Which pages appear to disinterest them?
- How much time do they spend on various pages?
- Which links do they visit or ignore?
- How easily do they navigate the website?
- Do they at any time demonstrate any confusion or frustration?

After observing the testing, ask the testers to complete a survey in which they can express their candid opinions about their experience at your website. In addition to identifying specific settings (such as browser version, screen resolution and size, and device type) the tester is using, your survey should include questions such as the following:

- Did the website's content satisfy your needs, wants, and expectations for content at the website?
- Was the website's content interesting and valuable?
- Was it easy or difficult to navigate the website?
- What improvements, if any, would you suggest for the website?
- Would you return to the website and recommend it to others?

You also should provide the same survey for testers who you or your observation team did not observe during the testing process.

Exploring How to Organize a Test Group

1. Review the audience profile you developed for your website. The profile should include age range, gender, educational background, geographic location, careers, income levels, and interests and activities. Review the identified target audience needs, wants, and expectations for website content.

2. Identify individuals you know who match your target audience's profile. Ask the identified individuals and other interested parties, such as friends, family members, and fellow students, to participate in the testing of your website.

3. Develop a questionnaire for the testers in which they can express their opinions about their experiences at your website.

After testing your website, seriously consider all comments and suggestions, both negative and positive. Implement any comments and suggestions that will further the original purpose, goals, and objectives; meet the audience's needs; and generally improve the website's value, functionality, and usability. Consider a second round of testing if the comments led to you making considerable changes. File away for future consideration all appropriate suggestions that you cannot implement at this time for valid reasons such as time or cost limitations. After you have made all corrections and adjustments to your website, you are ready to publish it to a live server.

DESIGN TIP Perform both a self-test and target audience testing on your website before publishing it to a live server. Fix any necessary issues that impede visitors' experiences.

Website Publishing

Once you have tested your website thoroughly and corrected any problems, you can make it available to your audience by publishing it to a live web server. Publishing your website to a live web server involves acquiring server space and uploading all of your website files — HTML and CSS documents, images, multimedia, and other related files — to the web server. If you are using a content management system that includes website hosting, you should explore the hosting requirements, costs, and services before starting work on your website. Before you begin your research into web server and hosting options, you should know the approximate amount of server space you will need and how frequently you will update content. Also ensure you have access to any tools, plug-ins, scripts, or capabilities necessary to display your content or support your website's interactive and multimedia features.

Server Space

In Chapter 1, you learned that a web server is an Internet-connected computer used to store webpages. A web server runs server software that displays webpages and their related files upon request from a browser. Thousands of **web hosting companies**, such as GoDaddy and iPage (Figure 7-1), offer server space for a monthly fee. Some accredited registrars that you learned about in Chapter 1, such as register.com and Network Solutions, also offer low-cost web hosting services. Your Internet service provider (ISP) also might provide a limited amount of server space as part of your monthly Internet access fee, which might suit your needs for a personal or small business website. If you are a student, staff, or faculty member, your school might provide server space on its web server, although such resources might come with restrictions; for example, the website content must be related to your research, school organization, or classes. Other web hosting companies cater to e-commerce websites that require a more sophisticated level of server support, such as shopping carts, comments features, and more.

Web servers can be dedicated, shared, or cloud-based. A **dedicated web server** is one that hosts only your website files. Dedicated servers typically are more expensive, but have the added security of being limited to only your website content. A **shared web server** hosts multiple websites. Shared servers are less expensive, but come with additional security risks, as well as potential size limitations as your website grows in content and features. **Cloud-based servers** offer virtual storage for not only your website content, but other files related to your business or personal life.

Q&A
What type of server should I request? You should ask your web hosting service whether your website will reside on a dedicated, shared, or cloud server. All have advantages and disadvantages related to cost, security, and reliability. To learn more, use a search engine to search for *dedicated, shared, cloud-based web server.*

Figure 7-1 Thousands of web hosting companies offer server space for a modest monthly fee.

To find the right web hosting service, you can ask business associates for recommendations. Ask them which hosting service they use, how long they have used the hosting service, and how they would rate the quality of the customer support provided. You can also research the web to learn about more web hosting service options and find reviews. After you narrow your choices, evaluate each potential web hosting service by learning about the cost, level of customer support, and technical requirements for the service level you require. You should get answers to the following questions:

1. What are the fees to host a personal or commercial website?
2. How much available server space will I have for my website? What does additional space cost?
3. What technical support do you offer, and when is it available?
4. Does the server on which my website will reside experience frequent nonscheduled outages? How long do the outages last?
5. What is the longest scheduled downtime on a monthly basis for maintenance and backup procedures?
6. Does the web hosting service offer support for e-commerce, multimedia, scripting languages, applets, servlets, or other elements related to my website and its pages? Does the web hosting service support the Secure Sockets Layer (SSL) protocol for encrypting confidential data? Are additional fees required for these capabilities?
7. How are my website files uploaded to the server? What is the procedure for updating and republishing pages to my website? Does the web hosting service limit the number, size, or type of files that I can upload?
8. Have your servers been subject to security breaches or hacking? If so, how often? What security measures are in place to ensure the security of my website and any customer or personal information?
9. On what type of server (dedicated, shared, or cloud) will my webpages reside?

Q&A

How do I get a domain name for my website?
In Chapter 1, you learned about selecting and registering a domain name for your website. You can go to an accredited registrar's website, identify an available domain name, and register it at the website for a fee. Accredited registrars include register.com and GoDaddy. Alternatively, some web hosting services might assist with acquiring a domain name for an additional fee or as part of the original setup fee for the hosting services.

Exploring Website Hosting Companies

1. Use a search engine to search for *web hosting* or similar keywords. Identify at least 10 web hosting services. Evaluate a mix of websites that offer domain name registration, hosting services, ISPs, and web hosting.
2. Summarize your research. Include the web hosting source, services offered, and cost. Select one service appropriate for hosting a personal website, one service appropriate for hosting a small business website, and one service appropriate for hosting a midsized to large e-commerce website. Give the reasons for your choices in terms of cost and services offered.
3. Submit your findings in the format requested by your instructor.

These questions can help you eliminate options and narrow down your choices to one or two that fit your needs. Once you choose the best option, you need to finalize and upload your website files.

DESIGN TIP Carefully evaluate potential website hosting services from accredited registrars, ISPs, and web hosting companies to make the best choice for the level of hosting services your website requires.

Uploading Website Folders and Files

To publish your website, you must upload all of the website files to the server specified by your web hosting service. For the initial website publication, you upload all of the folders and folder contents (HTML and CSS documents, images, multimedia files, and so forth) for all pages at your website. Later, when you need to make updates to your website, you only need to upload and overwrite any changed files. Before uploading your web folders and files, review the contents of your web folders. Move any unnecessary files to another location, such as original image or word-processing files or backup files, to save space on the server and to limit any extra time in loading pages in your website.

To upload your files, you can use your computer's operating system, FTP client software, or the publishing feature included in your WYSIWYG editor. **File Transfer Protocol (FTP)** is the standard protocol, or set of rules, for uploading or downloading files over the Internet, such as webpage files to a web server. If you are using a content management system, you will save files to the host company's web server as you create them. Before publishing any of the web pages, ensure that you have uploaded and saved all images and multimedia files to the web server. You must know the name and URL of the web server. Your web hosting company will provide you with a username and password in order to access the web server.

FILE MANAGEMENT SYSTEM   Your operating system's **file management system** organizes your documents and files into folders. You can use your file management system to upload your website files directly from your computer's hard disk to your host's web server. If you are using Windows, your file management system is File Explorer. Apple computers use Finder to organize files and folders. You can drag and drop files and folders from one window to another in Windows Explorer, as shown in Figure 7-2.

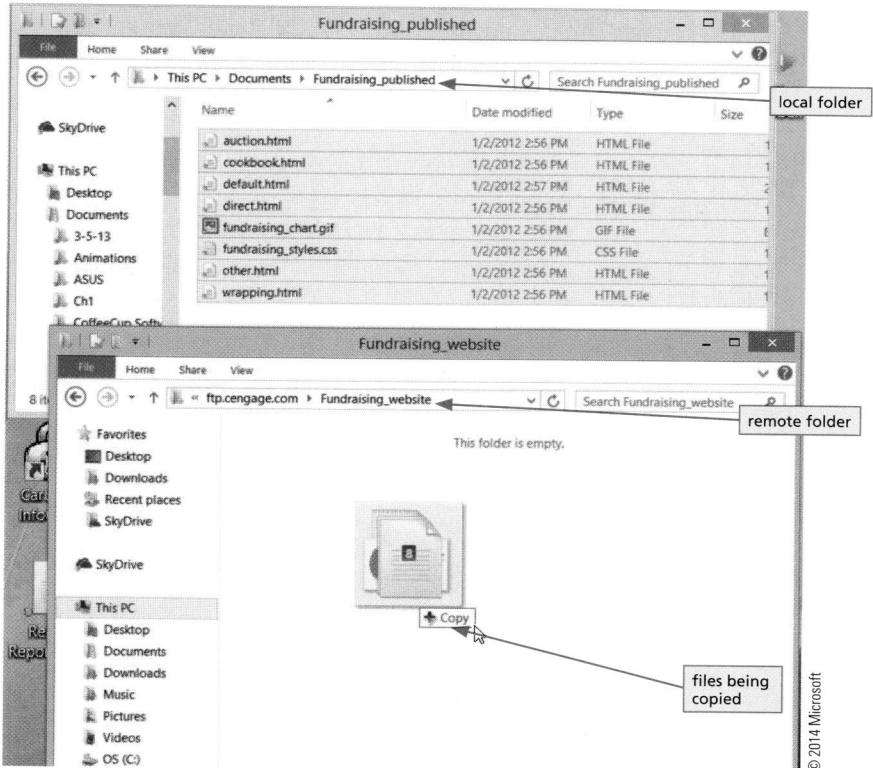

Figure 7-2 A file management system enables you to upload files to an FTP server by dragging and dropping between windows.

WYSIWYG EDITOR If you are using a WYSIWYG editor, such as Microsoft Expression Web (Figure 7-3), you can publish and update your website from within the program. As with other uploading methods, you need to arrange for server space and provide access information — name and URL of the remote server and your assigned username and password — before uploading your web folders and files.

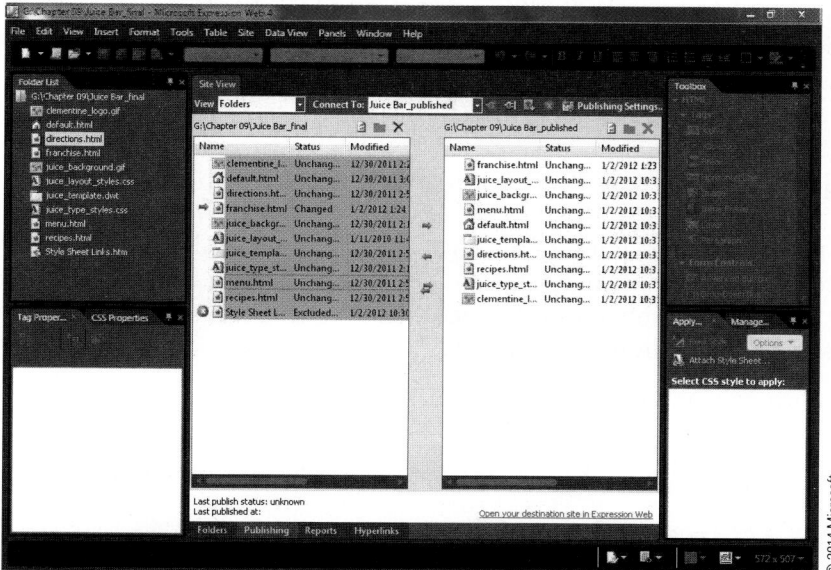

Figure 7-3 WYSIWYG editors also provide tools for uploading or publishing web folders and files to a web server.

FTP CLIENT   An **FTP client** is a software program that provides a user interface for transferring files using the FTP protocol, such as CuteFTP®, SmartFTP® (Figure 7-4), or FileZilla©. Typically, the FTP client user interface provides a split view of the folders and files on a local computer or device, such as the user's hard drive, and on a remote computer, such as the web server. You can use menus or buttons to initiate publication, or drag and drop files from the local computer or device to the web server location to begin copying the files from a local computer to a remote computer or vice versa. After you publish the website, you can **sync** the files, which makes sure that any changed files are the same on both servers.

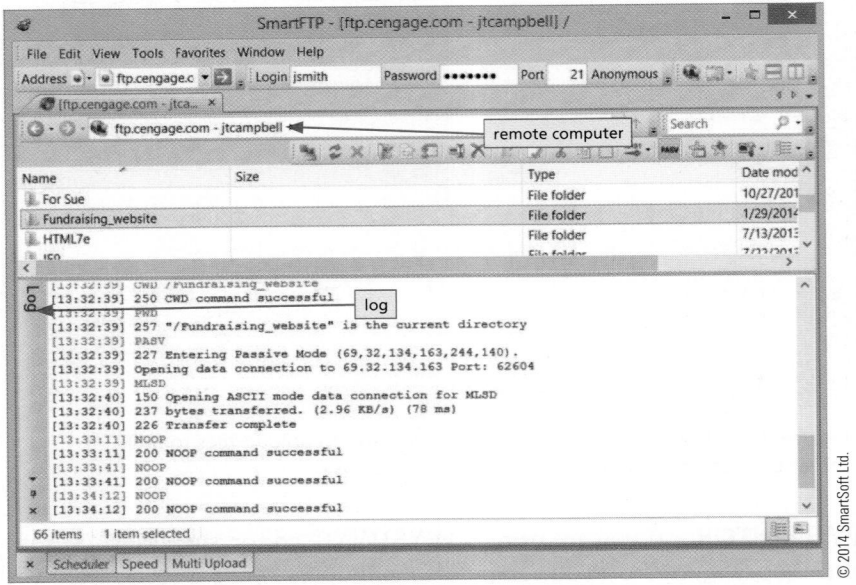

Figure 7-4 An FTP client transfers files between a local computer and a remote computer.

 File management systems, WYSIWYG editors, and FTP clients are three methods you can use to upload your website files to a live server.

Retesting Published Pages

After publication, you must monitor your website continually to ensure that it functions correctly and does not contain outdated information. Conduct a testing process similar to your prepublishing testing. Check the following elements when you publish your website, and periodically over the life of the website:

- Confirm that all images are displayed properly.
- Make certain that no broken links exist.
- Ensure all interactive elements, such as forms, function properly.

- Correct or update page file(s) on your local computer as needed, and then upload the corrected page file to the server.
- Skim the content, especially when it contains schedule or date information that may be time sensitive.

Test your website periodically after it is published to ensure that all features function properly and all content is up to date.

DESIGN TIP

Website Promotion

Once you publish your website, you need to promote it in order to reach the target audience. The amount of traffic you want or need to generate depends on the type of website you have. Attracting numerous visitors might or might not be a top-level concern for a personal website or blog. For an organizational/topical or e-commerce website, having a large number of visitors affects the website's success or failure.

To generate a high volume of traffic to your website, use both online and traditional promotional techniques. Take advantage of free social media platforms to establish an online community of subscribers and direct them to your website. To maximize your website promotion budget, consider using manual search tool submission, search tool optimization techniques, free link exchange, awards, and traditional word of mouth as ways to get your website noticed. If you are publishing an e-commerce website, you should consider increasing your promotion budget to add other paid online promotional tools to the mix: search engine paid or sponsored placement, a search tool submission service, an affiliate program, website advertising using an online advertising network, and opt-in email advertising.

Online Promotional Techniques

The Internet offers a variety of ways to announce your website and drive visitors to it. For example, in previous chapters you learned about the increasing importance of business blogs in promoting e-commerce websites. Other online tools for website promotion include social media platforms, search tool advertising methods (search tool submissions, search engine optimization, and search tool paid or sponsored placement), search tool submission services, affiliate programs, link exchanges, online advertising networks, RSS feeds, web-industry awards, and opt-in email advertising.

SOCIAL MEDIA Establishing an online web presence using social media is easy and free. You can use social media in a variety of ways, such as sharing updates, reminding customers of an event, creating a poll, linking to a photo, and more. Most websites have a social media navigation bar that provides website visitors with tools for following and sharing the website owner's social media presence and also allows visitors to share the website content using social media. Figure 7-5 describes several popular social media tools and how you can use them.

Q&A

What are web industry awards?
The Webby Awards and industry organizations such as the Web Marketing Association also recognize exemplary websites. If you decide to compete for an award, ensure that the award is relevant to your website's content and objectives. Many award websites recognize characteristics related to design, creativity, usability, and functionality. Some award websites focus on a specific industry or type of business.

Q&A

What are the latest website promotion techniques?
Social networking provides new ways to promote your website. Making a relevant comment on an article or blog post that includes your web address, using social bookmarking, and using inline linking are methods that became available in recent years. For more information, use a search engine to search for *website promotion techniques* and sort or filter the results to display the most recent information.

Q&A

For what purpose should I use hashtags?
Hashtags are text preceded by the # symbol and do not include spaces. Users of Twitter and other social media tools use hashtags to start or contribute to trending topics, such as a current event, live TV show, or other relevant topic. You can sort or search by hashtag to see posts or tweets about related content.

Social Media Websites

Platform	Uses
Facebook	Create a page for your website, business, or organization. Post status updates, photos, and links to webpage content. Build a community of users.
Google+	Manage your online and business profiles using the many expanding tools Google offers. Integrates with the Google search engine. Allows you to create events, groups, and hangouts.
Instagram	Post pictures or short videos that your followers can see, share, and comment on.
LinkedIn	Create a business profile for your website, organization, or company. Post links to articles of interest, and share updates regarding content postings, job openings, and more.
Pinterest	Create boards of 'pins,' which are images that link to webpages. Can use to share information about your products or related topics of interest.
Twitter	Attract followers to your profile. Post short messages or links to web and multimedia content. Share others' tweets and use hashtags to create and participate in trending topics.
YouTube	Create a channel for your website, organization, or business. Upload product demonstrations, speeches or lectures from employees, advertisements, and more.

© 2015 Cengage Learning

Figure 7-5 Social media platforms enable you to share content updates and create an online community.

YOUR TURN

Exploring Social Media Promotion Tools

1. Select three companies or organizations with which you do business or whose online presence you follow.
2. Visit each company's website. Make a note of whether the website has a social media navigation bar or otherwise promotes its social media presence.
3. Visit at least two of the social media profiles. What content does the website promote using social media? Did the social media presence enhance the website content?
4. List three specific ways you could use social media to promote the Regifting website.

Q&A

What is Google Panda?
Google Panda is an update to the Google search algorithm. Panda downgraded the relevancy of websites in search results based on poorly received or written content, or heavy reliance on ad content. For more information, use a search engine to search for *Google Panda*.

SEARCH TOOLS In Chapter 1, you learned about search engines and search directories and how these tools build their webpage databases or indexes. When your website appears in search engines' indexes, users can find your relevant webpages using specific keywords. You can wait for search engines' spiders to find your pages and add them to their indexes, which might take days or weeks. Alternatively, you can take the initiative and register your website's URL with major search engines and directories, such as Bing and Google. Some search engines require a fee to expedite your submission, while others are free.

SEARCH ENGINE OPTIMIZATION As you learned in Chapter 1, search engine optimization (SEO) refers to applying design and development techniques to your webpages to increase the possibility that they will appear near the top of a search results list for specific keywords. For example, you can increase the possibility of your webpages appearing in some search results lists by including meta tags and carefully crafting each page's title. Clearly worded webpage text, the density of specific keywords in your page text, and an impressive number of incoming links to your webpages are also elements of SEO. For medium to large e-commerce websites, it might be helpful to hire an SEO consultant to help direct SEO efforts.

In Chapter 1, you also learned about paid or sponsored search results placement as an online advertising tool. Search tool advertising programs, such as Google AdWords (Figure 7-6), and Yahoo! Small Business, as well as many social media platforms, blogs, and more, allow you to add a paid placement or sponsored listing for specific keywords to a search results page. You often pay for the advertising on a **pay-per-click** basis. If a user taps or clicks on your ad, you pay a small fee or share of any revenue generated.

TOOLKIT

SEO for web promotion
For more information about how you can use search engine optimization to promote your website, see Appendix D.

Q&A

What is keyword stuffing?
Keyword stuffing is adding or repeating commonly used search terms in a website in an attempt to increase a website's search rankings. Web designers recommend learning about proper use of keywords to ensure your website reaches its target audience. To learn more, use a search engine to search for *keyword stuffing ethics.*

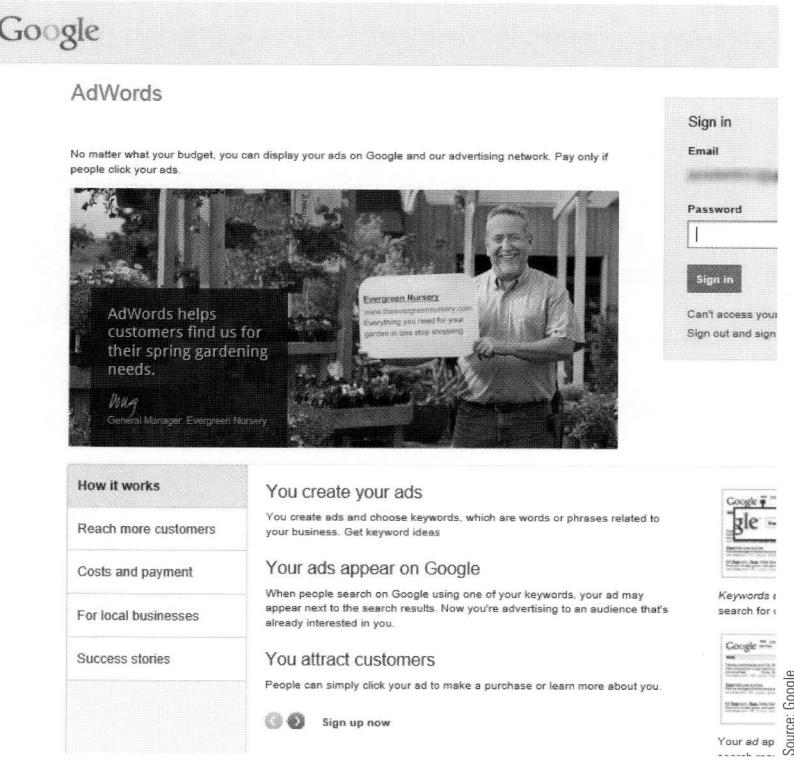

Figure 7-6 Search tool paid or sponsored placements allow website owners to advertise their sites based on a keyword search and then pay for the advertising on a pay-per-click basis.

Exploring Paid or Sponsored Placement Online Advertising

1. Use a search engine to find the online advertising webpages on the following websites:
   a. Google AdWords
   b. Yahoo! Small Business Search Advertising
   c. Facebook
2. Assume that you are part of the design and development team for a midsized e-commerce company. Your manager instructs you to recommend a paid or sponsored placement program for the company.
3. Use your research to make a recommendation based on price, services offered, and other significant program features. Submit your findings in the format requested by your instructor.

YOUR TURN

What is geo targeting?
Geo targeting determines the user's location by the ISP, IP address, Global Positioning System (GPS), or user-provided location information, such as ZIP code, and provides ad content relevant to the user's location.

SEARCH TOOL SUBMISSION SERVICES   Using a search tool submission service is an alternative to waiting for search engines to find and index your website or spending your own time registering your webpages with multiple search tools. A **search tool submission service** such as TrafficXS (Figure 7-7) is a business that registers websites with multiple search tools. SEO consultants often offer submission services. To use a submission service, you typically provide information about your website, such as its URL, a brief description of the website, and keywords to associate with the website. If you choose to use a submission service, take care to pick one that registers your website with the most frequently used search tools.

Figure 7-7 A search tool submission service is a business that registers websites with multiple search tools.

DESIGN TIP Manual search engine submission, search engine optimization of your pages, free link exchange, awards, and tools such as Twitter and Facebook are inexpensive techniques to promote your published website.

AFFILIATE PROGRAMS   An **affiliate program** is an e-commerce performance-based online advertising program in which a merchant website, called the **advertiser**, pays a fee or commission on sales generated by visitors driven to the website by links on other customer websites, known as **publishers**. Examples include Amazon.com Associates and the iTunes Affiliate Program. Figure 7-8 shows SimFreeSmartphones.com, an example of an Amazon.com affiliate. Affiliate program publishers place specially formatted links to advertisers' websites on their webpages. One type of affiliate program is **in-app advertising**, when an app, such as a game, includes advertisements for related products. Companies such as Criteo (Figure 7-9) offer services that create, distribute, and analyze in-app and mobile ads.

Figure 7-8 An affiliate program is an online promotional tool for site advertisers and a revenue-generating tool for site publishers.

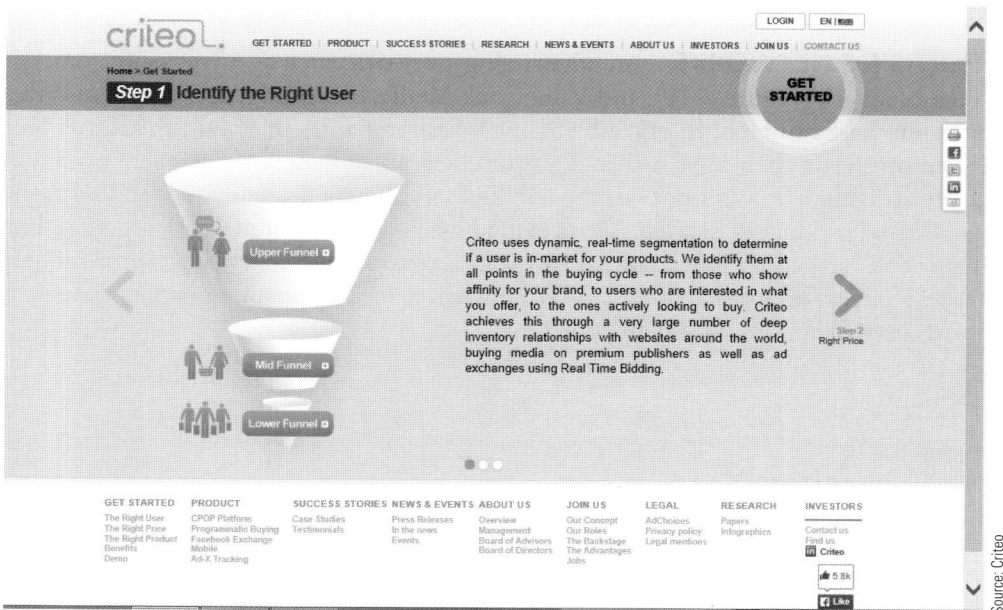

Figure 7-9 Some affiliate programs offer services to create in-app ads for multiple devices.

When a visitor clicks an affiliate link on the publisher's webpage, the advertiser's website (often a landing page) opens. If the visitor makes a purchase at the advertiser's website after arriving there from the publisher's website, the publisher receives a commission on the sale or a flat fee, depending on the affiliate agreement. Participating in an affiliate program is a useful revenue source and a good way for a business to drive traffic to its website. An **affiliate management network**, such as Google Affiliate Network, is a business that manages affiliate programs by helping to establish the relationship between advertisers and publishers, by monitoring visitors' click-throughs, and by processing commission or fee payments.

The criteria and rewards for becoming an affiliate program publisher vary. Although most affiliate programs accept applications from a variety of websites, even personal websites, the affiliate program accepts only those websites that meet the affiliate program's criteria.

Q&A

What are the benefits of affiliate programs?
Beyond the financial benefits, affiliate programs help build your website audience by targeting users who fit your audience profile. For more information, use a search engine to search for *affiliate program benefits*.

YOUR TURN

Exploring Affiliate Programs

1. Search the web using the search tool of your choice and the keywords *affiliate programs* or similar keywords to research affiliate programs from two points of view: as an advertiser and as a publisher.

2. Do any of the affiliate programs include in-app advertising? How do the fees and compensations differ between website advertising and in-app advertising?

3. Summarize your research. Discuss the advantages and disadvantages of being an affiliate program advertiser and a publisher. Discuss the role of an affiliate management network.

4. Assume you are part of the web design team for a large B2C website. What advice would you give the website's owner on participation in an affiliate program as an advertiser or as a publisher? Submit your findings in the format requested by your instructor.

Q&A

What is a link exchange program? A **reciprocal link** is a link between two website owners who agree informally to put a respective link to the other's website on their webpages. Reciprocal links work well when the companies are in related fields, but are not direct competitors. Some websites provide **link exchange programs** that offer reciprocal links free or at a cost to members. Members of a link exchange program can choose other member websites with which to exchange reciprocal links.

ADVERTISING NETWORKS   An **advertising network**, such as Advertising.com, Batanga Network (Figure 7-10), and ValueClick Media, brings together companies that want to purchase online or in-app advertising with companies that want to sell ads on their websites or in their apps. When a visitor clicks an ad from a webpage or from within an app, the visitor's browser goes to the ad's link target, which usually is a landing page for the advertised product or service. Ads provided by an advertising network are stored on an ad server and "served up" when added to a search results page or when a visitor requests a publisher's pages. In-app ads often appear between games in a gaming app, or when a user performs certain actions within an app.

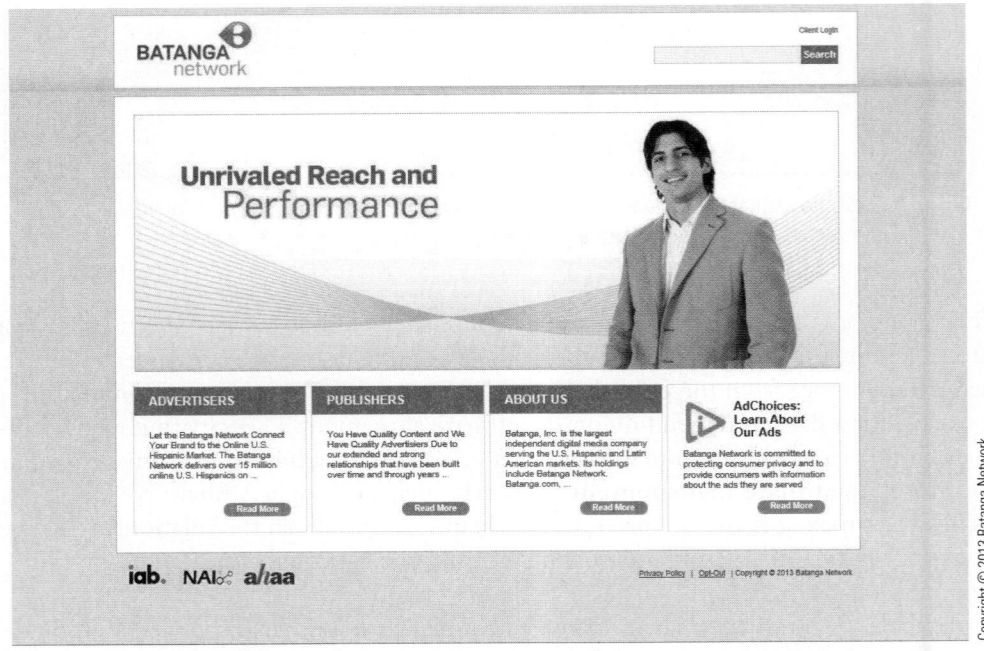

Figure 7-10 An online advertising network brings together website advertisers and publishers.

TYPES OF ONLINE ADS   The types of ads typically offered by an online advertising network include banner ads, pop-up and pop-under ads, and rich media ads. A **banner ad** is a rectangular webpage advertisement that links to the advertiser's website. Figure 7-11 illustrates banner ads on the Suzy Said home page. Banner ads are often horizontal; when a banner ad is a vertical rectangle, it is sometimes called a **sidebar ad**. The purpose of a banner or sidebar ad is to motivate visitors to click the ad, thereby driving traffic to the advertiser's website, in a process called a **click-through**.

Q&A   **What is a banner exchange website?** Similar to link exchange websites, banner exchange websites facilitate an exchange of banner ads among members.

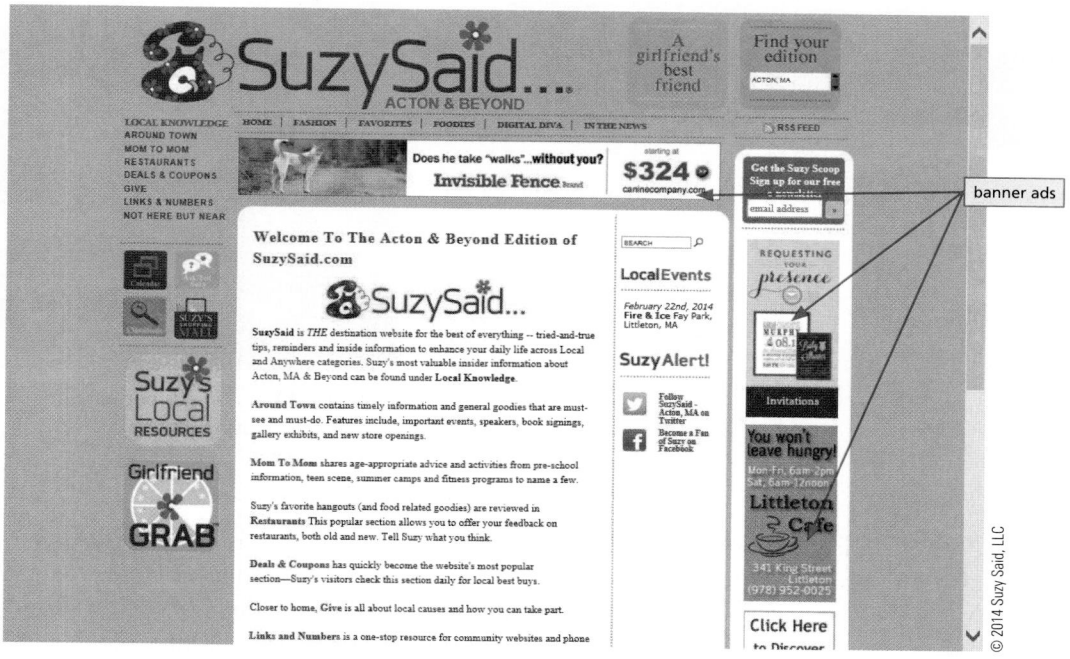

Figure 7-11 Banner and sidebar ads link to the advertiser's website.

Joining an online advertising network as an advertiser is a good way to ensure that your online advertising appears on a variety of appropriate websites; joining as a publisher is a way to generate revenue at your website.

DESIGN TIP

Other types of online ads include pop-up, pop-under, and rich media ads. A **pop-up ad** such as the Publishers Clearing House ad in Figure 7-12 opens in its own window on top of the page or app a visitor is currently viewing. Apps use pop-up ads also to request feedback and ratings for the app, or to join the app's Facebook page. Pop-up ads contain links that visitors can click to jump to the advertiser's website. Pop-up ads are so unpopular that today's desktop web browsers contain pop-up window blocking features, which are effective at blocking most of these types of ads. Some apps will offer an incentive to block ads, such as paying to get the premium version of an app. Within other apps, you cannot block pop-up ads, which typically display between games or moves in a game such as the Bingo Bash ad shown in Figure 7-13.

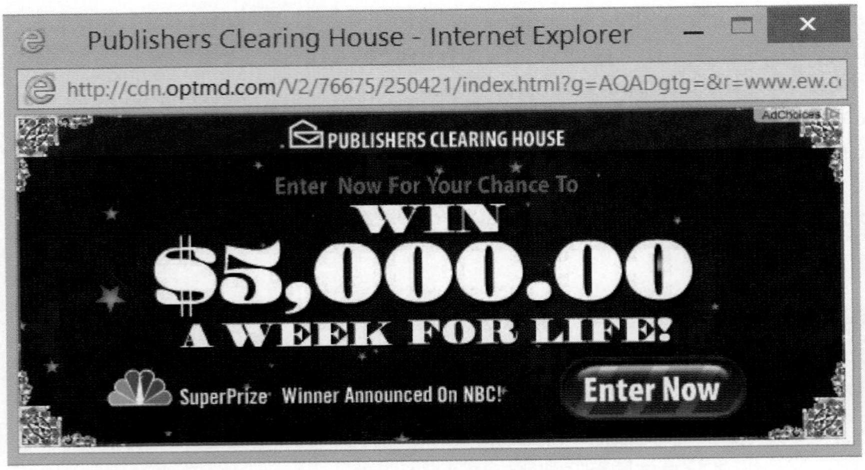

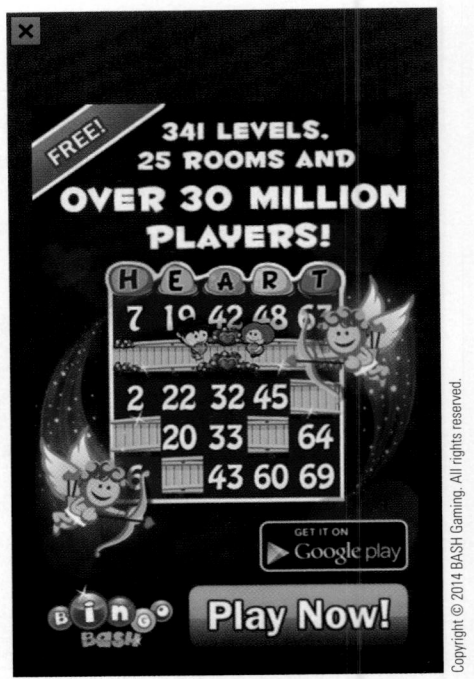

Figure 7-12 A pop-up ad opens in its own window on top of the current webpage being viewed in the browser.

Figure 7-13 In-app ads pop up periodically while you are using an app.

Q&A

What is a pop-under ad?

A **pop-under ad** opens in its own window underneath the browser and the current webpage. A visitor might not even be aware of the pop-under ad window until the browser window closes.

Rich media ads contain multimedia elements. This category of online ads includes **floating ads** that seem to float across the screen for a few seconds, **expandable banner ads** that grow larger when clicked, and **multimedia ads**. Publishers base the amount of money they charge advertisers for an ad on **impressions** (the number of viewers of the ad), or on the number of click-throughs to the advertiser's website. Your website hosting service likely will offer analytical tools that help you measure the success of your ads.

OPT-IN ADVERTISING Email and text messages can be a cost-effective way to promote a website's content, products, and services. **Opt-in advertising**, also called **permission-based advertising**, requires that the message recipient "opt-in" or formally agree to receive the email advertising. Opt-in email advertising begins with a visitor submitting his or her email address, cell phone number, and other required information and agreeing to receive messages. This arrangement is doubly beneficial — the recipient gets information he or she wants, and the advertiser can send a targeted message to a receptive audience. Although you hate to lose subscribers, always provide an option to unsubscribe. Many people dislike receiving email or texts, even from websites they visit frequently. Allowing customers to choose the frequency or type of advertisement you send them prevents you from losing them as customers, even if they choose to opt out as a subscriber. Figure 7-14 illustrates an opt-in email advertising message from Elements Massage.

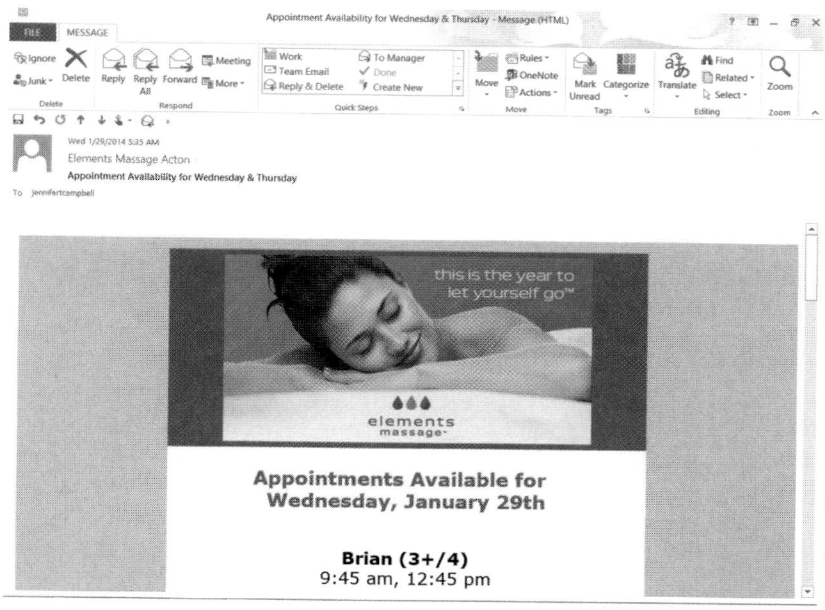

Source: Elements Massage

Figure 7-14 Opt-in advertising requires that the message recipient formally agree to receive messages from the advertiser.

Exploring Opt-In Advertising

YOUR TURN

1. Use a search engine to search for *opt-in text messaging ads* or similar keywords. Find two recent articles or industry blog posts that describe how these messages should be used to promote your business.
2. Use a search engine to locate two text messaging advertising services or consultants. Compare costs, services, and features of each.
3. View the policies regarding text message advertisements or app notifications from a company of your choosing. What types of ads do they send? How frequently?
4. Summarize your research and list five things that you learned that would help you come up with an opt-in advertising strategy for a small business.

DESIGN TIP

Be considerate and always provide a way for recipients to unsubscribe from opt-in email and text advertising messages and newsletters.

DESIGN TIP

Effective promotional techniques for an e-commerce website include the inexpensive techniques used for a noncommercial website, plus paid or sponsored search engine placement, affiliate programs, online advertising networks, opt-in email and text advertising, and promotional giveaways.

Traditional Promotional Techniques

You can use traditional techniques, including word of mouth, print materials, and promotional giveaways, to promote your website.

WORD OF MOUTH   Simply telling people about your website is an easy, free way to market your website. Inform family, friends, colleagues, and business associates of your website's URL and encourage them to check it out. Encourage others to use their personal social networks to publicize your website by linking to your webpage content in Facebook, liking your Facebook page, following your other social media profiles, and retweeting or reposting your social media posts.

PRINT MATERIAL   Your website's URL should appear prominently on all printed material you use, including stationery, business cards, brochures, reports, print media ads, signage, and magazines. Visitors interested in learning more details about your website's content, products, or services can visit the website to find the information they need.

PROMOTIONAL GIVEAWAYS   **Promotional giveaways** include such items as magnets, coffee mugs, coasters, t-shirts, caps, pens, memo pads, and calendars. Include your website information on all promotional giveaways. You can hand out promotional giveaways when meeting new customers or distribute them at trade shows, conferences, or other events.

Website Maintenance and Evaluation

The web is a dynamic environment where rapid changes in technology and visitors' expectations can cause websites to quickly look out of date. An effective web designer understands that web design is a continuing process and that the work of developing, creating, and maintaining a website is never really finished.

Ongoing Maintenance, Updating, and Retesting

You should maintain, update, and retest your website elements regularly. In addition to checking for problems, such maintenance keeps your website fresh and keeps your audience coming back by offering something new. As part of an ongoing maintenance plan, you should do the following:

- Add and promote timely content. For example, change photographs, add to/substitute text, publicize upcoming events, and offer timely tips or create a frequently updated blog. Use social media, opt-in email, and other methods to promote new content to your audience.

- Check for broken links and add new links. Ensure your website visitors can find content by maintaining a functional navigational system that includes links to the primary pages in your website, and including a search feature.

- Include a way to get user feedback, and then act on that feedback. Visitors' suggestions and criticisms can help you improve your website. Use analytics to track webpage views, sharing of your content using social media, and trending content.

- Evaluate and implement new technologies and adapt your content to new platforms or devices when they can further your website's objectives and increase its accessibility and usability, as well as fit into your website budget and meet your audience's expectations.

Some WYSIWYG editors and content management systems include the capability to update pages residing on the live server. Updating live pages carries the risk that your audience will see incomplete or undesired changes. Follow these steps for maintaining and updating your website:

1. Download the desired webpage from the web server to your computer, if necessary, to ensure you have the most current version of the page and can work offline without making changes live. If you are using a content management system, open the webpage editor and select the webpage you want to edit.

2. Update the webpage.

3. Preview the webpage in a browser and verify the changes appear as you want.

4. Upload the approved updated page to the server, replacing the existing page.

Evaluating Website Performance

When you created your original design plan, you first created a purpose statement and listed your website's primary and secondary goals and the necessary objectives. After publishing your website, you then begin the ongoing process of evaluating your website's performance toward achieving its goals and purpose. Evaluating the performance of a simple personal or topical website with one or two goals includes getting feedback from family, friends, classmates, and other members of the website's target audience. Most content management systems include methods to track and evaluate views and shares of your content.

Website performance evaluation is much more complicated for large, complex organizational or commercial websites with multiple goals and broadly defined purposes. Typically, these types of websites follow a formal evaluation plan that, in addition to ongoing testing and visitor feedback, might include benchmarking, web server log transaction analysis, and a review of other performance measures, often by third-party marketing professionals.

BENCHMARKING   A **benchmark** is a measurement of performance. For example, a benchmark for an organizational or e-commerce website might be to increase the number of visitors by 10 percent per month over the next 12 months. Comparing the benchmark with the actual growth in the number of website visitors each month can help a website's owner determine what, if any, changes to make at the website. A performance benchmark is not static. After evaluation against actual performance, you might need to adjust a benchmark to make it more realistic.

WEB SERVER LOG ANALYSIS   In Chapter 2, you learned that each time a browser requests a webpage from a web server, that request for a page is recorded in the server's transaction log. Web server log transactions provide a wealth of information, such as the following:

- The requesting computer's IP address
- The browser making the request
- The date and time of the request
- The URL of a referring link (the link the visitor clicked to jump to the website's page)
- The path a visitor takes from page to page through a website

Q&A

What are tracking cookies?
Tracking cookies are small text files stored on a webpage visitor's hard drive, usually without the visitor's knowledge. Web marketers use tracking cookies to monitor which websites the visitor visits and other visitor behaviors. Many visitors consider tracking cookies an invasion of privacy and most popular computer security software packages, such as Norton, locate and remove tracking cookies.

From the raw data contained in a web server transaction log, additional measures of visitors' behaviors can be evaluated using **web server log analysis software**. You can install web server log analysis software on your own servers or use tools provided by your hosting company. Many large organizations and e-commerce companies contract with professional marketers that focus on website performance evaluation. Professional marketers, such as VisiStat and webtrends (Figure 7-15), often provide a complete analysis package that combines a variety of data-gathering techniques, including web server log transaction analysis, with software that measures and reports on website performance. These performance measurements are web analytics.

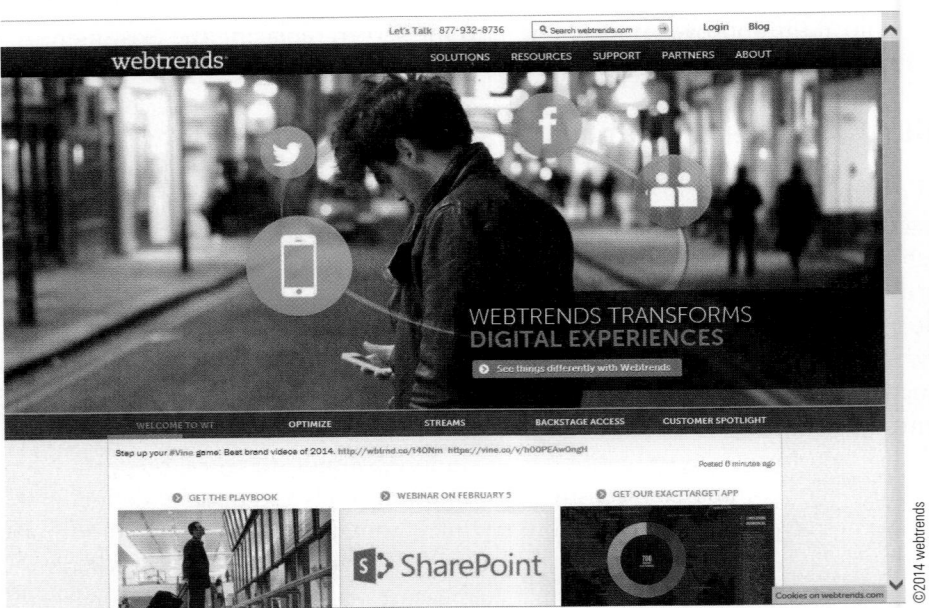

Figure 7-15 Professional marketers that focus on website performance offer products and services for determining website performance measurements.

WEB ANALYTICS   Developing **web analytics**, sometimes called **web metrics**, involves combining various types of visitor data — server log analysis, eye-tracking studies, tracking cookies, page tagging, sales data, and so forth — and then analyzing that data to discover how visitors act at a website. Typical web analytics reports contain a variety of measurements, such as unique visitors, repeat visitors, page views, click-stream analysis, and, for e-commerce websites, conversion rate.

A **unique visitor** is an individual visitor to a website. The unique visitor measurement can help determine the success of your website promotional efforts at driving visitors to your website. A **repeat visitor** is a unique visitor who visits your website more than one time during a specific time period. A small number of repeat visitors might indicate those who are visiting your website are not finding useful information or helpful features. The **page views** measurement determines page popularity. For example, if you have a page that receives few views, you might consider evaluating the page's content and retesting all the links to the page to see if there is a problem with the page. A **click-stream analysis** identifies how a visitor moves through your website by clicking from link to link and might also indicate how long the visitor stayed at each page. Finally, an important measurement for an e-commerce website is the **conversion rate** — the rate at which a visitor shopping at the website becomes a buyer of the website's products or services. To calculate the conversion rate, divide the number of completed shopping cart transactions by the number of unique visitors.

One factor in an e-commerce website's success is the number of sales made and the overall profit generated. However, it is also important to measure the number of visitors, the percentage of visitors who initiate a transaction, and the percentage of visitors who complete a transaction. Having a large number of visitors who do not initiate a purchase could mean that your advertising dollars attract the wrong audience or that there is something wrong with either the products themselves or the way they appear on the webpage. Although it is normal to experience a percentage of visitors who initiate but do not complete a transaction, if many customers are abandoning the purchase in the middle, it could indicate issues with the usability of your website. You must address, test, determine the cause of, and solve any usability problems.

By combining benchmarking, web server log analysis, and other web analytics with management expertise, the owners and managers of a complex organizational or e-commerce website can better understand the website's overall performance and take steps, if needed, to correct any problems or make necessary improvements.

Chapter Review

This chapter introduced you to testing, publishing, promoting, maintaining, and evaluating a website. You learned that prepublishing testing, perhaps using a staging website or a staging server, is an important step that web designers must take before publishing a website to a live server. To publish your website, you first must acquire server space from an ISP, content management system, web hosting company, accredited registrar, or other source. Then, you are ready to upload all your website files to a server using a file management system, WYSIWYG editor, or FTP client. After publishing your website to a live server, you should continue to test your pages for appearance and functionality on an ongoing basis.

You can use both online and traditional promotional techniques to make your target audience aware of your website. Online promotional techniques include social media, blogs, getting your website's pages into a search engine's index, using search tool paid or sponsored placement, using an affiliate program, creating a presence using social media tools, participating in an advertising network, and sending opt-in advertising. Traditional methods include old-fashioned word of mouth, inclusion of your website's name and URL on all printed materials, and promotional giveaways.

After you publish your website, the work continues as you update your website with current content, check for broken links, and implement new technologies. You also must continue to evaluate your website's ongoing performance against your stated goals and purpose using techniques such as benchmarking or web server log analysis, or contracting with third-party marketing professionals to develop your website's web analytics.

TERMS TO KNOW

After reading the chapter, you should know each of these key terms.

advertiser (186)
advertising network (188)
affiliate management network (187)
affiliate program (186)
banner ad (189)
benchmark (193)
broken link (176)
click-stream analysis (194)
click-through (189)
cloud-based web server (178)
conversion rate (195)
dedicated web server (178)
expandable banner ads (190)
file management system (180)
File Transfer Protocol (FTP) (180)
floating ad (190)
FTP client (182)
hashtag (184)
impression (190)
in-app advertising (186)
keyword stuffing (185)
link exchange program (188)
multimedia ad (190)
opt-in advertising (190)

page views (194)
pay-per-click (185)
permission-based advertising (190)
pop-under ad (190)
pop-up ad (189)
promotional giveaways (192)
publisher (186)
reciprocal link (188)
repeat visitor (194)
rich media ad (190)
search tool submission service (186)
self-testing (176)
shared web server (178)
sidebar ad (189)
spam (192)
staging server (176)
staging website (176)
sync (182)
unique visitor 194)
web analytics (194)
web hosting companies (178)
web metrics (194)
web server log analysis software (194)

TEST YOUR KNOWLEDGE

Complete the Test Your Knowledge exercises to solidify what you have learned in the chapter.

Matching Terms

Match each term with the best description.

____ 1. staging website

____ 2. hashtag

____ 3. click-stream analysis

____ 4. impression

____ 5. dedicated web server

____ 6. FTP client

____ 7. pay-per-click

____ 8. affiliate program

____ 9. cloud-based web server

____ 10. sidebar ad

a. A vertical banner ad.

b. Text used to start or contribute to trending topics.

c. An e-commerce online advertising program in which a website, called the advertiser, pays a fee or commission on sales generated by visitors driven to the website by links on other websites.

d. Identifies how a visitor moves through your website by clicking from link to link and might also indicate how long the visitor stayed at each page.

e. Virtual storage for your website content.

f. Software with a graphical user interface that is used to transfer files over the Internet.

g. Stores only your website files.

h. The measurement and analysis of visitors' actions at a website.

_____ 11. in-app ad

_____ 12. web analytics

i. A measure of the number of times an online ad is viewed.

j. The inclusion of advertisements for related products in apps.

k. A payment method for online advertising in which the advertiser pays a small fee each time a visitor clicks on an ad from the publisher's webpage.

l. A new or revised version of a website, on which you will conduct testing before publishing or republishing new web content.

Short Answer Questions

Write a brief answer to each question.

1. Discuss the processes of self-testing and target audience testing for a prepublished website.

2. Identify at least three options for acquiring web server space.

3. Define FTP and compare the use of a file management system, a content management system, a WYSIWYG editor, and an FTP client for uploading website files.

4. Briefly discuss why it is necessary to retest the pages at a published website and how to perform retesting.

5. Discuss at least three social media tools you can use to promote your website.

6. Explain how an affiliate program works as both an advertising program and a revenue generation program; give two real-world affiliate program examples.

7. Define the following terms as they relate to website promotion: geo targeting, hashtag, spam, and keyword stuffing.

8. Describe different types of online and in-app advertising techniques.

9. Explain why unsolicited advertising is an inappropriate method for promoting a website.

10. Explain the purpose of benchmarking and web analytics in evaluating website performance.

Test your knowledge of chapter content and key terms.

LEARN IT ONLINE

Instructions: Reinforce what you learned in this chapter with games, exercises, training, and many other online activities and resources. Reinforcement activities and resources are available at no additional cost on www.cengagebrain.com.

Investigate current web design developments with the Trends exercises.

Write a brief essay about each of the following trends, using the web as your research tool. For each trend, identify at least one webpage URL used as a research source. Be prepared to discuss your findings in class.

1 | Making Money Using In-App Advertising

As a website designer, you can use advertising to earn money to support your website. Research costs, methods, and effectiveness of in-app advertising. Find services that help you create messages and reach your target audience. How do these companies match user profiles with a company's products or goals? How would you use this approach as a website designer?

2 | Using Hashtags as a Promotional Tool

Research methods and recommendations for using hashtags to promote a website, company, or specific content. List five promotion techniques that you could use to make a website successful. Visit Twitter and see what business or technology topics currently are trending. View several related tweets and examine the types of users participating in the trend. How might a company participate or start a trend using hashtags?

Challenge your perspective of the web and web design technology with the @Issue exercises.

Write a brief essay in response to the following issues, using the web as your research tool. For each issue, identify at least one webpage URL used as a research source. Be prepared to discuss your findings in class.

1 | Web Analytics

Web marketers use a variety of techniques, such as using server logs, tracking cookies, and page tagging. These techniques enable the web marketer to identify website visitors' actions and then analyze these actions to develop the web metrics or analytics necessary to evaluate website performance. Some of these data-gathering techniques might be considered an invasion of privacy by many website visitors. Research the ways in which web analytics data is gathered and analyzed. Then create a presentation for your class that describes data-gathering and analysis methods and related privacy concerns. Discuss the effect of visitors' data gathering from two perspectives: as a website visitor and as a website owner.

2 | Security Issues

Search the Internet for articles that deal with security issues surrounding rich media ads and other online ads. Find recommendations for your browser settings. Check the settings in your browser. Summarize what you have learned about security concerns and recommendations. List the steps you took, if any, to protect yourself.

Use the World Wide Web to obtain more information about the concepts in the chapter with the Hands On exercises.

1 | Explore and Evaluate: SEO Companies

Use a search engine to locate two companies offering SEO consulting and marketing services. List the services and associated costs for each. If possible, find user reviews of each service. Explain which service you might use for a small business website, and why.

2 | Search and Discover: Affiliate Programs

Use a search engine to identify at least three affiliate programs. List the services and costs for each program. If possible, find user reviews of each program. Explain how you might use the program to market an e-commerce website.

Work collaboratively to reinforce the concepts in the chapter with the Team Approach exercises.

1 | Recommend Promotional Techniques for a New Informational Website

Join with two other students to create a team. Assume the team is charged with the responsibility of identifying free or low-cost online promotional techniques for a new informational website whose audience will be parents with young children interested in finding information on online educational programs and apps. Create a presentation for the website's owner that summarizes at least three online techniques the team recommends. Give reasons for your recommendations.

2 | Website Evaluation

Create three teams of students according to the type of website they designed: personal, organizational/topical, or commercial. Within each team, each member should present his or her website to the team for evaluation, explaining how he or she developed and implemented his or her website plan. Each team then chooses the top two websites in their group according to overall design and the degree to which each website achieves its stated goals and purpose. Next, have the entire class evaluate the top two websites from each team and select the one website whose design and implementation best fits its stated goals and purpose.

CASE STUDY

Apply the chapter concepts to the ongoing development process in web design with the Case Study.

The Case Study is an ongoing development process using the concepts, techniques, and Design Tips presented in each chapter.

Background Information

You are now ready to test, publish, and promote your own website. You will apply what you have learned about self-testing, target audience testing, online and traditional promotion techniques, and ongoing website maintenance and evaluation.

Chapter 7 Assignment

Create an outline that describes exactly how you will complete the following steps. If possible, actually test and publish your website.

1. Self-test your prepublished website. Create a team of testers and have them test your website. If necessary, have your testing team members simulate target audience members.

2. Select an appropriate web hosting service or content management system. Determine exactly how you will upload your files to the hosting service's web server. If possible, actually upload your website files to a web server using information provided by your instructor.

3. Identify the online and traditional promotional techniques you will use to promote your website. Create a mock-up of at least one method — an online or in-app ad, an opt-in advertising message, or a flyer announcing your website.

4. Develop a regular schedule for website maintenance, updating, and, when necessary, retesting.

5. Identify the methods you will use to analyze your website's performance against its stated goals and purpose.

A | HTML 5

Introduction

Hypertext Markup Language (HTML) is the original language used for publishing webpages. It is a nonproprietary format, originally based on Standard Generalized Markup Language (SGML). HTML code instructs web browsers how to display webpage content. Since 1990, HTML has been the standard technology for creating webpages, with HTML 4 being the last accepted update in 1997. The W3C introduced HTML 5 as a replacement in 2012; as of the writing of this text, it has not been fully adopted and implemented. This appendix covers HTML syntax, HTML tools, new features of HTML 5, and a list of HTML tags.

HTML Syntax

HTML uses tags such as <h1> and <p> to structure webpage content into headings, paragraphs, lists, hyperlinks, images, and so on. Most HTML tags follow the same basic structure *<name> attribute=value </name>*:

- **Start tag** — The start tag introduces the element by name. For example, *<ol>* is the start tag for an ordered list.
- **Attribute** — Many HTML tags have **attributes** that you can use to specify additional structural or formatting requirements. Tags can have several associated required, standard, and optional attributes. Many tags also use **event attributes**, which occur based on an action, such as *onkeypress* or *onclick*. An ordered list attribute example is *type*, which refers to the type of ordered list.
- **Value** — Values define the attribute. Not all elements require a value. Values appear after an attribute, and start with an equal sign. Ordered list type values include *=A* (capital letters), *=i* (lowercase roman numerals), and *=1* (Arabic numerals).
- **End tag** — The end tag follows the completed element. For example, *</ol>* is the end tag for a paragraph. Not all elements require an end tag. **Void elements**, for example *meta*, *embed*, and *link*, are elements that do not need an end tag.

HTML documents consist of a header and a body. The body contains the webpage content and structural information.

The header contains **meta data**, which is information about the document itself, such as the title. Header information appears between the *<head>…</head>* tags. Information in the header is not visible on the webpage. The browser uses meta data to display the webpage's title and description in the browser title bar and in search engine results. Search engines use meta data to add the webpage to the search index. The following list includes important header information to include:

- **Title** — The webpage's title appears in the browser's title bar and provides a description of the page's contents. Place the title between the *<title>…</title>* tags.
- **Language** — You must not only specify the document language (HTML), but also which human language you are using. Screen readers and other adaptive devices

use this information to ensure proper pronunciation and interpretation of webpage content. For example, you would use the following syntax for an HTML document written using British English: *<html lang="en-GB">...</html>*.

- **Description** — The page description appears under the webpage title when a search engine lists search results. The description should be one to two full sentences, and should include a complete webpage description. Both the description and keywords use the <meta name> tags. For example, a webpage description for a summer camp's home page might be: *<meta name="description" content="Camp Blue Ridge provides boys and girls ages 8 to 15 a summer wilderness experience. Activities include swimming, boating, hiking, horseback riding, archery, and more.">*.

- **Keywords** — Keywords are a list of words that describe the page content. Search engines use a webpage's keywords to locate results based on a user's search. Keywords for the summer camp could be: *<meta name="keywords" content="summer camp, blue ridge, boys camp, girls camp, wilderness, swimming, boating, hiking, horseback riding, archery">*.

- **External style sheet** — If your document relies on an external CSS document (style sheet), you must specify that in the document head. For example: *<link rel="stylesheet" type="text/css" href="mystylesheet.css">*.

HTML Tools

You can create HTML documents using a variety of tools: simple text editors, WYSIWYG editors, and developer toolkits.

- **Text editors** — Text editors are simple programs that enable you to write HTML code as text. Using a text editor requires knowledge of HTML codes and syntax. Notepad (Windows) and SimpleText (Mac) are default programs installed with your operating system. Komodo Edit, TextMate, and Bluefish are other text editing tools.

- **WYSIWYG editors** — Microsoft Expression Web and Adobe Dreamweaver are two sophisticated WYSIWYG editors that you can use to create complete and professional-looking websites without knowing or learning HTML code. WYSIWYG editors offer website and CSS templates, web preview tools, accessibility and other checking tools, and more.

- **Developer toolkits** — Appear IQ, Google Web Toolkit, and Worklight are examples of tools used to develop, distribute, and support web apps. Worklight, for example, includes several separate tools that enable you to develop apps, distribute apps to the cloud, create and manage an app store presence, monitor and maintain app security, and manage the web app server.

HTML 5

HTML 5 made many changes to the existing standards from HTML 4 and XHMTL 1.1 (extensible HTML), in an effort to combine them into one single markup language. One of the goals for HTML 5 was to remove support of some formatting tags that CSS typically addresses, including font. This results in smaller HTML files and removes potential for conflicts with CSS documents. Another focus for developers of HTML 5 was to include standards that would optimize HTML files for multiple devices, including those with less power than PCs or laptops, such as smartphones. HTML 5 also separated HTML from SGML, which changes and simplifies the way HTML files are processed. New tags such as *<video>* and *<audio>* remove the need for plug-ins, such as Adobe Flash, to view and play Rich Internet Applications (RIAs) such as multimedia files or gaming graphics.

The W3C plans to fully adopt HTML 5 by the end of 2014, although many web developers currently are implementing HTML 5 standards.

HTML 5 Tags and Attributes

The W3C constantly updates the HTML specifications by adding, deleting, and replacing tags. In the list below and on the following pages, italicized terms indicate where specific values, names, or elements are used. **Deprecated elements** — tags replaced with newer elements — do not appear. Most browsers still support many deprecated elements. A deprecated element is one that widely is replaced with another method of completing the same task, such as using CSS. As a web designer, you should keep up to date with current standards and trends.

The table on the following pages lists HTML tags and associated attributes.

What is an obsolete element? Obsolete elements are ones that web designers no longer use and current browsers do not support. This appendix does not list currently obsolete elements.

HTML Tags and Attributes

HTML Tag and Attributes	Description
<a>....</a>	Creates a hyperlink
download=*filename*	Specifies the hyperlink target to download
href=*url*	Specifies the target URL of a hyperlink reference
rel=*relationship*	Indicates the relationship going from the current page to the target
target=*name*	Defines the name of the window or frame in which the linked resource will appear
<address>....</address>	Defines information such as authorship, email addresses, or addresses
<area>....</area>	Creates a clickable area, or hot spot, on a client-side image map
coords=*value1, value2*	Specifies the coordinates that define the edges of the hot spot; a comma-delimited list of values
download=*filename*	Specifies the hyperlink target to download
href=*url*	Specifies the target URL of a hyperlink reference
hreflang=*language_code*	Specifies the language of the target URL
media=*media_query*	Specifies the media/device for which the target URL is optimized
shape=*shape*	Identifies the shape of the area, such as a circle
target=*name*	Defines the name of the window or frame in which the linked resource will appear
<article>....</article>	Defines an article
<audio>....</audio>	Defines an audio file

HTML Tag and Attributes	Description
autoplay	Specifies that the audio will start playing as soon as the browser or playback app has the necessary data to start
controls	Specifies which audio controls to display, such as a play or pause button
loop	Specifies that the audio will start over again every time it finishes
src=*URL*	Specifies the URL of the audio file
<base>	Identifies the base in all relative URLs in the document
href=*url*	Specifies the absolute URL used to resolve all relative URLs in the document
target=*name*	Defines the name for the default window or frame in which the hyperlinked pages will appear
<blockquote>....</blockquote>	Specifies text quoted from another source
cite=*URL*	Specifies the source of the quotation
<body>....</body>	Defines the start and end of a webpage
** **	Inserts a line break
<canvas>....</canvas>	Used to draw graphics using scripts
height=*pixels*	Specifies the height of the canvas
width=*pixels*	Specifies the width of the canvas
<caption>....</caption>	Creates a caption for a table
<cite>....</cite>	Indicates that the enclosed text is a citation
<col>....</col>	Organizes columns in a table into column groups to share attribute values
span=number	Sets the number of columns that span the <col> element
<colgroup>....</colgroup>	Encloses a group of <colgroup> tags and groups the columns to set properties
span=*number*	Sets the number of columns the <colgroup> element spans
<command>...</command>	Defines a command button such as an option button or check box
check	Specifies that the command should be checked when the page loads; only for type="option" or type="checkbox"
disabled	Specifies that the command should be disabled
icon=*URL*	Specifies an image that represents the command
label=*text*	Required for all command buttons; creates a text label for the name of the command
optiongroup=*groupname*	Specifies the name of the group of option commands that will toggle on when the command itself is toggled
type=*typename*	Specifies the type of command, such as option button, check box, or command

HTML Tag and Attributes	Description
\<datalist\>....\</datalist\>	Specifies a list of predefined options for input controls
\<details\>....\</details\>	Specifies additional details that the user can view or hide
open	Specifies that the details should be visible (open) to the user
\<div\>....\</div\>	Defines block-level structure or division in the HTML document
\<dl\>....\</dl\>	Creates a definition list
\<!DOCTYPE html\>	Defines the document type
\<dt\>....\</dt\>	Indicates that the enclosed text is a term in the definition list
\<embed\>....\</embed\>	Defines a container for an external application or interactive content (a plug-in)
height=*pixels*	Specifies the height of the embedded content
src=*URL*	Specifies the URL of the external application
width=*pixels*	Specifies the width of the embedded content
\<fieldset\>....\</fieldset\>	Groups related form controls and labels
disabled	Specifies that a group of related form elements should be disabled
form=*form_id*	Specifies one or more forms to which the fieldset belongs
name=*text*	Specifies the fieldset name
\<figcaption\>....\</figcaption\>	Defines a caption for a \<figure\> element
\<figure\>....\</figure\>	Specifies self-contained content, like illustrations, diagrams, photos, etc.
\<footer\>....\</footer\>	Defines a footer for a document or section
\<form\>....\</form\>	Marks the start and end of a webpage form
action=*url*	Specifies the URL of the application that will process the form; required attribute
autocomplete=*on* or =*off*	Specifies whether a form should have AutoComplete on or off
enctype=*encoding*	Specifies how the form element values will be encoded
method=*method*	Specifies the method used to pass form data to the server
target=*text*	Specifies where to display the form's results
\<h*n*\>....\</h*n*\>	Defines a header level *n*, ranging from the largest (h1) to the smallest (h6)
\<head\>....\</head\>	Delimits the start and end of the HTML document's head
\<header\>....\</header\>	Specifies a header for a document or section
\<hr\>	Defines a topic shift in an HTML page

HTML Tag and Attributes	Description
<html>....</html>	Indicates the start and the end of the HTML document
manifest=*URL*	Specifies the address of the document's cache or offline browsing
<i>....</i>	Sets enclosed text to appear in italic
<iframe>....</iframe>	Creates an inline frame within an HTML document
height=*pixels*	Sets the frame height to a value in pixels
name=*text*	Assigns a name to the current frame
src=*url*	Defines the URL of the source document that is displayed in the frame
width=*pixels*	Sets the frame width to a value in pixels
<img>....</img>	Inserts an image into the current webpage
alt=*text*	Provides a text description of an image if the browser cannot display the image; always should be used
height=pixels	Sets the height of the image to a value in pixels; always should be used
src=*url*	Specifies the URL of the image to be displayed; required
usemap=*url*	Specifies the map of coordinates and links that defines the href within this image
width=pixels	Sets the width of the image to a value in pixels; always should be used
<input>....</input>	Defines controls used in forms
alt=*text*	Provides a short description of the control or image button; for browsers that do not support inline images
autocomplete=*on* or =*off*	Specifies whether an <input> element should have AutoComplete on or off
checked	Sets option buttons and check boxes to the checked state
disabled	Disables the control
form=*form_id*	Specifies one or more forms to which the <input> element belongs
formaction=*URL*	Specifies the URL of the file that will process the input control when the form is submitted (for type="submit" and type="image")
height=*pixels*	Specifies the height of an <input> element (only for type="image")
list=*datalist_id*	Refers to a <datalist> element that contains pre-defined options for an <input> element
max=*number* or =*date*	Specifies the maximum value for an <input> element
maxlength=*value*	Sets a value for the maximum number of characters allowed as input for a text or password control
min=*number* or =*date*	Specifies the minimum value for an <input> element
multiple	Specifies that a user can enter more than one value in an <input> element

HTML Tag and Attributes	Description
name=*text*	Assigns a name to the control
placeholder=*text*	Specifies a short hint that describes the expected value of an <input> element
readonly	Prevents changes to the control
required	Specifies that an input field must be filled out before submitting the form
size=*value*	Sets the initial size of the control to a value in characters
src=*url*	Identifies the location of the image if the control is set to an image
type=*type*	Defines the type of control (text, password, check box, option, submit, reset, file, hidden, image, button)
value=*data*	Sets the initial value of the control
width=*pixels*	Specifies the width of an <input> element (only for type="image")
<ins>....</ins>	Identifies and displays text as having been inserted in the document in relation to a previous version
cite=*url*	Specifies the URL of a document that has more information on the inserted text
datetime=*datetime*	Specifies the date and time of a change
<keygen>....</keygen>	Specifies a key-pair generator field used for forms
disabled	Specifies that a <keygen> element should be disabled
form=*form_id*	Specifies one or more forms to which the <keygen> element belongs
name=*name*	Defines a name for the <keygen> element
<label>....</label>	Creates a label for a form control
for=*data*	Indicates the name or ID of the element to which the label is applied
form=*form_id*	Specifies one or more forms to which the label belongs
<legend>....</legend>	Assigns a caption to a fieldset element, as defined by the <fieldset> tags
<li>....</li>	Defines the enclosed text as a list item in a list
value=*value1*	Inserts or restarts counting with *value1*
<link>....</link>	Establishes a link between the HTML document and another document, such as an external style sheet
href=*url*	Defines the URL of the linked document
media=*media_query*	Specifies on what device type the linked document will be displayed
rel=*relationship*	Indicates the relationship going from the current page to the target

HTML Tag and Attributes	Description
sizes=*HeightxWidth*	Specifies the size of the linked resource; only for rel="icon"
type=*MIME-type*	Indicates the data or media type of the linked document (for example, text/CSS for linked style sheets)
<map>....</map>	Specifies a client-side image map; must enclose <area> tags
name=*text*	Assigns a name to the image map; required
<meta>	Provides additional data (metadata) about an HTML document
charset=*character_set*	Specifies the character encoding for the HTML document
content=*text*	Specifies the value for the <meta> information; required
http-equiv=*text*	Specifies the HTTP-equivalent name for metadata; tells the server to include that name and content in the HTTP header when the HTML document is sent to the client
name=*text*	Assigns a name to metadata
<object>....</object>	Includes an external object in the HTML document such as an image, a Java applet, or other external object; not well-supported by most browsers
data=*url*	Identifies the location of the object's data
form=*form_id*	Specifies one or more forms to which the object belongs
height=*pixels*	Sets the height of the object to a value in pixels
name=*text*	Assigns a control name to the object for use in forms
type=*type*	Specifies the content or media type of the object
usemap=*url*	Associates an image map as defined by the <map> element
width=*pixels*	Sets the width of the object
<ol>....</ol>	Defines an ordered list that contains numbered list item elements (<li>)
start=*number*	Specifies the start value of an ordered list
reversed	Specifies that the list order should be descending (9,8,7...)
type=*option*	Sets or resets the numbering format for the list; options include: A=capital letters, a=lowercase letters, I=capital Roman numerals, i=lowercase Roman numerals, or 1=Arabic numerals
<option>....</option>	Defines individual options in a selection list, as defined by the <select> element
disabled	Disables the option items
label=*text*	Provides a shorter label for the option than that specified in its content
selected	Sets the option to be the default or the selected option in a list
value=*value*	Sets a value returned to the server when the user selects the option

HTML Tag and Attributes	Description
<p>....</p>	Delimits a paragraph; automatically inserts a blank line between paragraphs
<param>....</param>	Passes a parameter to an object or applet, as defined by the <object> or <applet> element
name=*text*	Defines the name of the parameter required by an object
value=*data*	Sets the value of the parameter
<pre>....</pre>	Preserves the original format of the enclosed text; keeps line breaks and spacing the same as the original
<q>....</q>	Sets enclosed text as a short quotation
cite=*URL*	Specifies the source URL of the quote
<script>....</script>	Inserts a client-side script into an HTML document
asynch	Specifies that the script is executed asynchronously (only for external scripts)
defer	Indicates that the browser should defer executing the script
src=*url*	Identifies the location of an external script
type=*MIME-type*	Indicates the data or media type of the script language (for example, text/javascript for JavaScript commands)
<section>....</section>	Defines sections in a document, such as chapters, headers, footers
<select>....</select>	Defines a form control to create a multiple-choice menu or scrolling list; encloses a set of <option> tags to define one or more options
disabled	Disables the selection list
form=*form_id*	Specifies one or more forms to which the selection list belongs
multiple	Sets the list to allow multiple selections
name=*text*	Assigns a name to the selection list
size=*value*	Sets the number of visible options in the list
required	Specifies that the user is required to select a value before submitting the form
<small>....</small>	Sets enclosed text to appear in a smaller typeface
<source>....</source>	Specifies multiple media resources for media elements, such as <video> and <audio>
....	Separates sections in a document where no visible formatting change occurs
<style>....</style>	Encloses embedded style sheet rules for use in the HTML document
media=*data*	Identifies the intended medium of the style (screen, TTY, TV, projection, handheld, print, braille, aural, all)
scoped	Specifies that the styles only apply to this element's parent element and that element's child elements

HTML Tag and Attributes	Description
title=*data*	Indicates the title of the style sheet
_{....}	Sets enclosed text to appear in subscript
^{....}	Sets enclosed text to appear in superscript
<table>....</table>	Marks the start and end of a table
sortable	Specifies that the table should be sortable
<tbody>....</tbody>	Defines a group of rows in a table body
<td>....</td>	Defines a data cell in a table; contents are left-aligned and normal text by default
colspan=number	Defines the number of adjacent columns spanned by the cell
headers=*idrefs*	Defines the list of header cells for the current cell
<textarea>....</textarea>	Creates a multiline text input area within a form
cols=*value*	Defines the number of columns in the text input area
disabled	Disables the element
form=*form_id*	Specifies one or more forms to which the text area belongs
maxlength=*value*	Sets a value for the maximum number of characters allowed as input
name=*data*	Assigns a name to the text area
placeholder=*text*	Specifies a short hint that describes the expected value of an <input> element
readonly	Prevents the user from editing content in the text area
required	Specifies that the user is required to select a value before submitting the form
rows=*value*	Defines the number of rows in the text input area
wrap	Specifies how the text in a text area is to be wrapped when submitted in a form
<tfoot>....</tfoot>	Identifies and groups rows into a table footer
<th>....</th>	Defines a table header cell; contents are bold and center-aligned by default
colspan=number	Defines the number of adjacent columns spanned by the cell
rowspan=number	Defines the number of adjacent rows spanned by the cell
<thead>....</thead>	Identifies and groups rows into a table header
<title>....</title>	Defines the title for the HTML document; always should be used
<tr>....</tr>	Defines a row of cells within a table
<u>....</u>	Represents some text that should be stylistically different from normal text, such as misspelled words or proper nouns in Chinese
<ul>....</ul>	Defines an unordered list that contains bulleted list item elements (<li>)

HTML Tag and Attributes	Description
\<video\>....\</video\>	Defines a video element
autoplay	Specifies that the video will start playing as soon the browser or playback app has the necessary data to start
controls	Specifies that video controls should be displayed (such as a play/pause button)
height=*pixels*	Sets the height of the video player
loop	Specifies that the video will start over again, every time it is finished
muted	Specifies that the audio output of the video should be muted
src=*URL*	Specifies the URL of the video file
width=*pixels*	Sets the width of the video player

B Cascading Style Sheets (CSS)

Introduction

Appendix B discusses Cascading Style Sheets (CSS), which is a formatting specification used in HTML and XHTML documents. The W3C recommends using CSS standards. CSS also is the Web Accessibility Initiative's (WAI) standard for webpage element formatting and page layout.

CSS Benefits

The specific benefits of using CSS include the following:

Q&A

How widely used is CSS?
All browsers today offer varying levels of support for CSS, however, none offer total support for all CSS standards. Most professional web designers use at least some elements of CSS when developing webpages, to promote accessibility and usability, and to comply with industry standards.

- **Separation of structure and presentation** — The original purpose of HTML was to define the structure of a web document rather than the presentation, or appearance, of content. Using CSS to determine the presentation of the content allows a web designer to change a document's appearance without impacting the document's structure. Websites that use CSS for formatting can reduce overall file size because multiple webpages share the same formatting document.

- **Control over typography and page layout** — CSS allows for the specification of font formatting, leading (space between lines), tracking (space between words), and kerning (space between letters). Additionally, you can control margins, indents, and element positioning with CSS.

- **Ability to make global changes to a website** — With CSS, you can control the appearance of hundreds of webpages using a single style sheet. Editing the style sheet allows you to make changes to all the pages in a website quickly and consistently. This allows for flexibility in web design. Applying a new or edited CSS document enables you to make changes to a website's appearance that meet new accessibility standards or apply the latest RWD techniques.

Style Rule Syntax, Properties, and Values

Q&A

What if I make a syntax error?
CSS ignores improperly formatted declarations. If a webpage element does not appear as intended when viewed in a web browser, check the CSS document to ensure you have used the proper formatting and punctuation.

To use CSS to format webpage elements, you first define webpage elements by enclosing them in HTML tags in the HTML document, such as <h1>...</h1> to define first-level headings. You then can apply multiple formatting instructions to page elements at one time by assigning styles within the CSS document. CSS formatting uses style rules to define the appearance or location of webpage elements. A style rule consists of a *selector*, the element affected by the rule, and a *declaration*, the property:value pairs that provide the actual formatting instructions contained within a pair of brackets { }. Figure B-1 illustrates two style rule examples.

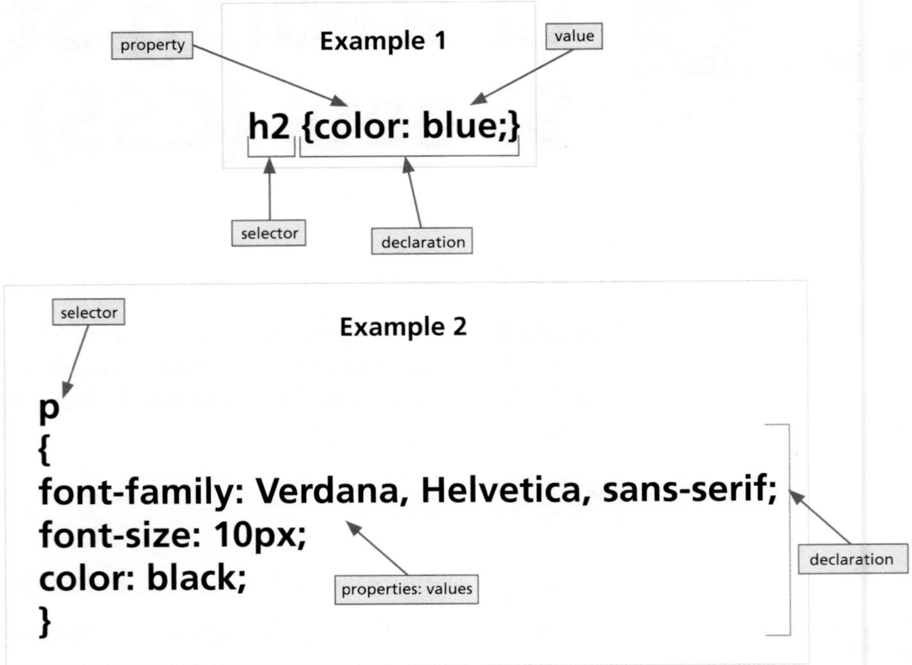

Example 1

property   value

h2 {color: blue;}

selector   declaration

Example 2

selector

```
p
{
font-family: Verdana, Helvetica, sans-serif;
font-size: 10px;
color: black;
}
```

properties: values

declaration

© 2015 Cengage Learning

Figure B-1 A style rule consists of a selector and a declaration containing properties and their values.

In style rule Example 1, the *selector* is the h2 heading style element and the *declaration* contains the color property and the blue value. This style rule specifies that all heading style 2 text will be blue. The style rule in Example 2 is more complex and uses a line-by-line arrangement of the style rule elements to improve readability.

In Example 2, the *selector* is the p element (paragraph text) and the *declaration* contains multiple property:value pairs. CSS syntax requires you to separate multiple values by a comma, as shown in Example 2, and multiple property:value pairs using a semicolon. The first property, *font-family*, specifies three values indicating three font choices for paragraph text:

- The Verdana web font — The preferred choice
- The Helvetica sans-serif font — An alternate choice if the user's computer or device does not have the Verdana web font
- An available sans-serif font — A default choice if the computer or device does not have access to either the preferred or alternate font choice

The second property, *font-size*, specifies the paragraph text font size as 10 pixels. The third property, *color*, specifies the paragraph text font color as black.

Pseudo-classes enable you to create special effects by specifying multiple properties for the same element, depending on the user's action or other criteria. You can use a pseudo-class to specify rollover effects for a navigation button or a link, for example. You can change the color depending on whether the user already has clicked a link in the browsing session, or when the user points to it, hovers the mouse over it, or selects it. The syntax for pseudo-class is selector:pseudo-class {property:value;}.

Each CSS property has its own rule about acceptable values, such as colors, numbers, percentages, predefined values, and so forth. For example, the *font-size* property in Example 2 could have an absolute size value stated in the number of points, inches, or centimeters; a size value stated in pixels, which is relative to the screen; a size value stated as a percentage of the base font size; or a size value stated as an em value.

Inline Styles, Internal Style Sheets, and External Style Sheets

You apply CSS style rules to a webpage in one of three ways:

- As an *inline style* inserted within the individual HTML tags on a page
- As part of an *internal style sheet* inserted within a page's HTML heading tags
- As part of an *external style sheet* linked to webpages with an HTML tag

Inline styles involve inserting the style rule within an element's HTML tag. You should use this method sparingly because inline styles have a number of disadvantages, including failure to separate content from design (which is the primary goal of CSS), increased webpage maintenance issues, and accessibility issues. Figure B-2 provides an example of an inline style as part of the <h2> </h2> tag pair. External style sheets are the most flexible because you can use them to apply formatting rules to multiple site pages.

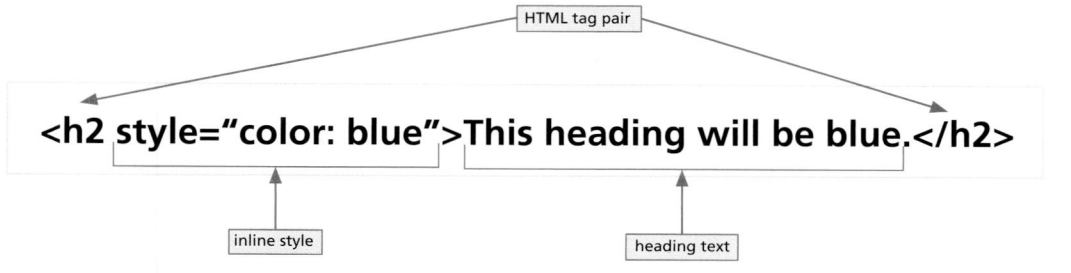

Figure B-2 Inline styles are inserted within an element's HTML tag.

Internal style sheets, or embedded style sheets, appear within a page's HTML <head> and </head> tag pairs along with other heading information, such as a page's title. Style rules in an internal style sheet only modify elements on the page that includes the rules. Figure B-3 illustrates an internal style sheet.

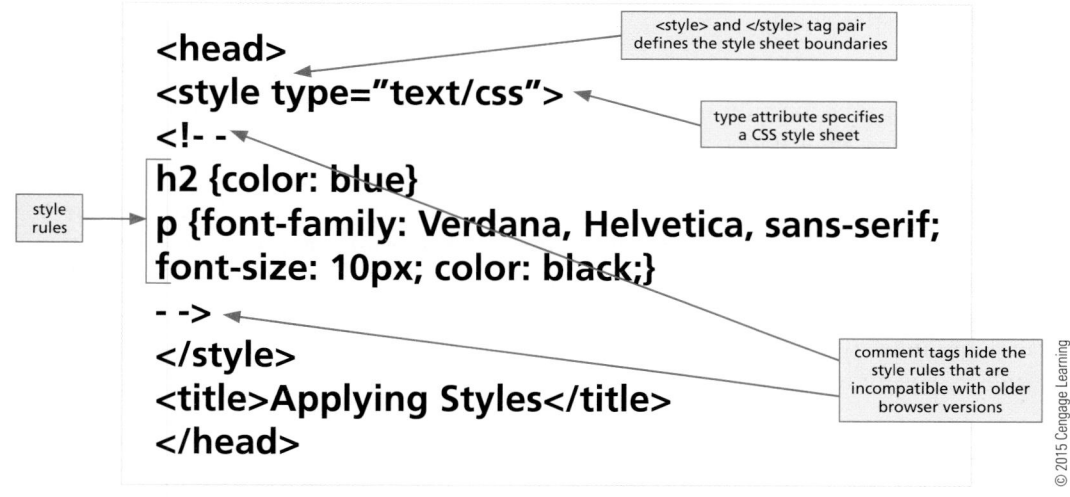

Figure B-3 Style rules in an internal style sheet only affect elements on the webpage in which the rules are embedded.

Q&A

When is it appropriate to use inline styles or internal style sheets? Although external style sheets are the most flexible CSS option, inline styles and internal style sheets enable you to make exceptions to specific instances of an element. To learn more, use a search engine to search for *using inline styles and internal style sheets*.

Are external style sheets available to purchase or download?
Numerous sources enable you to download and apply, or modify, a predefined CSS style sheet, or a style sheet template. Review any restrictions on its use, pay any associated fees, and give proper credit to the source. Make sure to find reviews of the vendor or provider to ensure that the CSS document is safe to use, and does not include any unwanted or potentially harmful code.

An external style sheet, sometimes called a linked style sheet, is a separate text document that contains style rules. Unlike an internal style sheet, you can apply the style rules in an external style sheet to one or more webpages by linking the pages to the external style sheet. External style sheets are a powerful tool for changing the formatting or layout of multiple pages at a site at one time simply by editing the style sheet. Figure B-4 illustrates the link to an external style sheet within a webpage's heading tags.

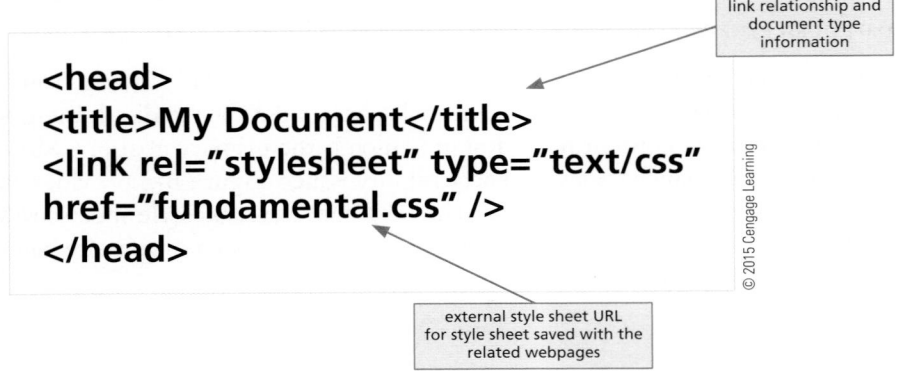

link relationship and document type information

```
<head>
<title>My Document</title>
<link rel="stylesheet" type="text/css"
href="fundamental.css" />
</head>
```

external style sheet URL for style sheet saved with the related webpages

© 2015 Cengage Learning

Figure B-4 The style rules in an external style sheet can be applied to one or more webpages by linking the pages to the external style sheet.

How can I develop my own CSS documents?
WebKit and Mozilla Gecko are examples of tools you can use to create and apply CSS documents. To learn more, use a search engine to search for *WebKit and Gecko CSS.*

Style Sheet Conflicts

A conflict might occur when more than one style sheet applies to a webpage element. For example, a web designer could use both an inline style and an external style sheet, both of which could contain style rules for the same page element. To resolve style sheet conflicts, browsers follow an order of precedence for applying the style sheets based on location, sometimes called a cascading order. In general, the order of precedence for a browser's application of style sheets from highest to lowest order is as follows:

1. Inline styles
2. Internal style sheet
3. External style sheet
4. Default browser styles set by the user

Are all properties inherited by child elements in CSS?
No. Fonts are an example of an inherited property. Borders are an example of a property that does not automatically apply to a child element. To learn more, use a search engine to search for *inherited properties* CSS.

In addition to the location of the style sheet, two other factors play a role in resolving style rule conflicts: inheritance and specificity. You can nest some HTML code elements by placing them within other code elements. In CSS, nested elements have a parent-child type of relationship in which certain parent element properties, such as the color property, can force their value on nested child elements when no separate style rule exists for the child elements. The child element inherits the value of the parent element. In general, when style sheets conflict, the more *specific* style rule takes precedence. For example, because an inline style modifies a *specific* HTML tag, the inline style overrides a conflicting style rule in an internal style sheet or an external style sheet.

The Evolution of CSS

CSS is an evolving set of standards, constantly evaluated to ensure its relevance as new technologies develop. The W3C approves and regulates CSS standards. Versions CSS3 and the still-developing CSS4 did not revise the entire CSS standards at once, but rather released updated standards in context-specific modules, such as media queries, or use of color. CSS3 is backwards compatible to previous versions of CSS, meaning that it uses the same syntax as previous versions, and therefore does not cause problems with devices or technologies that use earlier versions.

As with any web design standard, it is important to keep up with the latest developments. One example of a new CSS rule is the *rem*. As you learned in Chapter 5, a rem specifies font size as a percentage rather than a specific pixel size. Rems are an example of a CSS development created in response to the push to incorporate responsive web design (RWD) techniques in web design. By using rems to specify font size, you ensure that your webpages can be read using devices with varying screen sizes and resolutions.

Figure B-5 provides a quick reference for CSS properties.

CSS Properties Quick Reference

	Property	Description
Background		
	background-color	Specifies the background color in hex or word codes, as in body {background-color: #ffffff}
	background-image	Specifies the background image
Font		
	font-family	Specifies typeface
	font-style	Specifies the normal or italic style
	font-size	Specifies the size of the text as absolute, relative, a percentage, or by length
Text		
	text-align	Aligns text horizontally
	text-decoration	Adds underline, line-through, or other text decoration
	text-indent	Specifies the amount of the first-line indent from a paragraph's left margin
	color	Specifies text color

© 2015 Cengage Learning

Figure B-5 Commonly used CSS properties.

C | Responsive Web Design

Introduction

As you learned in earlier chapters, the goal of responsive web design (RWD) is to optimize your website for multiple device types and screen sizes. When designing a website, your primary focus should be to optimize the user experience (UX) of your website visitors. Website visitors dislike websites that require excessive scrolling, require the user to zoom in and out, include difficult-to-use navigation, and take a long time to load. RWD techniques help you create device-independent websites that deliver the best possible UX. In this appendix you will learn about RWD guidelines, RWD tools, considerations specific to mobile devices, and alternatives to RWD.

Responsive Web Design Techniques

As the number of smartphone and tablet users continues to increase, web designers often recommend a 'mobile-first' web design strategy. Creating a website that is optimized for mobile devices ensures that your audience can access relevant web content on their mobile device (such as a tablet or smartphone) or computer (desktop or laptop). Figure C-1 shows the Microsoft website on different devices.

Q&A

How does a web server detect mobile browsers? Browser sniffing technology typically is an embedded script, such as JavaScript, whose purpose is to inform the web server what type of browser and device the website visitor is using so that the web server can deliver the CSS and HTML documents that will provide the best UX. Browser sniffing is unreliable, so it is important to incorporate RWD.

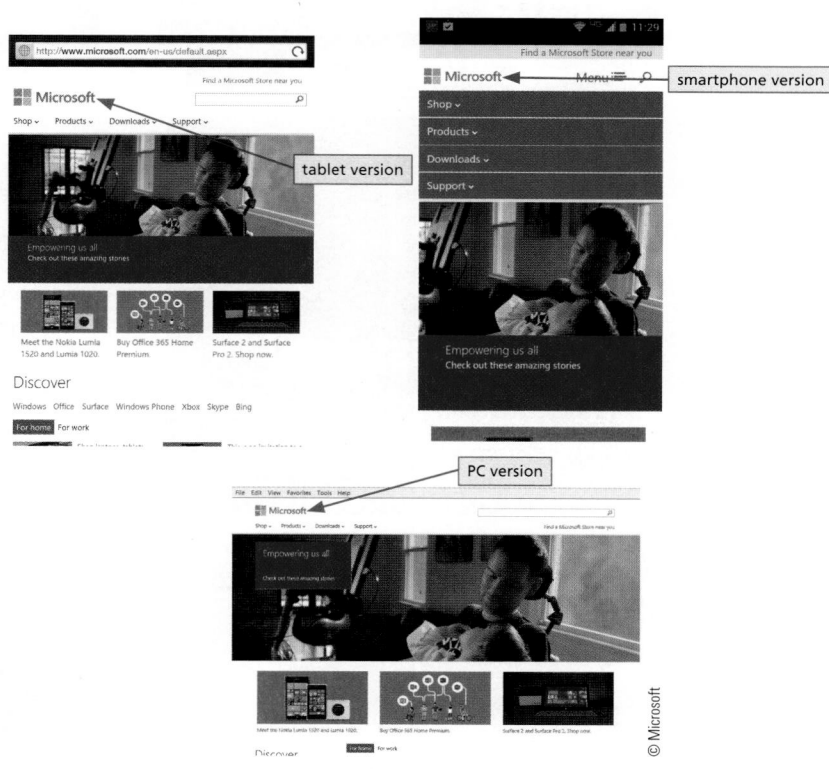

Figure C-1 RWD optimizes a website for multiple devices and screen sizes.

RWD not only addresses differing screen sizes, but also addresses differences in mobile browser capabilities. When designing a website, keep in mind the following examples of current RWD guidelines and techniques:

- Consider using a fluid grid-based layout for your webpages. You can use grids to move and resize webpage items to adapt to different screen sizes or devices.

- Using CSS for formatting is an important practice in RWD. You can use CSS to define flexible formatting specifications, such as font size as a percentage of the screen size.

- Be sure to use flexible image sizing. Instead of a fixed size (such as pixels), set the image size to a percentage of the screen area. In addition, compress image file sizes as much as you can without sacrificing display quality to ensure your webpage loads quickly in lower-bandwidth mobile devices.

- Consider mobile devices' differing navigation needs and restrictions. Most mobile devices use touch screens, which make using drop-down menu navigation difficult or, in some cases, impossible. In addition, with a smaller screen size, minimizing the navigation increases the amount of web content the user can see. Examples of mobile-friendly navigation include icons (called "hamburger" or "drawer" icons because of their appearance). A user taps or clicks the icon to display off-canvas navigation options, which appear to the side of the screen. In some cases, such as the Slate website shown in Figure C-2, the icon opens a new window that includes navigation to the main areas of the website.

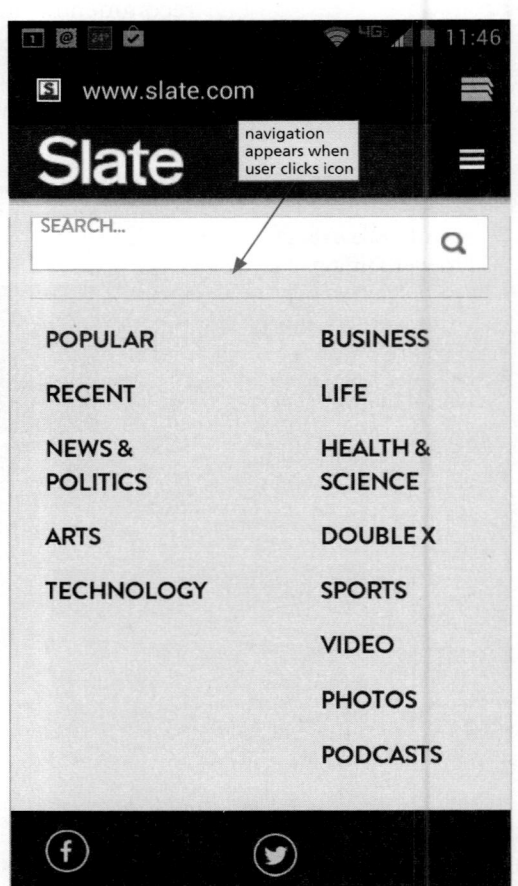

Figure C-2 Icons help maximize screen real estate by minimizing navigation.

- Carousels and slide shows enable you to maximize screen real estate, which is important when designing for smaller mobile screen sizes. Use touch-friendly navigation for your carousel or slide show, apply transition effects if desired, and consider providing thumbnails in addition to navigation so that users can tap or click a thumbnail to move directly to that content.

In addition to differences in screen size and bandwidth, mobile devices and some newer laptops have introduced other considerations that affect web design:

- Auto rotation — Most newer tablets and smartphones, and even some laptop or desktop monitors, automatically switch screen orientation depending on the angle of the screen. Auto rotation enables users to make the screen wider than it is long (landscape) or longer than it is wide (portrait) in order to best view the content.
- Touch screen — As previously mentioned, touch screens affect web navigation. Because there is no mouse or other pointing device, adding extra space around icons improves users' accuracy when tapping screen items with their fingers. In addition, most users are right-handed, so consider placing elements on the right side of the screen. In addition to selecting items, other gestures enable users to affect the screen, such as swiping (moving the view), pinching (to zoom in and out), and more. Recognized touch screen gestures differ between devices, and even within apps running on the same device.

It is important to test your website on multiple devices, screen sizes, screen orientations, and bandwidths. RWD is not an exact science, but the goal is to maximize UX by addressing obvious, known issues to the best of your ability.

Responsive Web Design Tools

Many tools exist that help you develop, optimize, and test your websites for RWD. The following are some current examples:

- Foundation — Free online framework software for developing responsive web design. Features include grid management, flexible navigation, user-interface elements, and the ability to incorporate CSS, JavaScript, and other web technologies.
- Adobe Edge — A suite of web development products that enable you to develop and test websites, use code or a WYSIWYG environment, and optimize web design elements such as multimedia and typography.
- Bootstrap — A mobile-first, open source web design framework that supports JavaScript, HTML, and CSS. Bootstrap includes templates and modules to create and manage forms, buttons, navigation, and typography.

Other Mobile Strategies

RWD is just one strategy for delivering web content on mobile devices. Advantages to RWD include the simplicity and cost reduction of managing and marketing a single URL and website, rather than separate mobile and computer versions of your website. Disadvantages to RWD include limitations on UX by relying on one website to satisfy users of all screen sizes and device types and possible incompatibilities with older browser versions.

Q&A
What other RWD tools exist?
As new technologies and devices become popular, RWD must adapt to meet new standards. New downloadable or cloud-based software and apps, as well as plug-ins, attempt to address these changes. To learn more, use a search engine to search for *RWD tools* and filter or sort to see the most recent results.

◁ **What is Adaptive**
ଧ **Web Design?**
ఠ Adaptive web design
(AWD) refers to
providing different
HTML documents
and style sheets for
different browsers and
devices. Responsive
Style Sheets (RESS)
refers specifically to
style sheets. These
documents reside
on the web server,
which uses browser
sniffing to determine
which version to use.
Using AWD is more
expensive and less
reliable than RWD.

Two other options include developing a mobile-specific website, or creating a native mobile app:

- Mobile website — Before RWD came into popular use, many companies created separate mobile and computer versions of their website. Proponents of this approach believe that UX is improved for all users because both mobile and non-mobile website visitors have access to a website that is specific to their device type. The disadvantages associated with creating mobile websites include the increased work and cost of maintaining and marketing multiple URLs and the fact that a mobile website version does not address differences among mobile devices.

- Native mobile app — In addition to or instead of using RWD or creating a mobile website, many companies and organizations, especially large e-commerce companies such as CVS (Figure C-3), create apps that users can download and use. One advantage to a mobile app includes increased UX because an app can include coupons or other features that users can access directly from the app, in-app purchasing, and text or other notifications. Native mobile apps are expensive to develop and maintain because they require different content and features than a website, and they must be developed separately for different devices. In addition, marketing a web app can be expensive.

Figure C-3 Creating a native mobile app provides the best UX, but can be expensive.

As with any web design technology or strategy, RWD is ever-evolving, so it is important to keep on top of all developments.

APPENDIX D | Search Engine Optimization (SEO)

Introduction

As you learned in Chapter 1, the basic goal of search engine optimization (SEO) is to write content and design webpages that will appear high in search engine rankings. The higher your search ranking, the more likely a website visitor is to tap or click the link to your content in the search results. As a website owner or promoter, you always should keep in mind that SEO also is about providing accessible content to your target audience — helping you reach your website goals. Understanding how search engines rank websites, as well as how to design webpages that increase your search rankings, will give you a better grasp on how to use SEO marketing. This appendix also introduces you to careers in SEO.

How Search Engines Work

Search engines use complicated, patented, ever-changing algorithms to create search rankings. **Search engine algorithms** instruct the search engine to locate and rank search results based on keywords and a variety of other factors. In addition to using programs called crawlers to locate webpages, search engines determine relevancy of search results based on page rankings, frequency of content updates, keywords and meta data, and number of inbound and outbound hyperlinks. In addition, search engines may use analytical tools to rank search results based on factors such as number of website visitors, trending topics, and more.

Google, Bing, Yahoo! and other search engines keep their search engine algorithms private. By not disclosing search engine algorithms, the search engines are attempting to prevent SEO marketers from manipulating web content to improve search rankings. Google updates its search algorithm approximately 500 times each year, requiring SEO marketers to follow best web content-writing practices rather than focusing exclusively on search engine rankings. Other trends and developments in search engine algorithms include:

- Personalized searches based on a user's previous search history
- Localized searches that provide results targeted to a user's geographic location
- Analysis of what terms people search for in order to improve the algorithms
- Increased focus on social sharing, by analyzing trending and commonly shared web content on social media platforms such as Facebook and Twitter
- Focus on natural language searches that use phrases or questions rather than keywords. For example, a keyword search might be: *SEO search engine rankings*. A natural language search for the same topic might be: *How can I use SEO to improve my search engine rankings*?
- Banning or removing webpages from the search index if they use manipulative or unethical SEO practices, ensuring the best search results for the users

Q&A

What is white hat and black hat SEO? White hat SEO techniques focus on creating content that will be helpful to the user. Black hat SEO includes hidden text, keyword stuffing, and other methods to manipulate search rankings. For more information, use a search engine to search for *white hat black hat SEO*.

SEO Techniques

SEO techniques are evolving constantly to accommodate new search engine algorithm practices and new web technologies and tools. Just as you do not want to publish websites that no one visits, you also are not meeting your website goals if your website is high in search rankings but its content is not of value to website visitors. Make sure to focus on creating and promoting your web content in a meaningful way that increases your website's chances of meetings its goals.

Common SEO techniques include:

- Using relevant meta data in the HTML document, such as keywords (meta tags), page descriptions, and page titles, to provide the most accurate depiction of your web content.
- Editing webpage content to include common search terms that will lead website visitors to your webpage.
- Adding links to and from pages within your website and to other webpages.
- Integrating your social media presence with your website by providing links to and from your profiles on different social media platforms.

SEO Careers

SEO careers require you to have knowledge of general marketing practices and web design, as well as to keep current with web marketing trends, search engines, and social media. Most SEO jobs require a bachelor's degree and some experience with either marketing or web design or both.

A related SEO career is **search engine marketing (SEM)**. SEM is a $20 billion business that uses paid and sponsored links to increase website traffic. Another related area of expertise is **social media marketing (SMM)**. SMM experts use social media platforms to expand a website's audience, such as by providing valuable, relevant content on its Facebook page or using Pinterest to entice followers to link to new products on the website.

An SEO job opportunity may require you to combine all of these skills, or have knowledge of how they all relate. Many SEO consultants and consulting companies exist to help small and large businesses with optimizing web content. In addition, many large companies who rely on web traffic to increase profits hire internal SEO experts. Some responsibilities of SEO, SEM, and SMM experts include:

- Creating and maintaining SEO guidelines for the website, including providing templates for web content and other digital assets
- Using web analytics and monitoring tools to evaluate success of the website's current SEO practices, and making recommendations for improvements in content, layout, or meta data. Creating reports and provide analysis for web analytics.
- Keeping up-to-date with SEO, search engine, social media, and Internet marketing trends
- Managing and maintaining relationships with other websites to provide mutual linking to website content
- Evaluating search results and search performance across the major search channels, including any differences in mobile search engine algorithms
- Comparing the success of the website with that of your competition by determining search rankings of competitive websites on different search engines

Index

3D virtual world: An online world in which participants live virtual lives using alternative personas. **7**

3G: Standards for mobile communications that support smartphone and laptop communications. **11**

4G: Standards for mobile communications that support gaming and streaming multimedia along with 3G specifications. **11**

A

absolute font sizes: Font sizes that might not change when visitors change their browser font size settings; measured in inches, points, centimeters, millimeters, and picas. **131**

accessibility
  design tips, 133
  image use, and, 133
  issues, web publishing, 62–63
  website design tips, 63
accuracy of website content, 51

active content: Webpage content created by a scripting language. **26**

Active Server Pages (ASP), 26
adaptive web design, APP 22
Adobe Dreamweaver, 112
Address bar, 15

advertiser: A website that pays a fee or commission on sales generated by visitors driven to the website by links on other websites; a website that operates an affiliate program; a website that purchases ads placed on pages at other websites. **186**

  types of online ads, 189–190
advertising, 185–191

advertising network: A business that brings together companies who want to purchase online advertising and companies with space at their sites to accommodate advertising. **188**, 189

Advertising Photographers Association of North America, 17

affiliate management network: A business that manages affiliate programs by helping to establish the relationship between advertisers and publishers, by monitoring visitors' click-throughs, and by processing commission or fee payments. **187**

affiliate program: An e-commerce online advertising program in which a website, called the advertiser, pays a fee or commission on sales generated by visitors driven to the website by links on other websites, called publishers. **186**

aggregator: A website or tool that displays preferred content from several sources such as RSS feeds, social networking tools such as Facebook pages and Twitter feeds, and social news websites such as Digg or StumbleUpon; a website's administrators instantly can alert followers to new content. **41**

alignment: The placement of webpage elements in fixed or predetermined positions, rows, or columns on the page. **50**

alternative personas: Animated alternative personas or virtual identities used for MMOGs or 3D virtual worlds or who provide welcome messages, sales support, or customer support at an e-commerce site. **157**. *See also* avatars

alternative text: A text description provided for a webpage image that appears if images are unavailable or turned off in the browser. **57**

animated GIF: Animated image format. **84**, 154–156

animated images: Moving images used to attract attention and enliven webpages. **84**

animation
  avatars, 157–159
  design tips, 85, 155
  gadgets, 159
  Microsoft Silverlight, 156
  overview, 153–154
  using on webpages, 84–85

animation frames: Boxes containing individual images that when displayed create the movement for an animated GIF image. **154**

animation with tweening: Animation in which the beginning and ending frames identify the original and final location and/or appearance of an image while the in-between frames are created by software. **157**

antialiasing: A technique for smoothing jagged edges by adding shaded pixels that make the image appear to have smooth lines and curves. **139**

app (application): Typically refers to programs that run on mobile devices (mobile apps) or the web (web apps). Apps are an integral part of Internet technology. **4**

applet: Small programs that are designed to execute in a browser and are sent to a browser as a separate file together with the related webpage. **166**

asymmetrical: An off-balance arrangement of webpage elements that creates a fun, energetic mood. **46**

Cascading Style Sheet (CSS): A W3C standard for applying common styles to webpage elements, such as fonts, margins, colors, element positioning, and more. **25**, 114, 124
CSS properties (table), APP 17
design tips, 25
evolution, APP 17
and formatting, 113–114
inline styles, APP 15
internal and external style sheets, APP 15–16
overview and benefits of, APP 13
and page layout, 116–117
style rule syntax, properties, values, APP 13–14
style sheet conflicts, APP 16
certifications, web design, 29
chat agent: A person who provides live chat interactivity at a website by answering questions or selling products or services in real time using live chat software and a chat window. **168**
checklist, site plan, 120–121
Chrome browser, 13–14
chunked text: Easy-to-scan webpage text in small text sections containing headings, subheadings, and bulleted lists. **51**, 52
click-stream analysis: A web analytic method that tracks how a visitor moves through a website from link to link and how long a visitor stays at each page. **194**
click-through: The act of clicking on a webpage ad or search tool paid placement to jump to the advertiser's site. **189**
client-side image map: An image map whose hotspot link information resides in the page's HTML code and whose links are processed by the browser. **104**
cloud-based server: Virtual storage for users' website content and other files related to users' business or personal life. **178**
cloud computing: An environment where files and software are stored and shared online. **4**

CNN.com, 44
collaborative workspace: Online workspaces in which people communicate with each other using text, audio, video, whiteboard, and shared files. **5**, 6
color
 link, 101–102
 schemes, 55, 112
 using in web design, 53–56
 and visual contrast, 110–113
color depth: The number of colors displayed by a computer monitor measured in bits. **54**
color matching software: Software that contains tools to create sample website color schemes based on color theory. **112**
color wheel: A basic tool for understanding the color spectrum as a design tool. **53**
comments feature, adding, 167–168
commercial website: A website owned by a business. **18**
communication, Internet usage, 4–7
complementary colors: Colors opposite each other on the color wheel. **54**
compression artifacting: Reduction of image quality during lossy compression. **143**
CompuServe, 139
connectivity advantage: The web's ability to immediately distribute and share content. **41**
Consumer Product Safety Commission (CPSC), 62–63
consumer-to-consumer (C2C) e-commerce: Online business transactions occurring between consumers. **9**
content
 determining website, 76–87
 dynamically generated, 85–86
 placement, 98–100
 public domain materials, 80
 repurposing, 80
 value-added, 79–85
content management system (CMS): A system that facilitates the management of web content development, including

authoring, reviewing, editing, and publishing. **28**
content repository: A content management system (CMS) database that contains webpage elements that are called up for inclusion in a webpage as needed. **28**
content writer/editor: An individual who creates and revises webpage text. **29**
contrast: A mix of webpage elements used to stimulate attention. **48**, 112
conversion rate: A web analytic method that determines the rate at which an online shopper becomes a buyer; calculated by dividing the number of completed shopping cart transactions by the number of unique visitors. **195**
cookies: Small text files stored on a web visitor's hard drive. **60**, 193–194
cool colors: The green, blue, and purple colors of the color wheel. **53**
copyright: An ownership right to intellectual property. **59**, 60
design tips, 82
and downloaded images, 137
and public domain materials, 80
copyright notice: The word "copyright," the © symbol, the publication year, and the copyright owner's name that appears on a printed or web publication. **59**
Corel PaintShop Pro X6, 56
corporate portal: A website that is run on a company's intranet and provides an entry point for employees and business partners into the company's private network. **21**
cost advantage: The ability to create and update webpages less expensively than creating and updating print media. **45**
crop: To select and remove an unwanted portion of an image. **141**

objects, such as shapes, curves, and lines, combined to create a single image. **138**

vertical portal: A website that functions as the starting point for finding information about specific areas of interest. **21**

video: Images with movement and sound. **83**

video blogging: Website that permits users to share and comment on personal and professional videos. **6**. *See also* video sharing

video sharing: Sharing video clips by posting them to a website. **6**

Vimeo, 6

viral, going, 7

virtual identities: Animated alternative personas or virtual identities used for MMOGs or 3D virtual worlds or who provide welcome messages, sales support, or customer support at an e-commerce site. **157**. *See also* avatars

virtual meeting space: A website that allows users to share text, audio, video, whiteboard notes, and files from their own desktops. **5**. *See also* collaborative workspace

virtual models: Animated avatars used by online retailers to allow shoppers to "try on" clothing. **157**

visual consistency: The consistent look and feel of a website created by repeating design features, such as color scheme and typeface, across all pages at a site. **109–110**

visual identity: The combination of design elements identified with a website and its publisher. **49**

W

W3C standards for CSS, 113

warm colors: The yellow, orange, and red colors. **53–54**

Weather Channel website, 84

web

accessibility standards, 62–63

and Internet, 4

surfing the, 3

ways of accessing, 10–16

writing for the, 50–53

Web 2.0: The next-generation web that supports web-based services. **2**

web accessibility: The design of websites with alternative features to ensure their accessibility by people with various types of special needs. **62**

Web Accessibility Initiative (WAI)

accessibility standards, 62

color usage guidelines, 112

font selection, 128

image maps, 103–104

link standards, 111–112

multimedia guidelines, 152

web administrator: The member of the website design team who might oversee a web development team that includes creative and technical roles. A web administrator must have familiarity with databases, markup and scripting languages, content development, creative design, marketing, and hardware. Sometimes the web administrator takes on the role of the system architect. **30**

web analytics: The analysis of various types of website visitor data to understand how visitors act at the site. **194**

web artist/graphic designer: An individual who creates original art such as logos, stylized typefaces, and avatars or props for webpages and 3D virtual worlds. **29**

web-based chat: Exchanging text messages in real time using a website chat room. **5**

web-based form: An online form used to gather information from visitors. **44**

web browser: A software program that requests, downloads, and displays webpages. **13**

web design

audio, video elements, 160–164

designing website's look and feel, 109–118

determining website content, 76–87

font selection and readability, 128–131

identifying target audience, 72–74

interactive elements, using, 164–169

multimedia. *see* multimedia

principles of, 46–50

roles, 29–31

site plan checklist, 120–121

specifying website's navigation system, 100–109

tools, 23–29

using color, 53–56

website development planning process, 70

website's purpose definition, 71–72

writing for the web, 50–53

web hosting companies: Companies that offer a variety of website hosting services on their servers or provide facilities for website publisher's servers. **178**, 179

web metrics: The analysis of various types of website visitor data to understand how visitors act at the site. **194**. *See also* web analytics

web designer: An individual who converts text, images, and links into webpages. **29**

web programmer: An individual who uses scripting languages to create dynamic and interactive webpage elements. **30**

web publishing

accessibility, usability issues, 62–63

audio elements, 160–162

cost, delivery advantages, 45–46

currency advantage, 40–41

interactivity advantage, 42–45

issues, 56–59

legal issues, 59–62

multimedia issues, 152–153

video elements, 162–164

web-ready image: An image for the web that has been edited and optimized to find the best balance between file size and image quality. **140**, 141–144

web-safe font: A commonly available font that most browsers can display. **130**